Normandy and Brittany

Also by Richard Snailham

The Blue Nile Revealed: The Story of the Great Abbai Expedition 1968 (Chatto and Windus, 1970)
A Giant Among Rivers: The Story of the Zaire River Expedition 1974–5 (Hutchinson, 1976)
Sangay Survived: The Story of the Ecuador Volcano Disaster (Hutchinson, 1978)

Normandy and Brittany

From Le Tréport to St-Nazaire

Richard Snailham

Weidenfeld and Nicolson · London

Published in Great Britain by
George Weidenfeld & Nicolson Limited
91 Clapham High Street
London SW4 7TA

ISBN 0 297 78599 0

Printed in Great Britain by
Butler & Tanner Ltd, Frome and London

Maps by Richard Natkiel Associates

Key to maps

 Place of interest

 Ecclesiastical building

 Airport

 Castle

 Ferry port

Contents

Acknowledgments

I am grateful to Brittany Ferries, Townsend Thoresen and P & O for their generosity to me and the care they took over my travel arrangements. All the trips made to Normandy and Brittany in the two years prior to publication went smoothly.

Most of the books used in the compilation of this guide came from or were temporarily acquired by the excellent library of the Royal Military Academy Sandhurst and I thank the Librarian, John Hunt, and his staff. Cathryn Barker, with whom I once walked across large tracts of desert in northern Kenya, typed a good deal of the text and Elaine Grahame typed much of the rest. I thank them both warmly for that. I am grateful also for the various kind acts of Matthew Bennett, Dr Peter Bloomfield, Captain Richard Folkes, Keith Simpson, Lieutenant-Colonel Jack Deverell and the half-Norman Jan de Klerk – all colleagues of mine at Sandhurst. Susan Snailum helped to piece together memories of our BBC trip to Brittany in 1978. I have been materially assisted, too, by Diana, Baronne de Bosmelet, Vincent and Lois Cole, Adrienne Hack, Tony Kenrick and Penny Watts-Russell. I am grateful to Sally-Anne Greville-Heygate, Selina Head and Victoria Southwell who went with me to Normandy and Brittany on separate occasions as photographer and offered advice and encouragement in fair weather and foul. Their skilled work appears liberally in the course of this book. Pauline Hallam of the French Government Tourist Office was prompt and ready with information. Marcia Fenwick, Esther Jagger, Martin Corteel and Jane Blackett helped to give my effusions some shape and consistency during the editing stage and I thank them.

Introduction

The borders separating Normandy and Brittany from each other and from the rest of France are ancient and well defined.

Normandy was hacked out by the Vikings, and in 911 the French king established his frontier with them about midway between Paris and Rouen. It was to run in a sweeping circle from the Channel coast, down the Bresle, across to the Epte and down it to the Seine, then westwards along a bit of the Eure and the Avre. These little-heard-of rivers still mark the border between Upper Normandy and the regions of Picardy and the Ile de France. The Norsemen fleshed out their territory further west by gradual conquest until they came to the kingdom of Brittany.

The Bretons occupied the great headland of ancient rocks, forests and bays washed on the northern side by the tides of the Channel and on the south by those of the Bay of Biscay. The coming of the Normans caused their land frontier in the north to be fixed along the little river Couësnon, which to the abiding annoyance of the Bretons runs into the Channel, leaving the great spiritual and architectural treasure of Mont-St-Michel narrowly in Normandy. South of this there was a certain vagueness, but what the Bretons call Bro Roazan (the Land of Rennes) certainly included Forjera (Fougères) and Gwitreg (Vitré). Bro Naoned (the Land of Nantes) formed part of old Brittany and overlay both sides of the lower Loire around the city of Nantes. At the Revolution it became Loire Inférieure, then Loire Maritime, and since 1958 has been taken from Brittany and incorporated in the new Pays de la Loire region. I have compromised by considering in this book only the parts lying north of the Loire and west of Nantes.

The two provinces are as distinctive as their histories have been different. William the Conqueror, who ruled Normandy for fifty of his fifty-nine years, conquered England too, but his tombstone remembers him as 'Duke of Normandy, King of England', in that order. His successors were rather more obviously Kings of England, and after Henry II's time more involved with Anjou and Aquitaine; they relaxed their grip on Normandy until King John, in 1204, was driven out of it altogether. Although the English claim to the Duchy was not given up, the King of France, Philippe le Bel (1285–1314), made it a French province. English kings invaded constantly – the small port of St-Vaast-la-Hougue on the Cotentin saw the incoming armies of Edward III, Henry IV and Henry V, and by 1418 Normandy was again in English hands. But Joan of Arc encouraged Charles VII to fight back and at Formigny, in 1450, the English were seen off for the last time.

In the more settled years of François I (1515–47) the Normans could take advantage of the exuberant fertility of their soil, build their exquisite Renaissance châteaux and trade with the New World out of Dieppe, Honfleur and Le Havre. The Wars of Religion, the Revocation of the Edict of Nantes and the Revolution of 1789 all had their impact on the province, but its essentially rural peace was never severely shaken until the Allied invasions of 1944 wrought such violent destruction.

Brittany was independent of France for longer than Normandy and less bound up with English territorial ambitions. To begin with it was called Armorica, when a Celtic people, the Gauls, came in from the east to supplant an earlier, megalith-building, druid-led society. The Gauls succumbed to the Romans in 56 BC and four centuries later barbarian invasions, again from the east, drove out the Romans and brought in shiploads of Romanized Britons from Cornwall. Armorica became Brittany or Little Britain (Britain thus became Great Britain). The Christianity of the people was reinforced by an influx of saints from Ireland, Cornwall and Wales: Malo, Pol, Ronan, Efflam, Brieuc, Gildas, Samson, Tugen, Tugdual and their like.

In the ninth century Brittany became an independent duchy, then a kingdom. For centuries she was ravaged by conflict – overspills from the Hundred Years' War, then internal succession problems. Duchess Anne married Charles VIII in 1491, and then Louis XII; her half-French daughter Claude married François I and in 1532 ceded her duchy to France, to the undying regret of Breton nationalists, a tiny minority of whom believe that Brittany could still be a little Switzerland in the west.

Like the Normans, the Bretons from St-Malo, Roscoff, Brest and Lorient took to the sea as fishermen, discoverers, pirates, privateers and traders. In 1794 Breton Royalists known as Chouans rose unsuccessfully against the Revolution. In both world wars Bretons responded loyally: World War I saw a greater sacrifice from Brittany than, proportionately, from other parts of France; in World War II some backed the wrong horse but others, like the islanders of Sein, resisted the Germans immediately and wholeheartedly.

To adduce national characteristics is dangerous, provincial ones only marginally less so. Normans and Bretons are traditionally peasant people, but that means much less nowadays than it did before World War II. For example, the modern Norman peasant has often quadrupled, even quintupled, his output of dairy produce and has prospered accordingly. The Breton peasant farmer of the Bigouden will have built himself a smart new wood and ferro-concrete *pavillon* and rented out his old, stone, single-storey *penty* to holiday-makers.

But there are differences between Norman and Breton in much the same way as there are between Devonian and Cornishman. The true-born Breton is a Celt, with close racial and linguistic affinities with the Cornish and Welsh. Théodore Zeldin tells us that in 1900 these small, black-haired men were on average 3 ins shorter than their Cornish cousins. A typical Norman is likely to be an amalgam of Viking and Gallo-Roman, with admixtures of Saxon, Flemish and French: like the English, something of a hybrid. In temperament he is disparaged by other Frenchmen as being slow-witted, and comes close in British eyes to the conventional characterization of the Yorkshireman – obstinate, belligerent and tight with money – though his countryside of rolling downs and white chalk cliffs is nearer, perhaps, to Sussex. But this is being too anglomorphic. What are they like in themselves, the Normans and Bretons? The poet Hilaire Belloc described the old Normans as 'little, bullet-headed men, vivacious and splendidly brave.... [They] awoke all Europe [and] were like steel when all other Christians were like wood or like lead.... They were not formed or definable at all before the year 1000; by the year 1200 they were gone.' But their descendants are still there, farming, fishing, teaching nutrition at Caen University, producing videos at the Akai factory in Honfleur, Jacomo perfumes in Deauville or nuclear power at Flamanville.

Bretons used to be of just two kinds – men of the sea and men and women of the land. Fishermen, naval officers and coastguards lived in the Armor, 'the land of the sea'. Foresters, potato growers and horse-breeders came from the Argoat, 'the land of the woods'.

Lapped about so comprehensively by the sea, Bretons have for centuries ventured beyond their watery horizons – at least since the Veneti came close to beating Julius Caesar's galleys in 56 BC. Atlases have their quota of Breton names – Kerguélen, the Kermadec Islands, the Malvinas, Cape Breton Island. The word 'penguin' (French *pingouin*) is probably Breton in origin, and French has absorbed the Breton word for 'seagull' – *gwelan* has become *goéland*. Forty-five per cent of French fish comes from Brittany – mainly cod, mackerel and saithe – and a Breton is Minister of the Sea. In the summer months eighty thousand yachts lie round Brittany's coasts, and Eric Tabarly is as well known to the English-speaking general public as Robin Knox-Johnston or Chay Blyth.

The Breton as landsman is less easy to epitomize. Nowadays he (or indeed she, for women have always worked on the land just as hard as their menfolk) is not necessarily the conservative, inefficient, obscurantist, muddle-headed peasant of popular myth. Five thousand agriculturalists in Léon are now protected by the Société d'Intérêt Collectif Agricole (SICA), Europe's biggest vegetable co-operative. At the regular auctions at St-Pol-de-Léon two hundred tractors per hour draw their trailers through the sheds and every year upwards of two hundred thousand tonnes of cauliflowers and one hundred thousand tonnes of artichokes are sold there.

On land or at sea the Breton is nowadays increasingly less likely to be speaking the attractive, lilting Breton language. It has always possessed such localized dialects that Breton often had to speak to Breton in French to be understood. In 1930 there were one and a quarter million Breton speakers. Now, out of a population of about three and a quarter million people, about six hundred thousand may understand *Brezoneg*. There are sixty hours of broadcasting per week in Breton on Radio Breizh Izel and, where there are staff to offer it, Breton is now a taught and examinable subject in schools. It no longer carries the social stigma that young Breton speakers felt in the 1930s when they were made to hang wooden sabots around their necks; indeed, among some of the *jeunesse*, often left-wing, it enjoys cult status. But despite all this, it continues to diminish in use as the older generations die and the younger ones become more mobile.

Youenn Gwernig, a popular Breton folk singer, often takes his family to Welsh-speaking friends in Dyfed. The similarities between Welsh and Breton have perhaps been overstated, but although the families converse in English there is some common ground between Celt and Celt. *Gath wen* (white cat), for instance, sounds much the same in both languages. Noticing the family pet by the door and interested in these linguistic links, Youenn asked, 'How do you call your cat over here?' The Welshman leaned forward and stretched out a hand. 'We say "Pss, pss, pss" generally.'

Some knowledge of French is obviously vital for the visitor but a smattering of Breton can be helpful too, if only to explain placenames. As Cornwall is the land of Tre-, Pol- and Pen-, so Brittany is all Plou-, Ker- and Lan-. I have found it makes more sense of things to know that Plou-, Plo- or Pleu- means 'parish of', while Ker- means 'fortress or house of' and Lan-, Lann- or Lam- signifies 'church of'. To these and other prefixes a great many varieties of endings can be added, most of them proper names like -Maria and -Jean. Plougastel, therefore, is 'the parish of the castle', Kernevez 'the new house' and Lampaul 'St Paul's church'. Breton can produce oddities like Coat-pin (woody headland) or Hen-goat (ancient wood), which conjures up awful visions of farmyard error.

Of course the language of gastronomy is French and Breton will not help you much in a restaurant in Quimper. Naturally the menu is likely to be strong on seafood. You may find yourself tempted by shellfish such as lobster, crayfish, crab, oysters from Morbihan and Cancale or the rivers Auray and Belon, shrimps, mussels, clams, scallops, sea spiders, cockles, winkles, ormers and haliotes. *Homard grillé* or *à l'armoricaine* (often mis-spelt *à l'américaine*, some say intentionally by a Parisian *restaurateur* to attract the transatlantic gourmet, and now often styled Lobster American) is the princeliest dish of them all, and stuffed clams and mussels (*palourdes* and *moules farcies*) come high on the list, with the simpler *moules marinières* and *bigorneaux* (sea snails) as cheaper favourites. Fish of all kinds are available – tuna from Audierne, Lorient sardines, Loire shad, skate, brill, whiting, turbot, plaice, mackerel and herring. *Cotriade de poisson*, made from conger eel or whatever is left over, is a traditional fish stew served with potatoes and onions, and there are freshwater fish too – salmon from the Odet or the Aulne, and from the Loire trout and the pike which goes to make up the memorable *brochet au beurre blanc*. Vegetables feature prominently: cauliflowers, onions and artichokes appear in soups and other dishes.

The sheep that graze the salt meadows produce the *gigot de pré-salé* eaten with white beans, and Nantes duckling is famous. Cream and butter are plentiful and rich but local cheeses are few: Nantais, also known as *fromage de curé*, and St-Agathon. Perhaps Brittany's best-known specialities are *galettes* and *crêpes* – pancakes with a bewildering variety of fillings, savoury and sweet. To wash all this down there is cider in plenty – from Pleudihen, Fouesnant, Clohars and St-Féréon. Wine is made, too: Brittany produces Muscadet in what is now the Pays de la Loire. I think the wine from the Vallet region is the best, but try St-Herblon, Ancenis or Bouzille. From the area of the Gulf of Morbihan comes Rhuys wine, sounding disconcertingly Japanese, but it needs four people and a wall to drink this, they say – one to pour it, another to drink it, and two to hold him against the wall to stop him collapsing.

Of the two provinces Normandy bears the palm, gastronomically speaking. Cream, butter, cider, fruit and seafood are the key constituents of Norman cooking as of Breton, but Normandy has cheeses too, and Calvados. All the fish, with or without shells, that have been identified with Brittany are also brought into Norman harbours. Salt-meadow mutton comes from the Atlantic-facing side of the Cotentin. The best butter is produced around Isigny, the best cheeses in the Pays d'Auge, excellent cream everywhere.

In the Caen region they make *andouillettes*, whose name first charmed me in the 1960s when I remember ordering them without the least idea what they were. They sounded fluffily feminine, coquettish even. Could they be slivers of tangy seafood in little envelopes of flaky pastry? I was a bit set aback when the buxom Norman waitress brought me two enormous, evilly curved sausages tied at the ends like sections of inner tube. When I punctured the tough casing of the first one it split open with an audible gasp of relief and released a pungent bouquet which suggested a long incarceration. The contents seemed to be mainly large pieces of white fat and gristle held together by some dark, powerful, indefinable mix of meat and vegetable, heavily spiced. I have since eaten milder Norman sausages with greater enjoyment, and would still advocate an adventurous approach to the menu.

The best-known Norman dishes are probably *tripes à la mode de Caen, sole à la Dieppoise* and *poulet vallée d'Auge*. But also to be found on good menus are such rarer delicacies as *faisan à la Normande, timbale de langoustes au porto* (crayfish in port), *caneton à la Rouennaise,* or *alose de Seine farci* (Seine shad stuffed and baked). Everything is cooked in lashings of cream, butter, cider or Calvados – *à la Normande* generally means that some permutation of these has been involved. Of cheeses, the triple tiara is made up of Camembert, Livarot and Pont l'Evêque – but there are many others. Delicious tarts are prepared from the humble apple and pear. Much wine is drunk in Normandy but none made there. Cider is both made and drunk, and upwards of thirteen hundred stills produce Calvados (after a battle with the excisemen, Bulmer's have just got the go-ahead to produce apple brandy in Britain). *Pommeau,* an apéritif made from apple juice and Calvados, is worth tracking down. All in all, Normandy and Brittany are great places to eat. The temptations start early in the day and by mid-morning I am generally to be found slipping into a *pâtisserie.* Lunch and dinner, glorious prospects, lie ahead. These two provinces are no place for fatties unless they are happy to stay fatties. But then, after an enjoyable but exhausting day's tour of Norman fortifications, or taking in the salty, invigorating air of the Breton coast, the gastronomic pleasures of this part of France will be well deserved.

Normandy

1 Inland from Dieppe

The Pays de Caux, the Pays de Bray

For several years I never saw Dieppe in daylight. As an impoverished student I often came over from Newhaven by train ferry, which involved a night crossing and a pre-dawn arrival and was the cheapest route. I may have stuck my head out of the carriage window to see the moon on the Bassin Duquesne, or sidings full of *fourgons* with their curiously humped roofs, but my principal memories are of clankings and shuntings, long waits and bad smells. Finally there would be a shrill shriek from the Nord Pacific, now coupled on, and with a jerk it was off to Paris.

Dieppe is the closest entry point by rail or car to the capital: 168 kms compared to Le Havre's 205. Sealink carries you over in about three and three-quarter hours. Although at one time in recent years during the transition from rail to car traffic the service seemed on the point of collapse, it is flourishing now, with six departures daily from each end in high season and over six hundred thousand passengers a year using it. Of the four principal entry ports to Normandy it is the most exciting, and for visitors from London and the south-east of England generally the most convenient.

For thousands of incoming Britons the long, undulating line of white cliffs, so similar at a distance from the ones they have just left behind, and the notable landmark of the church of Notre-Dame-de-Bon-Secours on the skyline, is their first view of France. The ferry enters the welcoming jaws of the pierheads and then glides for some minutes past the curved scimitar of shingle beach, the broad green lawns of the promenade, then the busy streets, houses and restaurants of the old town itself, before tying up at the Gare Maritime on the Quai Henri IV. Yachtsmen have the same experience of penetrating directly to

16

the heart of an essentially Norman town, and they ultimately moor near the busy Quai Duquesne.

Dieppe is a trinity: port, town and seaside resort. The port is another trinity: Port de Voyageurs, Port de Pêche, Port de Commerce. The very name Dieppe, from a Germanic word meaning *deep*, comes from the fact that at all states of the tide this has always been France's best Channel haven. The Vikings and the Normans used it, as did the English who held it at various times in the fourteenth and fifteenth centuries. In 1644 the diarist John Evelyn wrote: 'The port is commodious, but the entrance is difficult.' Packets from the village of Brighthelmstone, now Brighton, ran across in the eighteenth century, and have done so from Newhaven since the early nineteenth.

The fishing port has declined somewhat – the 25,000 tonnes a year landed before World War II dropped to half that by 1978 and more now comes into Concarneau or St-Malo than into Dieppe. But the quality remains high: turbot, bass, brill, scallops and, of course, sole. It would be sacrilege to be in Dieppe and not enjoy *sole à la Dieppoise* with its cream and white wine sauce, mushrooms, shrimps and mussels.

Dieppe is still a considerable commercial port. The names of the quays give clues to its history: Quai de Québec – Dieppe superseded St-Malo and Honfleur in the early development of French Canada; Quai de Tonkin – the Indo-Chinese connection; Quai de Norvège – timber; Quai de Maroc – fruit and *primeurs* (early vegetables) from Morocco; and Quai des Indes – most of the bananas that the French consume arrive here from the Lesser Antilles in the West Indies. Dieppe and neighbouring Arques have their industries, so there is an export trade too.

The town lies wedged between port and sea and yet seems curiously unaffected by either. The area between the fish market and the Boulevard de Verdun, along the promenade, is a maze of streets and eighteenth-century houses that you could pick up and plonk down anywhere in Normandy. The churches of St-Jacques and St-Rémy, grey and peeling now, have been steadily extended since the twelfth century and have survived all wars. There is a smartly turreted fifteenth-century castle on the hill, from which it looks as if Snow White might emerge at any moment.

Dieppe's greatness began with the discoverers and privateers of the sixteenth century. The *Dieppois* were among the earliest fishermen to get on to the Newfoundland cod banks. Although he was a Florentine, Giovanni da Verrazano, who skirted the coast of eastern North America and discovered Manhattan in 1523–4, sailed out of Dieppe. He had been financed by Jean Ango, a native of the town who carried out a personal war against the Portuguese in the early sixteenth century. Ango became very rich and built a smart wooden town house, which no longer exists, and a delightful stone retreat at nearby Varengeville – the Manoir d'Ango (open from Easter to the end of October during normal hours). Among Ango's protégés were Jean Parmentier, who sailed to Newfoundland and Brazil, and Jean Fleury, who in 1521 seized a Spanish treasure fleet on its way back from Mexico. These men, French counterparts of Drake, Hawkins, Raleigh and Gilbert, preceded them by half a century and made Dieppe very rich. At this time the elaborate carving of Indian and African ivory was begun; some fine examples of this craft, for which Dieppe is famous, can be seen in the castle museum.

All this activity was interrupted in the late seventeenth century when Louis XIV revoked the Edict of Nantes, thus reimposing penalties on the Protestant Huguenots. Most of the great Dieppe *armateurs* were Huguenots and many of them fled, taking their entrepreneurial skills into exile. In 1694 the English, in the person of Admiral Lord Berkeley, bombarded and almost totally devastated the town, which is why it is so uniformly eighteenth-century today. One of the buildings destroyed was Jean Ango's old town house, though a beautiful Renaissance doorway was rescued from it and placed in the church of St-Jacques, where it now forms the entrance to the sacristy. Its remarkable feature is a frieze with dancing figures of American Indians. To see scenes of the New World on such an early Renaissance work is like finding a Roman coin in Shanghai or a Chinese pot on the Kenya coast – you are astonished at the idea, but then realize that it is perfectly explicable.

Early in the nineteenth century something occurred in Dieppe which was to alter its character yet again. Queen Hortense (Hortense de Beauharnais, wife of Louis Bonaparte, Queen of Holland and mother of Louis Napoléon) rented a house near Dieppe for a fortnight in the summer of 1813. Some new bathing-machines, modelled on ones seen in England in the 1790s, had just been installed and the Queen made arrangements to use one. She put on a chocolate-coloured woollen bathing-dress, ankle-length and fastened tightly at the neck. Police held back astonished crowds as she walked along the seafront and entered a machine. Two sailors carried it into the sea and immersed it several times. It must have been a claustrophobic and rather frightening business and the Queen only did it twice more. Nonetheless, the idea caught on. A bathing station and casino were built in 1822. The Duchesse de Berry made sea bathing fashionable after 1824. What George III had begun at Weymouth in the 1780s and the Prince Regent was currently doing at Brighton was echoed in Dieppe in the 1820s and 1830s. In 1848 the railway line from Paris to Rouen was extended to Dieppe, which now became not just a favourite cross-Channel watering place and a virtual English colony, but the gateway to Paris.

The Gare St-Lazare, so brilliantly painted by the Impressionist Claude Monet, was a gateway too – out of Paris. Artists flocked to Dieppe, from Jacques-Émile Blanche and the Isabeys to Picasso and Braque – Georges Braque is buried at nearby Varengeville in a tomb designed by his pupils, and his stained glass Tree of Jesse is in the church there. British artists came as well – Turner, the young Richard Bonington, and the man who made Dieppe his own and lived there from 1899 to 1905, Walter Sickert. Edward, Prince of Wales (later Edward VII), paid court to the Duchess of Caracciolo and was godfather – possibly also father – to her daughter Olga. The royal yacht would be anchored at sea and Tum-Tum would come ashore in a launch to the Villa Olga.

Half a century later, during World War II, another landing party came on to the beach with very different objectives. At dawn on 19 August 1942 the 2nd Canadian Division and three Commandos – some six thousand men – attacked Dieppe. It went badly. Only at Varengeville did Lord Lovat's commandos gain their objective. Dieppe itself was spared from any preparatory bombardment, a humane act but also one designed to permit easy tank penetration along rubble-free streets. But the Churchill tanks never made it: they stuck badly on the beach, and when I saw its two distinct shelves and steep shingle ramps up to them I could understand why. The German strongpoints wrought havoc. The Canadian regiments were decimated, and only three men from the Royal Regiment of Canada escaped from Puys. In all there were 3,670 casualties. The Museum of 19 August 1942 is 2 kms along the D75 towards Pourville and stands on the site of a radar station, one of the objectives of the raid. Documents, uniforms and vehicles are on show during normal opening hours in summer only.

The Dieppe raid also involved an assault on the medieval castle, built in 1435 when the English pulled out at the end of the Hundred Years' War. It has now been restored and contains an excellent museum for a wet day: its exhibits include ivory carvings, paintings, maritime memorabilia of all kinds, and the composer Saint-Saëns' first piano.

But the streets of Dieppe are their own museum. I found a good vantage point in the Grande Rue, a pedestrian thoroughfare when the market is there on a Saturday morning. There are good shops and great baulks of timber to sit and rest on and watch the world go by. Alternatively you could do this in the Café des Tribunaux, which has not changed much since the time of Oscar Wilde and Aubrey Beardsley.

Dieppe, much more so than Cherbourg and Le Havre, is a place well worth staying in for its own sake – thousands do. But excursions can be made, and of course it is a gateway from which many roads radiate – south to Rouen and Paris, southeast into the Pays de Bray, north-east to Le Tréport or west to Fécamp.

The museum dedicated to the raid of 19 August 1942, the Manoir d'Ango, the church and churchyard at Varengeville are all in the same general direction and could form part of a day's outing to the Ailly lighthouse. It is, however, a very popular stretch of coast, much used by the *Dieppois*, and on one warm spring Sunday I found every car-sized space to the side of the road already occupied, with a family picnic in progress, and the car park at the lighthouse noisy and littered. For tranquillity you have to go inland, though not necessarily very far.

The Château de Miromesnil is due south of the town, just off what is in effect the Dieppe ring road. Clear signs direct you from the D54 to the *'Lieu de Naîssance de Guy de Maupassant'* – which it is not. The writer's parents, snobs both, had rented rooms at Miromesnil so that their child might be born in suitably grand surroundings, but the birth, on 5 August 1850, occurred prematurely in the family home at Fécamp. True, the boy was taken for some time to Miromesnil and the room in which the family stayed, today a bathroom, is shown. Owned now by the Comte and Comtesse Bertrand de Vogüé, the château was built by Jacques Dyel and his nephew Jean in the early seventeenth century on the site of a medieval fortress destroyed after Henri IV's victory at Arques. The contrast of pale red bricks and yellowish stonework is a pleasing one and the château is set in thick beech forest. It is open from May to mid October in the afternoons, except Tuesdays.

Arques, where in September 1589 the then Protestant Henri IV defeated the Catholic League under the Duc de Mayenne, is not far off; it is now known as Arques-la-Bataille. The site is marked by a simple obelisk in the lee of the western end of the hilltop Forêt d'Arques. Military history enthusiasts can approach it by any of the *routes forestières* which climb up the hill. More interesting to me, though, was the ancient castle of Arques (see p.118), in which Henri was besieged before the battle. One of the very few Norman castles in existence before 1066, it was begun in 1038 by William the Conqueror's uncle, another Duke William. The English held on to it until 1204, and claimed it again from 1419 – its extremely deep moat perhaps helped to ensure that it was always the last bastion to fall. After long years of neglect and some further damage in World War II (the Germans built some V1 rocket sites near Arques) it is at last being restored.

Going north out of Dieppe you cross the swing bridges to the old fishermen's suburb of Le Pollet, and the fast but boring D925 to Le Tréport. I turned off on to the undulating and badly signposted coastal route, but only a few of the seaside villages struck me as worth bearing in mind for the future. To get to the first one, Puys, requires quite a long Z-shaped deviation in Le Pollet, for the Rue Cité de Limes is now one-way only, for inward-bound traffic. Limes, incidentally, lies on the high ground behind the beach at Puys – not so much a city, more a Gallo-Roman settlement abandoned in the 1400s. Puys itself has a short shingle beach at the end of a long narrow valley between the cliffs. I found it quiet and pleasant, but no more. Alexandre Dumas *fils* made it popular after 1870; the present-day Auberge du Vieux Puits was his home and its prices reflect this connection.

There follow a succession of rather undistinguished villages beginning with B – Bracquemont, Belleville with its hideous church, Berneval-le-Grand where Oscar Wilde wrote *The Ballad of Reading Gaol*, and Berneval-sur-Mer. The roads are potholed, and access to beaches is difficult. No doubt this keeps holiday traffic away and ensures that quiet corners survive. There must be attraction for some in this bit of coast, since new estates of holiday and retirement homes have sprung up on the ruins of 1942. St-Martin-Plage is very bungaloid, and Penly is nondescript. Between them comes Electricité de France's new Centre Nucléaire de Penly, of great importance to the French national grid, no doubt, but a bit of a blot on the coastline.

Then, by way of pleasant contrast, comes Biville-sur-Mer, a very appealing village with some neat, slate-hung cottages whose inhabitants still drape mattresses out of their bedroom windows to air. There is a village pond complete with swans, an attractive church on its edge and a tiny *mairie* in what looks like half a garage. The only problem with Biville is that it is not particularly *sur-Mer*.

At Tocqueville-sur-Eu the restaurant Le Quatre Pain has earned itself a Michelin rosette, one of only four in all Seine-Maritime. You can also eat well at Criel-Plage and Mesnil-Val, the adjacent villages, but although a lot of caravanners seem to congregate here the beach at Criel is not so pleasant. A levée of large boulders has been made along it through which the river Yères is led into the sea by a large square conduit. The presence of numbers of happy-sounding seagulls offshore suggests that a cleaner place to swim might be up the coast at Mesnil-Val. Criel has the rather dour, brick-built, scruffy look that I associate more with parts of Picardy, which is very near this northern corner of Normandy. Mesnil-Val faces south-west towards the afternoon sun and behind it is a high chalk cliff, the last before the mouth of the river Bresle, and from the top there are fine views of the Channel and ultimately Le Tréport.

Nearer to Paris even than Dieppe, Le Tréport is cheerful, breezy, unsophisticated and beloved of British coach tour operators whose predominantly elderly clientèle pick their way cautiously over the large shingle at the top of the shelving beach. The food and drink are good (try the Café des Parisiens on the harbour front), there is a fairground, and nothing too cultural to have to visit: perhaps the late sixteenth-century church of St-Jacques,

Routes from Dieppe

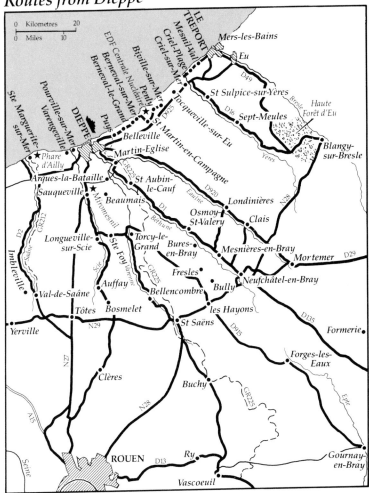

high on a mound and dominating the port, but that is all. Over the Bresle in Picardy is the companion town of Mers-les-Bains, where the Hotel Picardie has a good reputation.

Le Tréport began life in Roman days as Ulterior Portus, from which its name can be seen to derive. Not quite so clear is how Augusta, 3 kms up the Bresle, became simply Eu. It is an interesting, bustling, ancient frontier town, known, in the same way that we say 'New York City', as 'La Ville d'Eu' (to stand at a railway station ticket window and just say 'Eu' might suggest that you had not made your mind up). To guard an early river crossing point Rollo, first Duke of Normandy, built a castle here in which he died in 932. There was a cathedral here on the site of the present collegiate church of Notre-Dame-et-St-Laurent in which in 1052 Duke William contracted the controversial marriage with Mathilda, daughter of the Count of Flanders, which led to their excommunication and, indirectly, to the building of the great Caen abbeys (see p. 111–13) as their act of expiation. Harold, brother-in-law of Edward the Confessor, was received here on his way to visit William in 1064. The present church was built between 1186 and 1230 and dedicated to Our Lady and St Lawrence O'Toole, an Archbishop of Dublin who died there in 1180 and is interred there. Was Joan of Arc allowed to pray there, I wonder, on her way from Compiègne to be burned at Rouen in 1431? It is a fine church, sensitively and successfully restored by Viollet-le-Duc in the nineteenth century. Down some steps in a side chapel off the south ambulatory is a superb fifteenth-century entombment with painted and gilded figures whose sorrow is vividly portrayed as they surround the dead Christ.

Eu, though steeped in history, is much restored. If you drive in from Le Tréport the first thing you will see behind a bank of chestnut trees is the dignified stone and brick Château d'Eu. It is largely a 1902 reconstruction and never arouses much enthusiastic comment. Henri, Duc de Guise, began it in 1578 but only the right wing of his château survives. Extensively damaged by the Revolutionaries in 1795, it was rebuilt in 1821 by Louis-Philippe, Duc d'Orléans. When he was crowned king in 1830 Eu became his favourite residence, and he entertained Queen Victoria and Prince Albert there. Fire later ravaged it, but after yet more restoration it now acts as the Hôtel de Ville and also houses the Louis-Philippe Museum. This is full of the atmosphere of he 1840s, with glass, a collection of stuffed animal heads, furniture (some of it Brazilian, for the Comte d'Eu who restored it in 1902 was the son-in-law of the Emperor of Brazil, Don Pedro II), Gobelins tapestries and fine parquet floors – which is why no stiletto heels are allowed. Although the museum is advertised as being open from April to October (except Tuesdays) during normal opening hours, you have to join

Château d'Eu

one of the guided tours which take an hour and leave on the hour. If you have to wait, the park, designed by Le Nôtre, is worth a look.

While you are at Eu you may be able to spare some time for the chapel, built in 1620, of a Jesuit college founded here by Henri de Guise in 1573. It is down a lane leading off the Place Carnot. Two splendid but empty marble mausolea remain, built for Henri and his wife. Another pleasant excursion is to the Forêt d'Eu: find the D49 exit, which runs off the tree-lined Boulevard Thiers. You will head out past the supposed site of the old city of Augusta into rolling forest and farmland. The D58 and D126 lead to various pretty *routes forestières* in the upper woods. You may then either visit Blangy-sur-Bresle and continue up the attractive D49 flanking the river, or drop into the lush valley of the Yères which can be followed back to Criel and the sea. From Sept-Meules to St-Sulpice is as beautiful picnic country as I have ever seen – or, if you prefer, the Moulin du Becquerel at St-Sulpice is a decent restaurant.

Most motorists seem to head out of Dieppe in a generally south-easterly direction for Paris. The main road is the D915 which has plenty of good, fast stretches. It passes through Les Hayons (nothing of a place, but an important crossroads), Forges-les-Eaux, Gournay-en-Bray and Gisors. But I prefer quieter roads and enjoy seeing something of the Pays de Bray, so over the years I have tried other routes leading out of Dieppe, rather like the bones of a skeletal hand pointing, ultimately, towards Paris. The northernmost finger is the D920 to Envermeu and Londinières, following the pleasant valley of the Eaulne. Envermeu, a horse-breeding centre where Walter Sickert lived after 1911, has a good choir in its sixteenth-century church. Londinières is a good stopping place, with the Forêt du Hellet close at hand and Mesnières-en-Bray with its château (see below) in the next valley. A peaceful route on towards Paris would be the D1314 and D36 (turn off at Clais) to Mortemer, which is not the Mortemer of the abbey in the Forêt de Lyons (see pp. 105–6) but the ancestral home of the noble family of the Welsh Marches. Here Duke William beat the French King Henry in 1054 and the first Mortimer, Roger, fought for him. The D36 runs on to leave Normandy at Formerie.

*   *   *

Another route from Dieppe is the D1 to Neufchâtel-en-Bray. This rather busy road follows the Béthune upstream from Archelles (sixteenth-century manor house) to St-Aubin-le-Cauf (eighteenth-century château), to Osmoy-St-Valéry (La Valouine, a seventeenth-century manor house). None of these, sadly, is open. So with a glance across the valley to Bures-en-Bray, which is a sort of Norman Chesterfield with its curiously warped church spire, head for the plum of them all – Mesnières-en-Bray. It is really worth turning off, in fact, in Bures and heading for Fresles, in order to approach Mesnières from the most impressive angle. Just over the level crossing is the entrance of what has been since 1848 a school, the Institution St-Joseph, run by the Fathers of the Holy Spirit. An imposing stairway leads to the *cour d'honneur*, flanked by robust towers. This Renaissance château is open for guided tours on Saturday and Sunday afternoons only from mid-April to the end of October.

After this you could well refresh yourself in Neufchâtel-en-Bray, a largish town 5 kms further on. The *bondon*, a small drum of soft cheese, is its speciality. On one trip through Neufchâtel I noted in my book, 'like anywhere else'. This was not a disparagement; I meant that it has all the delights – a ruined medieval castle ('new' in Henry I's time), a town centre decently rebuilt after the war, a church begun in 1130 but with bits and pieces from all periods up to the sixteenth century, a theatre and a folk art museum – that befit the one-time capital of the *vicomté*.

After Neufchâtel there are at least three possibilities – east to Aumale, on the frontier of Normandy, south-east by the D135 towards Beauvais, or to join the main Gournay-Gisors-Paris road at Forges-les-Eaux. I did not see much sign of *forges* nor of *eaux* here, but it is built on a watershed near the sources of the Epte, the Andelle and the Béthune, and iron-bearing springs well up through the black clay which all round here shows through the Pays de Bray's carapace of chalk. Cardinal Richelieu and Louis XIII brought Anne of Austria, the Queen, here in 1632 to try to end eighteen years of apparent sterility. She took the waters but Louis XIV was not born for a further six years. There is a spa park, but the forges were Gallo-Roman and the town today is more of an agricultural centre.

Gournay, on the Epte, is another frontier town. At Ferrières-en-Bray next door the Gervais establishment churns out thousands of kilos of Petit Suisse cheeses. The happy conjunction in the mid-nineteenth century of a local farmer's wife, a visiting Swiss cheesemaker and Charles Gervais, an entrepreneur from Les Halles in Paris, gave birth to a lasting, thriving business.

The third route to Paris from Dieppe is the forest route, a pleasant drive south as direct as the others but far more wooded. It runs close to the best route south for walkers, the Sentier du Pays de Bray. Motorists should take the D154 to Arques-la-Bataille and up the valley of the Varenne to Torcy. The trees lining both sides of the road are the outliers of the Forêt d'Eawy (pronounced in three syllables, *ee-ah-vi*). Cross the main D915 and keep on the D154; the forest, so beloved of Walter Sickert, is on your left for the next 20 kms. You can branch up into it and find the almost straight *route forestière*, the Allée des Limousins, running roughly south-east. From Saint-Saëns the D38, D41 and D46 lead to the Forêt de Lyons.

In the outskirts of the Forêt just north of the N31 you will find Ry, a large village whose fame is founded entirely on a literary myth. It claims to be the Yonville-l'Abbaye of Gustave Flaubert's novel *Madame Bovary*. When a writer constructs a complete geographical setting for his characters, readers immediately want to know whence came the inspiration, and places that are easily identified seem to enjoy the cachet conferred on them: Casterbridge is Dorchester and Cranford is Knutsford. Dylan Thomas enthusiasts all know that Llaregyb is Laugharne (and a Milk Wood Restaurant and trips round the bay in the *Polly Garter* confirm it). Although Flaubert denied, categorically and more than once, that there was any single Yonville-l'Abbaye, this honour is claimed by Ry and the original Emma Bovary is said to have been Mme Delphine Delamare, the second wife of a doctor once taught by Flaubert's father, head of the Hôtel-Dieu hospital in Rouen. Unfortunately for this theory the origins of *Madame Bovary* can clearly be seen in some of Flaubert's youthful effusions, and the most obvious early treatment of the plot was written in 1837 when Delphine was still a schoolgirl at the Ursulines convent. Flaubert probably got some of his background for *Madame Bovary* from Buchy, 15 kms north of Ry, or from Forges-les-Eaux, but nevertheless it is at Ry that you will buy the postcards, see the Bovary house, the chemist's shop, and indeed the monument to Flaubert. The Bovary Gallery is in a restored cider factory, open weekends and Mondays from Easter to the end of October.

You can also go from the coast to the Forêt de Lyons on foot, taking the GR225 from Puys on the coast to Martin-Eglise, heading straight across the hump of the Forêt d'Arques (do not forget the 1589 monument on the side of the hill) to the Bois de Pimont, Forêt du Croc and the Forêt d'Eawy – it is woodland all the way. After Saint-Saëns, you walk across fields and down lanes south to Buchy where the path heads east to cross the Andelle near the pleasantly named village of Fry. It swings back again into the Forêt de Lyons, near the Château de Vascoeuil, where the historian Michelet lived and wrote (open afternoons April to November and in the mornings also at weekends).

There is also a slow, lorry-free route from Dieppe to Rouen which follows the river Scie. Take the N27 south to Sauqueville, where you should turn off for Longueville. The D13, rather difficult to find on the map, runs clear through to Rouen, via Clères. There are not many places where you can drive freely into the bailey of a deeply moated, eleventh-century feudal castle. I once did this at Longueville-sur-Scie, a beautifully romantic, overgrown ruin sitting above the town. It would be a superb place for a quiet picnic lunch, if you have stopped in Dieppe or Arques to pick up the ingredients – some *charcuterie*, a tomato or two, a Camembert, a *baguette*, fruit, wine and some delicious *pâtisserie* to top it off. To find the castle, take the D149 for Ste-Foy and Torcy-le-Grand. It is signposted and down a lane past the school. Its first owner was Gauthier Giffard, Seigneur de Longueville, who carried the gonfalon for William the Conqueror at Hastings. One of his sons became the Count of Buckingham. Later on it fell to Bertrand du Guesclin (see p.187); then Dunois, the Bastard of Orleans, owned it. Now it belongs to the townsfolk of Longueville, two of whom were quietly scything the hay in the bailey when I drove in.

Continuing up the Scie along the D3 you will come to the busy little town of Auffay whose centre on market day (Friday) is clogged with typical French stalls and farmers in workaday blue arguing in the middle of the road while their mongrels chase each other's tails. A small deviation down the D96 will bring you to the Châteäu de Bosmelet. It is a brick and stone Louis XIII edifice, with the usual indications of nobility – a chapel and a *colombier* (every pigeon house in France had to have a royal warrant). It is impossible to see from the road but, if forewarned, the *châtelaine* will open it to groups from twenty to fifty strong between May and October. The château was knocked about by German soldiers in the 1940s and the ramps for V1 rockets which they were putting up in the grounds were bombed by the Allies, but the Baronne de Bosmelet has done it all up with care.

Further down the D3 Clères would be a good place for a break. It offers a range of attractions – kangaroos, vintage cars and flamingos. A Renaissance château, rebuilt in 1865 in neo-Gothic style, is surrounded by a park in which in 1920 a bird zoo was established – about two thousand birds of over 250 species wander about uncaged. There are a few mammals, too – and quite a lot of *Homo sapiens sapiens*, because it is very convenient for school parties from Rouen, and the size of its car and bus park stretching down the D6 testifies to its popularity.

But my favourite is just next door, in a rather ramshackle corner house opposite the market hall. This is Jackie Pichon's Musée d'Automobiles, open all day, with seventy-five cars dating from 1894 to 1968 and many armoured vehicles from World War II. Pichon is in the Military Vehicles Conservation Group (MVCG) which was so prominent at the fortieth anniversary celebrations of D-Day. Here you can see, squashed together, cluttered, dusty, littered with variegated notices and exhortations, some beautiful, precision-built beasts whose names form a catalogue of French automobile achievement – an 1894 Panhard et Levassor, a 1901 Georges-Richard, a 1901 De Dion Bouton, a 1905 Chenard-Walcker, a 1910 Delage and a 1911 Unic. The collection includes a 1910 Delaunay-Belleville like the one from which President Poincaré inspected the troops in 1914, and others of more recent date, such as a 1962 Facel Vega. It is very appropriate that this little museum should be situated here, because it was near Rouen that in 1884 the first four-wheel car with a four-stroke petrol engine was driven in France, the invention of Edouard Delamare-Deboutteville and Léon Malandin.

From Clères you have the choice of the D3 or D155 to Rouen.

The N27 is the fastest route from Dieppe to Rouen (under an hour), due south and straight as a Roman legionary's spear –

The fortified manor house of Imbleville

but almost totally lacking in interest. You could add to it and still not be too late arriving in Rouen by following the valley of the Saâne. Take the D925 west for about 12 kms to St-Denis-d'Aclon, then turn left on to the D152 and D2. The Saâne is pure enchantment and the so-called 'pearl of the Saâne' is the fortified manor house of Imbleville. It lies athwart the river north of the village and when I first came upon it in the evening sun it seemed to me the most perfect gentleman's habitation I had ever seen. Built in 1491, the fortified court was opened up in 1842. There are towers, polygonal and round, a separate gatehouse with vestigial drawbridge, and the whole ensemble is surrounded by a moat drawn from the Saâne and exquisite formal gardens. It is not open, but no matter – a grass walk leads from the road down the north side and *hoi polloi* can gawp over the hedge at the good fortune of the Comte and Comtesse de Boigne, its present owners.

The final radial road out of Dieppe is the one for those destined for Fécamp or any of the other watering places on the Alabaster Coast. First on the D75 comes Pourville-sur-Mer, a pleasant town with the usual bizarre seaside architecture. There is a good restaurant here – Au Trou Normand – which every guide mentions. The shingle is enormous and difficult to walk over and the cliffs on both sides are sheer. The road swings inland through wooded Varengeville and then drops to Ste-Marguerite-sur-Mer and Quiberville which struck me as noisy and rather rubbishy. St-Aubin was worse, little more than a vast car park behind the sea wall. The next village is an agreeable change: Sotteville-sur-Mer is, in fact, some distance back from the cliff edge, with a charming church and pleasant lanes. You can drive along one of them through green fields to a notch in the cliff from which steps lead down to a shingle beach and, at low tide, interesting patterns of exposed rocks.

Veules-les-Roses is quite a little town and more animated. Roads lead down through trees to a sandy beach. There is a curious church here, and watercress beds. Victor Hugo, returned from exile in Guernsey, spent the last holidays of his life here between 1879 and 1884 at the house of his friend Paul Meurice, overlooking the sea. A miniature Dunkirk took place on these sands in June 1940 when three thousand British and French troops, cut off by the Germans, escaped by sea.

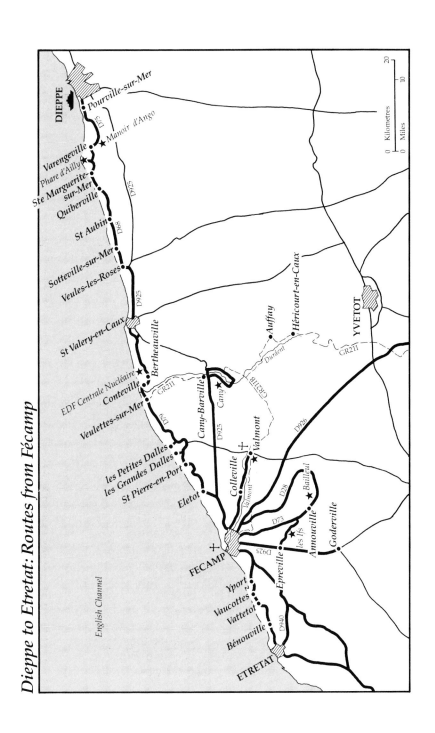

Dieppe to Etretat: Routes from Fécamp

English Channel

DIEPPE
Pourville-sur-Mer
D75
Manoir d'Ango
Varengeville
Phare d'Ailly
Ste Marguerite-sur-Mer
Quiberville
D925
St Aubin
D68
Sotteville-sur-Mer
Veules-les-Roses
D925
St Valery-en-Caux
Bertheauville
EDF Centrale Nucléaire
Conteville
GR211
Veulettes-sur-Mer
D79
Cany-Barville
Cany
les Petites Dalles
les Grandes Dalles
St Pierre-en-Port
D925
Eletot
Valmont
Colleville
Valmont
FECAMP
Yport
Vaucottes
Vattetot
D940
Bénouville
ETRETAT
Epreville
les Ifs
Annouville
Goderville
D925
D73
Bailleul
D28
Durdent
Auffay
Héricourt-en-Caux
GR211
YVETOT
GR211
D926

20
10
Kilometres
0
0
Miles

Bigger and livelier is the port and holiday resort of St-Valéry-en-Caux, a tidal port which cuts deep inland. It has had to be rebuilt from the ruins of 1940, when some three thousand men had to surrender to the Germans on the beach, and on the tops of the flanking cliffs there are monuments to those of the 51st Highland Division who died.

At Conteville Napoleon once planned a port, and the French government, less shy about these things than many other countries, has now built a nuclear power station there. Veulettes-sur-Mer is in the next valley at the mouth of the Durdent, which must be at its least pretty here as it meanders over a flat, midge-ridden plain through the shanties and awful white boxes that line the seafront.

The piece of coast which follows, however, I find particularly attractive. Still there are the high white cliffs riven by long, wooded valleys, each with its sleepy, unspoilt village. The main road to Fécamp undulates and zig-zags along at the heads of the valleys. I dropped first into Les-Petites-Dalles in its pleasant, deep ravine off the main road, leading to another notch in the cliffs. It was peaceful and *raffiné*. There are two or three hotels and interesting cliff walks past fragments of the Germans' old Atlantic Wall. Les-Grandes-Dalles, next, seemed even smaller than Les-Petites. A Z-shaped avenue of trees lined the route to a charming, even quieter place; I am not clear how St-Pierre-en-Port got its name, as it lies on the cliff top. Then, after Eletot, I swung round a corner to find the docks and town of Fécamp spread out before me.

There is a danger in letting subjective judgments, conditioned by mood, weather, time of day, season and the like, sway one's verdict, but I have to say that when I first saw Fécamp I found it cold and grim and northern. I arrived in that dull hour when the shops, abbey and distillery had all just shut, and my first impressions of the narrow, rather mean streets of the old town with their pitted surfaces, unmarked crossroads and poor signposting were not good. There is a big port, for general trade and the cod fishing industry, and the vast, ornate distillery and Musée des Bénédictines, built around the shell of the old abbey, draws big crowds. It has a long history (see page 102) and was important in Norman times – all four Dukes Richard as well as Emma, Edward the Confessor's mother, were born there. The abbey church of the Trinity is undoubtedly the finest church in the Pays de Caux and so makes a visit to Fécamp essential for lovers of architecture. The town offers good facilities for yachtsmen and land-based holidaymakers, too. There is a good length of shingle beach, a casino but not many good hotels. Guy de Maupassant was born and brought up here and later sited Mme Tellier's establishment at Fécamp, though it was in fact in Rouen. The municipal museum has a good general collection, and is strong on local art and furnishings of the eighteenth and nineteenth centuries, faïence, model ships and local Gallo-Roman finds.

Next to Dieppe, Fécamp would be the best place on the Channel coast of Seine-Maritime for a week of interesting tours. Cany, Valmont, and Bailleul are all under 20 kms away and are in the first rank of places to see.

The Château de Cany is due east of Fécamp and only 14 kms south of St-Valéry-en-Caux. Try to come upon Cany from the south, although it may seem awkward. I went to Cany-Barville, took the D268 out of the town and turned right where it joined the D131. That way I saw the château as it was meant to be seen, from the bridge looking down the Durdent, which is very attractive here. To get into the château I had almost to complete the circle by heading up the D131 towards Cany-Barville. It is a beautifully preserved ensemble in the rather austere late Louis XIII style, built between 1640 and 1646 by François Mansart. Everything is highly formal. From lawns with rectilinear paths you cross between two flanking pavilions (one a chapel) and over a moat into a large square court in front of the château. It is open from July to October (except Fridays) during normal opening hours. The interior is specially interesting – at the Revolution it was all placed under distraint by the shrewd owner and so the contents escaped dispersal. Much of what you see consists of original seventeenth- and eighteenth-century paintings, furniture, *boiserie* and Chinese porcelain.

Valmont, 11 kms up the D39 from Fécamp, offers two delights, though not, sadly, for the price of one: château and abbey (see page 105). The château and its grounds have now been converted into a leisure park, so you will probably not be alone in your visit. It is an odd mixture of Norman, late medieval and Renaissance. Château and abbey were founded by the

35

d'Estoutevilles, a redoubtable family whose progenitor, one Estout – which means 'robust' or 'powerful' – was given the task of guarding the approaches to holy Fécamp by Rollo as early as 912. A descendant, Robert, fought at Hastings and features in the Bayeux Tapestry. Another, William, Cardinal-Archbishop of Rouen, took part in Joan of Arc's trial. Louis defended Mont-St-Michel against the English. Later, in the mid sixteenth century, the François I wing was added as part of the new humanism, but the château was soon afterwards abandoned, to languish until the local authorities took it over in 1973. Most of the d'Estoutevilles are buried in the abbey, which is down in the town, across the river and railway, and difficult to find. Just *one* notice in the main street would help. There is a ruined church with a Renaissance apsidal end and some convent buildings from the 1680s. It was suppressed in the Revolution but is now maintained and open daily, except Wednesdays and winter Sundays (the château is open on Saturday and Sunday afternoons in summer and Wednesdays in July and August).

It would be pleasant to walk out to Valmont or Cany, and from Fécamp the GR211B follows the course of the river Valmont to both places. The GR211 starts at Veulettes-sur-Mer and traces the Durdent through Cany to Auffay (not the small town on the Scie, but the site of a closed though visible brick and flint château), then to Héricourt-en-Caux where the British like to eat at the Auberge de la Durdent, to Alleville-Bellefosse of the giant oak, and finally to Ste-Gertrude and Caudebec on the Seine, thus cutting right across the 'nose' of the Caux.

For Bailleul you could take the D73 out of Fécamp – if you can find it – or, more easily, the D925 Le Havre road, but turn left at Epreville. This road, the D11, goes over a railway bridge by the station at Les-Ifs and in trees on the right you will see a small (closed) château of mixed vintage, mainly Louis XIII. Still on the D11, after Annouville, look out for a lodge gate on the left and a semi-circular car park opposite. This is Bailleul. You should do everything in your power to visit this château, which is set in a park of chestnut trees and rises four-square from the gravel almost totally unaltered since it was built in 1543 by Bertrand de Bailleul. Its situation, its exterior and interior are all of high quality. The façade and rear have some delicate touches but the two sides are severe, blank faces broken only by galleries on the first floor and rows of oval *oeil-de-boeuf* windows, now glazed but perhaps designed as vestigial gunports. It is square in plan and four square pavilions are incorporated at each corner. They have steeply sloping tiled roofs in axe-head style with beautiful contemporary lead figures of Justice, Force, Prudence and Temperance crowning each pavilion. Although the whole edifice has a fortress look it was clearly intended not for defence but as a token of the more settled, spacious times of François I.

The present Marquise and her family live in Paris, except in July and August. They employ a guide of a kind found increasingly often in châteaux these days. Owners take on a widow from the nearby village, sometimes a former nanny or housekeeper, who is trained up to recount the history of the château to visitors. They are a dignified breed of lady, sometimes a mite frosty, and do not take too kindly to interruptions or questions. I was on my own at Bailleul and the lady guide stood at some distance and addressed me as if I were a crowd of thirty, *'Le château était construit en mil cinq cents ...'* The visit included the Salle de Garde, an external gallery, two or three finely furnished bedrooms and the *pièce de résistance* – the two-storey salon in the centre of the house, with its internal gallery. It is a miraculous still life, the cluttered yet elegant eighteenth century caught in amber. Fine Brussels tapestries hang on the walls and here and there a Memling, a Rembrandt and a Hobbema or two. The family, who hailed from Abbeville in the Somme valley, has included many notable members, like Nicolas de Bailleul who became Surintendant des Finances in the 1640s. It is thought to have connections with the Scots Balliol family, who produced two kings of Scotland and the thirteenth-century founder of Balliol College, Oxford.

Your final excursion from Fécamp will take you along the coast to Etretat. The D211 and D11 hug the coast and bring you first to Yport. Like all the small resorts on this coast it clothes both sides of a valley winding down to a shingle beach. The streets are very narrow, many of them *sens unique*, and in summer suffer excruciating jams. I only really saw it because I became trapped up a side street – a delivery van had blocked most of the road and a Dyane had tried to mount the pavement to get round it and had broken down. The only solution was to go off and have lunch. La Croquette, on the way down to the sea, looked pleasant for a modest snack. Les Embruns, on the attenuated front, looked grander. I chose the nearby La Sirène, one of the Logis de France chain, principally because I could see a free table overlooking the sea. The patron, Bertrand Tauvel, offers good value for money. Yport is a pleasant, quiet resort, very 'north France' – plenty of flint and brick, including its modern church.

I drove round many wooded hairpin bends to Vaucottes – neat and private-looking and at the end of a spur road leading down to the tiniest of turning circles overlooking shingle; then to Vattetot-sur-Mer, a pretty, leafy, rather smart village on the cliff top. And so I arrived in Etretat, the northernmost point of my circuit from Le Havre (see p. 75). It is not possible, thankfully, to arrive in this jewel of a place very easily, so it retains its peaceful, end-of-the-line air. The nineteenth-century writer Alphonse Karr once said, 'If I had to show a friend the sea for the first time I would choose to do so at Etretat.'

2 Le Havre and the Seine Valley

The Côte Fleurie and the Pays d'Auge

Modern Le Havre is first and foremost a port and commercial centre, though it began life as a naval base. François I built it up to replace the old harbour of Harfleur at the mouth of the Seine where Henry V had landed his men in 1415 before Agincourt. It was called Franciscopolis, but thankfully that name proved too much for Norman tongues to manage – it became known simply as 'The Harbour' and still is. From here in 1545 François prepared to launch his assault on Henry VIII's fleet in Portsmouth. It was during the course of the ensuing skirmish that the accidental sinking of the *Mary Rose* – so successfully raised in 1983 – occurred.

While the English have been reminding themselves of this rather shame-making mishap, in which Sir George Carew's flagship turned turtle in fair weather in full view of the king, nobody has recalled, least of all the French, that almost the same thing happened to François I before his fleet, an armada of 225 vessels, left Le Havre. On 6 July 1545 François dined with his admiral, Claude d'Annebault, on the flagship, the *Carraquon* – just as Henry was to do aboard the *Henri Grace à Dieu* with his admiral twelve days later. While François went on shore and stood watching his fleet weigh anchor, disaster struck the *Carraquon*. Fire spread from the galley and could not be extinguished. The admiral got away just before the powder store blew up and the whole ship foundered. So somewhere off Le Havre is another *Mary Rose*, but its remains are probably charred and long dispersed by the tide. It was just not d'Annebault's day, for he transferred to another carrack which promptly grounded near Honfleur. The mouth of the Seine is treacherous, which is why today it is one of the best dredged and marked of channels.

Incoming Townsend Thoresen ferries berth near the city centre at the quay once used by British Rail vessels. Car-drivers tend to ignore Le Havre and follow the beckoning signs out of the city to the Tancarville bridge, Rouen and Paris. This is a pity, for Le Havre – France's second port after Marseilles – deserves at least a few moments of a visitor's time.

Europe's worst damaged port in 1945, it had to be completely rebuilt, and Auguste Perret, who taught Le Corbusier, presided over its rebirth in the last eight years of his life. The old city, designed in the sixteenth century by an Italian, Bellarmato, was on a grid-iron pattern and so is Perret's, though on a grander scale. His streets are wide and windswept with blocks of re-inforced concrete well set back. This sounds Orwellian and cheerless and, depending on the weather and your mood, you may find it so. But it is a city of people – the top parts of the concrete cubes are all lived in – and it has animated shops, restaurants and hotels. Do not expect to find them in the same profusion as in older French cities, however. Le Havre is built on generous lines and you should make your tour by car. I recall the difficulty I had, going ashore from a yacht, in finding a *boulangerie* among the identical-seeming blocks behind the Boulevard Clemenceau.

It was while on this bread run that I discovered the remarkable church of St-Joseph. Conical, like Liverpool's Catholic cathedral, it points a defiant finger to heaven, is lit by a myriad pieces of stained glass and has a central altar. You cannot fail to notice it. It is on the Boulevard François I but early arrivals by ferry should note that the church does not open until ten.

If you have come by an overnight boat you will find that between half-past seven and eight the streets are marvellously empty, the light clear and the vistas quite imposing. Turn into the tree-lined Avenue Foch, a fine, cobbled boulevard angled by Perret so that it looks symbolically out to sea through the Porte Océane. Inland, it leads to the vast Place de l'Hôtel de Ville. Six ten-storey towers spring from the three-storey buildings that line its sides. It is all very symmetrical, Scandinavian and predictable, but it has power. To the south, Place Gambetta and Place Général de Gaulle overlook the Bassin du Commerce, now given over to pleasure craft. These squares have a striking war memorial and some very futuristic buildings in the Espace Oscar Niemeyer where conferences, concerts and plays take place. Further south still, overlooking the harbour, is the excellent André Malraux Fine Arts Museum. Local talent features strongly here – the Fauvist Raoul Dufy, who was an *Havrais*, and Eugène Boudin, born in Honfleur across the water, who fathered the Impressionist movement. His pupil Monet, together with Jongkind, Pissarro, Renoir and Sisley, have many paintings hanging here, though not necessarily their best. As you look across the Seine from the Fort de Ste-Adresse above the city you can see why it was that Impressionism began here in this misty, luminous world of water, sandbanks and distant, smudgy coastline. Monet would have been just as happy with today's dawn view of orange flame flaring from the silver pipes of the petro-chemical installations towards Honfleur.

But Le Havre is not just modern architecture, commerce and brute industry. A century ago the Goncourt brothers wrote, 'We went to spend a month sea-bathing at Ste-Adresse near Le Havre', and you could still do so today. Ste-Adresse on its hill is the smart end of the city, where shipping magnates keep an eye on the Bourse and count their francs. The beach is lined with little white boxes, like headstones in a war cemetery, for the *Havrais* to change in and sit outside. The Musée de l'Ancien Havre is situated in a restored seventeenth-century house which somehow escaped the bombings. A plaque outside identifies it as the home from 1676 to 1727 of Méssire Michel Dubocage de Bléville and his son. It is a lucky survivor and stands in the St-Francis district in the heart of dockland. There is some Roman material, but it mainly seeks to trace Le Havre's story from 1517, and particularly its maritime achievements. It has normal opening hours but is closed on Monday and Tuesday.

The sea has long brought prosperity to Le Havre. It began in the days of the American War of Independence when France sustained the revolting colonists with a lively import–export trade. Strong links with the United States have developed. It was to Le Havre that the first transatlantic steamboats came from New York in the mid-nineteenth century and from Le Havre that the last of their line, the *France*, habitually sailed. Ironically it was the American bombardment that destroyed the city in

September 1944, but it was their aid that enabled it to become a working port again by 1950.

But like most people, eager to get out of the industrial murk and into France, I feel a slight sense of relief as I leave Le Havre behind. The traffic heading east on the N182 thins out, and the road runs under the line of white chalk cliffs clothed in the soft deciduous woodland that fringes the northern bank of the Seine for much of its length.

An historically famous old town, Harfleur was once the principal port on the northern shore but now forced inland by siltage and reclamation. There it lies, the scene of Henry V's first continental action – 'Once more unto the breach, dear friends, once more . . .', with the church of St-Martin deep inside the *zone industrielle*, a still extant link with the bloody siege of 1415.

Harfleur is a bit too close to Le Havre to detain anyone for very long, as is Tancarville, though the latter does have three points of interest. The village nestles at the foot of a chalk spur dominated since the tenth century by a castle commanding the Seine. A twelfth-century donjon still stands and there is a ruined Renaissance wing. Various bits of the rather untidy *château féodale* seem now to be privately occupied, but the bailey is open and there is a smart restaurant, the Relais de la Pierre Gante, overlooking the river. The Tancarville canal, which enables barges to travel from the port of Le Havre inland towards Paris without being exposed to hazards of the estuary such as westerly storms, shifting sandbanks and the now much-diminished bore, rejoins the river proper at this point. The constant passage of large freighters heading for Rouen – Russian, Dutch, German and even Chinese – can be observed from the D982 at the point where the estuary ends and the river begins. But looming over all is the stupendous suspension bridge which has put the name of Tancarville securely on the map. Before 1959 there was no bridge below Rouen and laborious ferries linked north and south banks. Now, from the same chalk abutment on which the castle stands, this single span carries traffic at a height of at least 48 m over its 1,400-m overall length to the Marais Vernier and the Plaines d'Eure. Completed in three and a half years with no loss of life, it has cut about 150 kms off the journey from Le Havre to Caen.

Much of the traffic swings on to the D179 link road to the

autoroute (A13) for Rouen and Paris, but on this trip I was looking for an attractive corner in which to base myself to look at this part of Normandy. At the south end of the Tancarville Bridge I turned right. You can double back on yourself and either head for Caen or take the coast road via Honfleur and the Côte Fleurie to Trouville and Deauville. Leaving the flat green polder of the Marais Vernier I was astonished at the sight of an inland lighthouse high on my left, the Pointe de la Roque, on the tip of a spur which, like a prognathous lower jaw, does not quite fit against the upper one at Tancarville. After crossing the river Risle I turned right on to the D312 for Honfleur. Conteville, home of Herluin, William the Conqueror's stepfather, is pleasant and quiet, with a celebrated restaurant, the Auberge Vieux Logis. Berville comes next, optimistically adding *sur-Mer*. The 'sea' here is the Seine, barely a kilometre wide, and the road down to it peters out scruffily amid gipsy caravans and rubbish, rather like the Thames at Canvey Island. Further on, the road becomes a miniature corniche and the attractive ruins of the Abbaye de Grestain lie to its right. Here, in this house founded by her husband Herluin in 1050, are the remains of Arlette, William's mother, her husband and her son, Robert de Mortain.

There is rarely a dissenting voice about Honfleur. When I was there one April I found it magical; the spring weather and the thin out-of-season crowds helped. Its approaches are a bit of a mess, but suddenly there is the Vieux Bassin, the splendid little dock with a backdrop of glorious houses, shops and cafés on three sides. The houses are narrow, attenuated, slate-roofed and slate-hung in places. Honfleur is the port from which sailed the great Norman expeditions of the sixteenth and seventeenth centuries, rivalling Dieppe and preceding Le Havre's days of greatness. Samuel Champlain, not the discoverer (that was Jacques Cartier of St-Malo) but the founder of French Canada, sailed there from Honfleur several times after 1608, as a plaque on the town wall attests. Canada became virtually a Norman colony. To accommodate this growing trade Louis XIV's Norman-born minister, Colbert, built the Vieux Bassin in 1681. Honfleur is still a working port and industrial centre, hence the Bassin de l'Est and the Bassin Carnot which flank the town to the east and the sprawl of factories surrounding it. But the inner core is charming, containing fine old streets with interesting, often rather *luxe*

shops. From the Governor's House, or Lieutenance, and the old
Caen gate, walk up the Rue de Logettes and follow the line of
the Vieux Bassin round.

On the way I stopped for the remarkable old church of Ste-
Catherine. In 1453 after the final defeat of the English in the
Hundred Years' War the townsfolk decided to thank the Lord for
their departure by building a church. Stonemasons were so busy
everywhere that the local shipbuilders turned to the task with
their axes and in the 1480s–90s produced a church made entirely of wood. It is in effect the hulls of two carracks upside
down and side by side. Standing separately above it is a bell-
tower with stays like a ship's mast but protected by slate.

The entry ticket for this bell-tower also admits you to the
Eugène Boudin Museum. Honfleur would make an ideal centre
for a one- or two-week holiday – by no means an original observation – because in the event of wet weather it has three
excellent museums. The Eugène Boudin contains early Impressionist works, most of them painted around Honfleur, while the
Museum of Old Honfleur comprises two in one: the Maritime
Museum in the church of St-Etienne by the Vieux Bassin and
the nearby Folk Art Museum in the former salt warehouses.

My 1909 Baedeker reminds me that before the building of the
Tancarville Bridge Le Havre and Honfleur were linked only by
steamer 'twice or thrice daily in $\frac{1}{2}$ hr'. Eugène-Louis Boudin was
the son of a skipper of one of these mid-nineteenth century
steamers. He became an artist by a series of chances and was
sent off to study in Paris on a grant from the far-sighted burghers
of Le Havre. He ended up as guide and mentor to artists such
as Monet, Jongkind, Courbet and Corot, who first came to the
quiet little port of Honfleur in the 1850s and who founded the
Impressionist school. They tended to gather in the Ferme St-
Siméon of Mère Toutain, whose fields overlooked the Seine from
rising ground just outsde Honfleur and who plied them with
inexpensive fish soups, *moules marinières* and cider. Here they
were enchanted by the quality of the light, the blue skies, the
blossom on the apple trees and the shimmer of the sea. Mère
Toutain's farm is now a pricey and prestigious hotel and restaurant.

I found nowhere in Honfleur very cheap, mainly because
droves of Parisians tend to congregate there at weekends to
gorge themselves on seafood. However, as in other popular parts

The old harbour of Honfleur (Selina Head)

of France, it is possible either to spend a fistful of francs on an excellent, memorable meal, or to find a smaller place not mentioned in any food guide where you will eat almost as well for much less. Serendipity generally helps out here. A dismaying tendency has crept in among French hoteliers, however, to insist that if you lodge with them you must also dine with them: there may be nothing wrong with their menu but it is a little constricting. (There are, of course, no such limitations on where you eat lunch.)

On Whit Sunday and Monday the sea is blessed at Honfleur and a procession carries votive ships to the coast. The Seamen's Festival ends with a mass in front of Notre-Dame-de-Grâce, a strange church of heterogeneous style on a beautiful site above the town. The Conqueror's father founded it, and Champlain and others worshipped there before their great voyages to the New World.

Honfleur has no good bathing beach, and if you want to swim you must drive westwards. An attractive road takes you for 15 kms along the Normandy corniche. It is undulating, narrow and traffic-thronged. Cricquebeuf – a good Viking name – has a fine twelfth-century church. Villerville is pretty and has a sandy beach. But Trouville is the best place, for its fine, pale golden strand. On a brilliantly hot day in April I wandered across the wooden *planches* to find it virtually empty. In 1870 Claude Monet painted two ladies in ankle-length bombazine and cheeky little tip-tilted hats, sitting on wooden chairs and reading *Le Monde* under their parasols. Now you may find superbly tanned *Parisiennes* stretched behind canvas windshields – for this coastline is known for its breezes – wearing only a bikini bottom and a Sony Walkman.

Trouville, like its grander neighbour Deauville, has frequently gained a place in historical footnotes – largely through the attentions of the occasional king or emperor and a great many painters and writers. In 1417 Henry V, bent on the conquest of Normandy, despatched an army to the then small village at the mouth of the Touques. It remained a tiny fishing community until Charles-Louis Mozin exhibited paintings of it at the Paris Salon of 1834. Alexandre Dumas *père* gave it favourable mention and in 1836 Gustave Flaubert spent his first holiday there and fell in love. As wealthy French families established summer villas, hotels, bathing-machines and a casino appeared. The overthrown King Louis-Philippe hid in the Rue des Rosiers before escaping to Honfleur and then England after the 1848 Revolution. Whistler, Courbet, Boudin and Monet were among those who came to paint in the later nineteenth century. The Empress Eugénie, with Napoléon III and their entourage, had often holidayed in Trouville and been painted by Boudin. In 1870, at the time of the Franco-Prussian War, she fled there by coach like Louis-Philippe, and a friend found room for her on a yacht bound for England.

Sea-bathing and the seaside resort may have been invented by the English but the French put it all on canvas, and Trouville is the quintessential artist's beach with its vast white sands, naked children, jetty, shrimp pools and ships on the distant horizon. It is more than that, though. Trouville is L-shaped and the great casino on the corner, where you can not only gamble but eat, see a film or enjoy thalassotherapy, divides it into two. Facing the sea is the quiet beach with its boardwalks, the huge façade of the Trouville Plage Hotel and big houses in tiers behind. Round the corner are the raffish Touques-side restaurants and shops facing Deauville. Trouville is more animated and down-to-earth, and yachtsmen will often walk a good kilometre from their Deauville berths to dine there.

Deauville was a later, conscious development. Under the direction of the Duc de Morny the marshland opposite Trouville was drained, a racecourse built and streets laid out in a grid-iron pattern. Villas proliferated and down the 600-m-long Promenade des Planches some very smart establishments were set up: the Pompeian Baths, the Soleil Bar, the Port Deauville marina (fairly recently) at the eastern end, and acres of tennis courts. Often known as the 21st *arrondissement* of Paris, it glitters in high summer and the season comes to an end with the Grand Prix de Deauville on the last Sunday in August. As a rather sea-stained yachthand I once felt distinctly out of place changing money in the foyer of one of the *luxe* hotels. It is the haunt of both *jeunesse doré* and elderly dowagers with thin ankles taking their tiny long-haired dogs for a walk. But things certainly happen there: it seems to be trying to make up for the featurelessness of its site and its lack of historical roots by organizing a constant round of frenetic activity, cultural, sporting and social.

*   *   *

Beyond Trouville-Deauville, which share a railway station under that name, the Côte Fleurie seems a bit of an anticlimax. Bénerville-sur-Mer and Blonville-sur-Mer certainly suffer by comparison, with their sand-blown promenades and slightly run-down shanties. But Villers-sur-Mer is pretty. The vast villas, which might only be used for three weeks in the year by some Paris industrialist, exhibit a bizarre mix of styles – mock Tudor, Scottish Baronial, ecclesiastical Gothic – often all in the same building.

Next comes Houlgate, which sounds faintly Belgian and is an attractive resort with an extensive beach, good walks eastwards to the Vaches Noires promontory, and a pleasant wooded hinterland. In the town is a small monument to those who set off for England with William the Conqueror in 1066.

The marshalling of his great fleet of perhaps eight hundred ships and army of probably more than seven thousand men actually took place at next-door Dives-sur-Mer. This one-time port on the river Dives is now no longer *sur-Mer* and its seaward end is disfigured by a railway line and copper alloy foundry. But this was William's Portsmouth where for several months before his September D-Day he prepared and trained his men and kept them in order – itself no mean feat. His Tactical HQ was the castle at Bonneville-sur-Touques, inland of Trouville, and the inner side of the surprisingly large fifteenth-century Notre-Dame de Dives is covered with an immense nominal roll of all his principal captains. Among them is the minstrel Taillefer, who asked William's permission to be the first to set foot in England and who rode self-sacrificially to his death on Senlac Hill. By an odd quirk of history his name means 'cutter of iron', and when the tables were turned in 1944 and the Allies landed in Normandy the commander-in-chief was Eisenhower, whose name, in German, also means 'cutter of iron'.

Notre-Dame and its colourful churchyard-cum-garden is a pleasant oasis in a busy town of tiny, traffic-choked streets. The seventeenth-century Hostellerie Guillaume-le-Conquérant at 2 Rue d'Hastings, and the even earlier covered market hall, are worth a look.

Just as Trouville spawned Deauville so in 1860 across the Dives a new seaside resort was created at Cabourg, and the two are now often jointly referred to as Cabourg–Dives. Based on a 4-km-long promenade by a superb beach, the town of Cabourg

fans out protractor-like in a series of radiating streets linked by
two concentric inner ring roads. Ornate, toytown houses sit behind the shade of trees. This is a select, if somewhat faded,
watering place: no traffic roars along the seafront Promenade
Marcel Proust, formerly the Promenade des Anglais. Proust frequently refreshed himself at the Grand Hôtel in the centre, as he
did at Trouville, and used both places as models for his 'Balbec'.
Most of *A la Recherche du temps perdu* and *A l'Ombre des
jeunes filles en fleurs* was derived here.

On the way from Tancarville to Cabourg you will have crossed
the Risle, the Touques, the Dives and a number of lesser streams,
and by no means all the delights of this area lie along the coast.
All the resorts described so far are backed by countryside full of
charm and interest. You are in the rich Pays d'Auge here, and it
merits a good look.

South-east of Dives the pretty castle at Cricqueville-en-Auge,
completed in 1584 in stone and brick, can be seen but not
visited. Almost all the villages hereabouts have the suffix *en-
Auge* because this is the Vallée d'Auge, the home of the celebrated *poulet vallée d'Auge* – chicken in a thick sauce of cream
and Calvados. You might try to find this delicious dish at
Beuvron-en-Auge, just to the south, at the Pavé d'Auge or the
Boule d'Or. Afterwards climb up to Clermont-en-Auge and walk
it all off while enjoying the excellent views over the Dives valley.
Not far away in a south-easterly direction is the former Cistercian monastery of Le Val Richer, where Thomas à Becket was
exiled for six years. Bought and restored by the historian Guizot,
who lived there from time to time until his death in 1874, it is
kept just as he left it, but can only be visited by applying in
advance.

This whole area, which has always been prosperous, is thick
with châteaux and manor houses. On the Michelin map the symbol for a château, a solid black rectangle with projecting towers
at each corner, is everywhere. One of the best is the Italian-style
Château de Canon, built in 1764 and set in beautiful parkland
west of the Dives. Sadly, there is no visiting except in groups
with prior permission. From Beuvron-en-Auge I did a leisurely
château-crawl across the Dorette and up the Vie, a gentle tributary of the Dives, and looked at Victot and Crèvecoeur-en-Auge
where there is a group of castle buildings (eleventh to sixteenth

centuries) housing a museum of Norman architecture and the Schlumberger Museum devoted to – of all things – the search for oil (to pour through those machicolations?). It is open afternoons only, April to September, except Wednesdays. Next came two extremely beautiful moated manors – Grandchamp-le-Château and Coupesarte. This took me south-west towards Livarot, where I imagined that I could smell the pungent, orange-coated cheese produced there.

Livarot is a good centre for cheese enthusiasts – Camembert is to the south and Pont l'Evêque to the north. There are pleasant tours round about. To the east, along the D4 towards Caen, is St-Pierre-sur-Dives. It has a fine old abbey church whose first curé was the martyr St Wambert, killed by the Normans in 872. It also has a superb medieval market hall: of thirteenth-century date, it was sadly destroyed in 1944, but has been faithfully restored down to the last chestnut peg. As you head west the pleasant view of the upper Dives valley is marred by a giant factory where cheese boxes for the whole region are made. Four kilometres south of St-Pierre at Vendeuvre is a château in whose orangery will be found a museum of miniature furniture, open every afternoon from May to the end of August.

Back in Livarot there is another attractive drive south via the D579 to Vimoutiers. On the way you pass through Ste-Foy-de-Montgommery and near it is St-Germain-de-Montgommery. Never mind the spelling – this is the family seat of the British Field-Marshal Viscount Montgomery. In a curious way Monty's Norman name has been re-imported, for what was once Colleville-sur-Orne, near Ouistreham, became Colleville-Mont-gomery after 1944. Vimoutiers is a neat, modern-looking place, considerably rebuilt since the war and with evident civic pride. It is of obvious interest for gastronomes, being the centre of a region that produces the best Calvados in Normandy, although oddly it is just outside the department which shares its name; and the statue of Mme Harel, the inventor of Camembert, was put up – by four hundred American cheesemakers from Van Wert, Ohio – next to Vimoutiers' rather ugly church. The cheese is made here and every Easter week there is a fair.

There are ten classified regions where the excellent apple brandy is distilled, but the *appellation contrôlée* stuff is the Cal-vados du Pays d'Auge. A *digestif*, it is best employed to fill *le trou normand*, the gap between courses at lunch or dinner,

The Dives Valley: Pays d'Auge

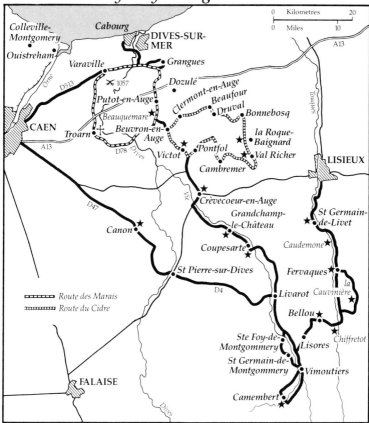

when it is said to revive the jaded palate and encourage the loaded stomach to further activity. The Chevaliers du Trou Normand, a gastronomic society, hold their meetings at Vimoutiers.

Camembert, the soft milky cheese produced in flat cylinders with an edible white rind, evolved in the late eighteenth century at Marie Harel's farm 5 kms south of Vimoutiers. The process sounds easy – milk from which a third of the cream has been skimmed off is heated to 30°C, rennet added and water taken off. The mixture is then ladled into moulds and kept at 25°C. I dare say there are intricacies and refinements.

On the way back to Livarot, turn up the D268 to Lisores where there is a museum devoted to the Argentan-born Cubist painter

Fernand Léger, who died in 1955. A little further on is the charming, half-timbered sixteenth-century manor house at Bellou – the only place I have ever seen with a dovecote wired up for a telephone. Chiffretot and La Cauvinière are similar manors nearby. Fervaques, north-east of Livarot on the D64 as you head north down the Touques valley, is a more substantial sixteenth-century structure of brick and stone. But the best of them is a little way on, nearer Lisieux. St-Germain-de-Livet, which can be visited, is a century earlier but also in a chequerwork of brick and stone, with rooms furnished in varying styles through to early nineteenth-century Louis-Philippe.

Orbec, where Debussy was inspired to write *Jardins dans la pluie*, is further east along the D4 and would make an equally pleasant base. It has been bypassed, so its Rue Grande, with a fine Flamboyant church in the middle of it, is quieter now. Further down, where the main street narrows, is the highly regarded restaurant Au Caneton, where the duck comes, inevitably in this region, with apples.

My youthful memories of Lisieux are of the grey-white dome of a modern basilica and the rather cloying atmosphere, heavy with sentiment and sanctity, of a shrine to the young Alençon girl, St Theresa of the Infant Jesus of Lisieux, who died here in 1897 aged twenty-four and was canonized in 1925. The cult of St Theresa escapes me, but no doubt this is the flawed, uncharitable view of a Protestant. Shops selling that peculiar art form, the religious souvenir – *Cadeaux, Maison du Rosaire* –are ubiquitous but there is much besides to draw the visitor, of whatever faith, to this former cathedral city. Catholics certainly flock there by the thousand, especially from Brittany.

The Gallo-Romans called it Noviomagus and it was the capital of the Lexovii and an important junction of the Roman road system. It was a see in the sixth century and Bishop Arnoult married Henry II and Eleanor of Aquitaine there in 1152 – the marriage that took England into central and south-western France and affected Anglo-French relations for four hundred years and more. The present church of St-Pierre, begun in 1170 and said to be the oldest example of the Gothic style in France, had an amazing escape from the bombardment of 1944. It is a fine building with a Lady Chapel built in the 1430s by Bishop Cauchon, fresh from the trial of Joan of Arc.

The Touques Valley

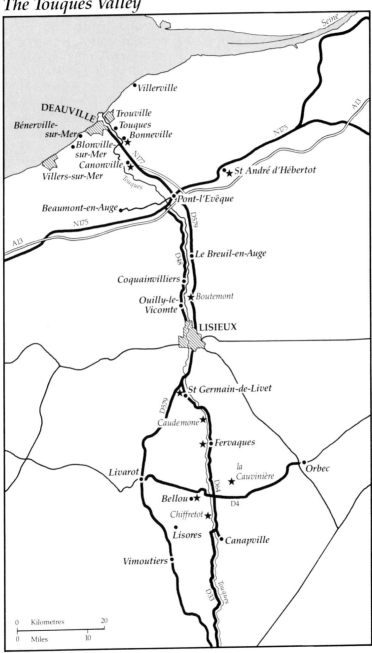

Seine

Villerville

DEAUVILLE
Bénerville-
sur-Mer
Trouville
Touques
Bonneville
Blonville-
sur-Mer
Canonville
Villers-sur-Mer
N177
Touques
N175
A13

St André d'Hébertot

Beaumont-en-Auge
N175
A13
Pont-l'Evêque

D579
Le Breuil-en-Auge

D48
Coquainvilliers
Ouilly-le-
Vicomte
Boutemont

LISIEUX

D579
St Germain-de-Livet
Caudemone
Fervaques
Livarot
la
Cauvinière
Orbec
D64
Bellou
D4
Chiffretot
Lisores
Canapville
Vimoutiers
Touques
D33

| 0 | Kilometres | 20 |
| 0 | Miles | 10 |

Heading north down the Touques valley you have alternatives: the D579, which is the former N179 (it is worth mentioning some former road classifications because quite often the old signs are still there); and the D48. Both are attractive riverside routes, the latter through Ouilly-le-Vicomte with its restored tenth-century church, and the former past the Château de Boutemont. The D48, beyond Ouilly, passes through Coquainvilliers, where, except at weekends, you can see Calvados being made at the Boulard distillery, in the Moulin de la Foulonnerie.

These roads lead to the third Auge cheese town – Pont l'Evêque. In fact, there are several *ponts* here – over the Touques, the Calonne and the Eau d'Yvie – one of which was built by an eleventh-century bishop. Modern bridges help to carry the A13 autoroute which has a complex junction at Pont l'Evêque from which a spur road leads off to Deauville. The cheese, actually made at Le Breuil-en-Auge, is rectangular, soft, strong, golden-coloured and much more venerable than Camembert, being first noted in 1230. The town was another victim of the Liberation, but the Flamboyant Gothic church of St-Michel with its square tower survived, as did a sixteenth-century Dominican convent and the Hôtel de Montpensier and the Hôtel Brilly, which houses the syndicat d'initiative. It is a pretty town, and flat green fields hem it in on all sides. All the villages around have interesting features – such as St-André-d'Hébertot with its beautiful seventeenth- and eighteenth-century château and Beaumont-en-Auge, 6 kms down the D118 to the west, which offers a good view over the Touques valley and two museums – one devoted to the physicist Laplace who was born in the Place de Verdun in 1749.

Returning to Deauville–Trouville by the Touques, you pass Canapville (confusingly the second village of that name in the same valley) where the bishops of Lisieux, until they were suppressed in 1802, kept up a charming manor house. Duke William's castle at Bonneville, and Touques, a port long before the time of Trouville, are worth looking at.

The final valley to be explored is that of the Risle (nearest of the three to the Seine) and its attractive tributary, the Charentonne. It can be reached from Le Havre via Foulbec on the N178, then the D312 to Pont-Audemer – an excellent first-night stopping point from the boat. It is a most attractive town, athwart two arms of the Risle, whose interconnecting channels give it an almost Venetian appeal. It retains the unfinished eleventh-century church of St-Ouen, the Renaissance stained glass in whose side chapels was much admired by both Victor Hugo and Proust, the picturesque but expensive Auberge du Vieux-Puits, and the Cour Canel with its half-timbered houses. The castle overlooking the town to the north saw the first use of cannon in France when du Guesclin besieged it and the fleeing James II, defeated at the battle of the Boyne, lodged in the town on his way to Paris in 1690.

Heading up the east bank of the Risle you go through Corneville, which was the setting of a nineteenth-century operetta and has a carillon to remind us of it. Appeville-Annebault has a château built by the unlucky Admiral Claude d'Annebault, whose flagship was burned under him off Le Havre, and Montfort offers an eleventh-century ruined castle.

The Risle runs between the flat Lieuvin plateau to the west and that of the Roumois to the east. There are many tempting diversions. At Boissy-le-Châtel, 9 kms east of the river off the D124, is the fine Château de Tilly, built of stone lozenges and brick in 1500 and open to the public. About the same distance to the west, off the D137, is the eighteenth-century Château de Launay with its exquisite dovecote. But for those who choose the Risle simply as the route south it would be a pity to miss its most notable glory, the working abbey of Le Bec-Hellouin, a few kilometres east of Launay. It is a stunning survival, made famous by Lanfranc (see p. 103).

Another 6 kms upstream is Brionne, overlooked by a Norman donjon (see p. 117). William the Conqueror besieged the Duke of Burgundy in this castle between 1047 and 1050, during which time he met Lanfranc, the man who was later to serve him so well as Prior of the Abbaye aux Hommes at Caen and as Archbishop of Canterbury.

If you take the D137 out of Brionne for Le Neubourg you will come to Harcourt, a very English-sounding place, and the original home of the English family of that name. There is a twelfth-century feudal castle here much rebuilt and flanked by fourteenth-century towers, open every afternoon except Tuesdays from mid-May to mid-September, and surrounded by an arboretum developed since 1828 by the Académie d'Agriculture de France.

Drive on through the tiny village of Ste-Opportune-du-Bosc, where there is a World War I memorial extraordinary even for the genre: a very warlike, helmeted *poilu*, ringed in by a chain suspended from spent howitzer shells. Signs are already guiding you towards another château which is in the not-to-be-missed category, Le Champ de Bataille. It sounds medieval but is seventeenth-century, built in the Italian manner, mainly in the 1690s, for the Comte de Créqui. It passed by marriage to the Harcourt family and after some vicissitudes to the present Duc d'Harcourt, who has furnished it impeccably and opened it to the public. I found the grounds, one sunny Sunday, taken over very attractively by a *Concours d'Attelage*, and carriages, traps, diligences, cabriolets and their horses were all assembling for the afternoon's driving. What was the *bataille*? A rather murky affair in 935 between the army of Duke William Longsword (commanded by Bernard the Dane, who later built the first castle on the site of Harcourt) and Riouf, Comte de Cotentin.

Le Neubourg, with its wide streets and lovely fat church in the centre, is the nearest town and the heart of a district – the Plaine de Neubourg – which Michelin describes as 'open and monotonous'. I rather like it: the map makes real sense here – all the villages shown on it are visibly around, their squat churches, yew trees and farms seeming to sail along the horizon like misty oil tankers coming up the Channel.

If, on the other hand, you were to take the N138 from Brionne out to the south-west you would come to Bernay on the Charentonne, on the edge of the Pays d'Ouche. Two adjacent buildings encapsulate the story of this cattle-breeding centre: the former abbey, now town hall, and its abbey church. William the Conqueror's grandmother, Duchess Judith of Brittany, founded the abbey in 1013, and the church, now newly restored, was built between 1015 and 1040. Further on up the Charentonne, on the N138, is the smaller town of Broglie, once Chambrais. It is the home of that princely family, Piedmontese in origin, which has produced three Marshals of France, a Nobel prizewinner for physics and numerous statesmen and diplomats.

On the road from Bernay to Conches-en-Ouche (see p.167), the D14/D140, is Beaumesnil, one of the most splendid châteaux in Normandy and a suitable high note on which to end this journey up the Risle. Almost pyramidal in profile, it is a perfect, unusually rich example of the Louis XIII style, built in 1633–40.

The Risle Valley

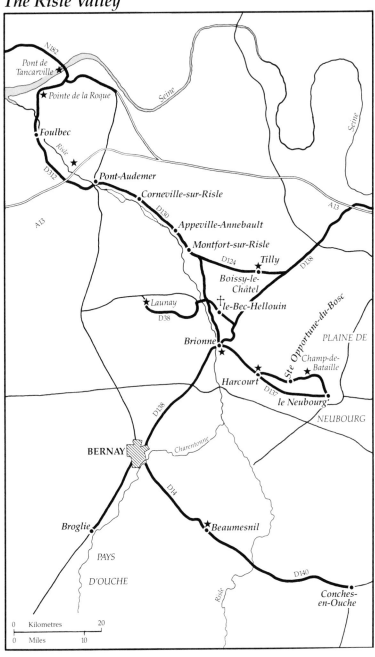

Pont de Tancarville

N182

Seine

Pointe de la Roque

Foulbec

Risle

D312

A13

Pont-Audemer

Corneville-sur-Risle

D130

Appeville-Annebault

Montfort-sur-Risle

D124

Tilly

A13

D138

Boissy-le-Châtel

Launay

le-Bec-Hellouin

D38

Ste Opportune-du-Bosc

Brionne

PLAINE DE

Champ-de-Bataille

Harcourt

D137

le Neubourg

D38

NEUBOURG

BERNAY

Charentonne

D14

Broglie

Beaumesnil

PAYS D'OUCHE

Risle

D140

Conches-en-Ouche

0   Kilometres   20

0   Miles   10

Unhappily it is not open to the public but the grounds are, though not in August – an odd inversion of the norm.

Another delightful way in from Le Havre is by the beautiful Seine valley. There are essentially three routes – up the river itself by boat; by road along the south bank; and by road along the north bank. The last two routes can be tackled by vehicle, by bicycle or on foot. Let me take the river route first.

It is 120 kms from Le Havre to Rouen and if you take careful note of the tides it is an easy passage there and back. When it is high water at Le Havre it is low water at Rouen and vice versa. You can catch the flood tide up the river and make the passage all in one day if you keep motoring at about 6 knots through the water. The water itself is flooding at 5 knots, and so at 11 knots you should cover the distance in eight hours or so. Leave Le Havre six hours before high water and you will be two or three hours up the river before the procession of barges, ocean-going freighters and container ships begins to overtake you and bob you up and down in their wash. You can, of course, stop, and bad weather in the form of fog may force you to, but there are not many moorings and anchorage in the Seine mud is not always very safe. An old hazard, the Seine bore or *mascaret*, is now negligible thanks to dredging and deepening of the channel; the Bar du Mascaret and the Rue du Mascaret in Caudebec are reminders of its former significance.

The 25-km Canal de Tancarville from the Arrière Port at Le Havre to the Tancarville Bridge is a tedious succession of locks and overpasses but the remaining 95 kms is full of interest: first the Tancarville suspension bridge and the Château de Tancarville on its chalk spur to the north. Quillebeuf, once a busy port, lies opposite and is linked by ferry to the smelly and unpleasant industrial complex of Port Jérôme. Then a piece of the old Mulberry harbour from Arromanches is seen to starboard and flat, alluvial fields and the Château d'Etelan amid trees to port. At Villequier, one of the prettiest riverside towns, the *mascaret* can still be treacherous. Larger vessels slow up to change pilots here. Caudebec-en-Caux, equally pretty, would be a good place to stop – perhaps on the way downstream, when it will take you two successive ebb tides to come down, riding out three to four hours of flood in between. Next you will shoot the impressive new Pont de Brotonne and head south-east for the second time.

The Seine Valley

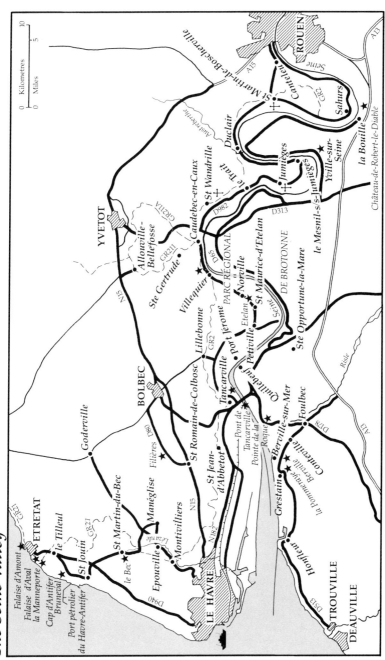

More factories stand opposite La Mailleraye and Le Trait, and there is another smart little inter-departmental ferry at Yainville. Distant views of the great abbey at Jumièges (see p. 100) follow, and another ferry. You are now on the last tight loops before Rouen. A ferry at Yville precedes a long, straight run north to Duclair. Turning south again, you will pass the Abbaye de St-Martin-de-Boscherville. La Bouille, with its much-favoured restaurants, lies below the picturesque ruins of the Château de Robert-le-Diable. Then you are on the final run past the Forêt de Roumare to Rouen – the port side beautifully wooded, the starboard a filthy agglomeration of factories and oil refineries. At Croisset, where the port of Rouen begins, you might just make out the dingy, grey stone pavilion which is all that is left of the estate where Gustave Flaubert lived and wrote.

Now the southern road route. This would be a very pleasant cycle ride – the Seine only drops 16 m between Vernon on the Normandy–Ile de France boundary and the sea, and that is over 100 kms as the crow flies.

There is also excellent walking in the valley. The long-distance footpath GR23 runs from the Tancarville Bridge, round the edge of the Marais Vernier into the Forêt de Brotonne, which it crosses from west to east to strike the Seine again opposite Port Jumièges. It follows the south bank for a while and then cuts off the next meander by running down the southern edge of the Forêt de Mauny to La Bouille. This could take you three days. A *variant*, GR23A, crosses by ferry to Jumièges to join GR2. These routes are marked on the Michelin 1:200,000 series, Sheet 55, but the topographical guides published by the FFRP–CNSGR (see bibliography) are more detailed. Lovers of wildlife should note that much of the lower Seine is now within the Parc Naturel Régional de Brotonne, which, though only a fifth of the size of the Normandy–Maine park, preserves much of architectural and natural history interest. The Tancarville Bridge carries you from Le Havre straight into the park, to the Marais Vernier, an area of drained marshland full of undisturbed flora and fauna. You can see from the bridge that this fen is round and that its southern half is flanked by a steep, semi-circular chalk cliff. The ends of this cliff, each with a lighthouse on its tip, protrude like horns towards the Seine itself. The Marais Vernier is a former bend in the Seine, filled with alluvium and since the early seventeenth century progressively drained. Henri IV brought in the Dutch who constructed the Digue des Hollandais along the diameter of the circle. Groups wanting to explore its wild life more closely can spend a day in the Réserve Naturelle des Mannevilles, clumping around in wellington boots with a biologist. Enquire from the Parc Naturel Régional de Brotonne, 2 Rond Point Marbec, 76580 Le Trait. Guided tours leave from the Place de l'Église in Ste-Opportune-la-Mare.

For motorists there are pleasant, quiet roads along the southern bank. Along the way they have rather little of intrinsic interest in themselves but they offer views across to the excitements on the northern side. Quillebeuf would be your starting point. Incoming Vikings built a port here (the '-beuf' suffix is nothing to do with cattle but means a *buth* or booth – a small building). It remained a whaling port until after the Revolution – in the story of which it merits a footnote, for the *Télémaque* is thought to have sunk just offshore in 1790 with the French crown jewels on board. Follow the road along the river bank, turning always to the left. Aizier, with its Romanesque church, is on the edge of the Forêt de Brotonne. The D95 and D65 bring you to Vatteville, where there is an old mill and some fine glass in the church. Beyond the Pont de Brotonne is La Mailleraye, and across the Seine some fine views of Jumièges. Here you have to take the busy D313 inland before finding a by-road to Yville, where there is a good eighteenth-century château. Follow the river line until Duclair is opposite, then you must cross the plateau by the D64 to Bardouville before dropping down to the water's edge again. From there to La Bouille is a long stretch where you feel very much a part of the river's life. Navigation lights are built into the side of the road and on a dark afternoon one December I watched Chinese and Russian cargo ships follow each other up the home stretch, the Chinese, a long way from Qingdao, lining the bridge deck in amazement at the rows of smart restaurants and houses in La Bouille. This village, linked by *vedette* to Rouen, makes a quiet, civilized hideaway from which forays to the busy city can be made.

The northern bank offers more life and interest and it, too, can be walked. The GR2, the Sentier de la Seine, runs from Le Havre to Les Andelys. For fit medievalists it would make a good pilgrimage route. From Montivilliers it skirts Harfleur, goes through

St-Jean d'Abbetot to Tancarville, Lillebonne, Villequier, Caudebec, St-Wandrille and Duclair, then from St-Martin-de-
Boscherville through the Forêt de Roumare to Sahurs, where it
takes you by ferry over to La Bouille and Elbeuf and rejoins the
northern bank, having by-passed Rouen.

I have in fact followed most of this route by car as well. It is
10 kms from Tancarville to Lillebonne, which lies in a valley set
back from the Seine. This is an ancient port, the Roman Julio-
bona, chief town of the Caletes (from which derives Caux, the
name of the region) in Roman days at the end of a spur road
from Paris and Rouen. The familiar notice on the outskirts of the
town gives you the necessary information – *Théâtre Antique, Donjon de XIIIe s., Eglise de XVIe s.* The Roman theatre, from the
first and second centuries, is the biggest in northern France.
Overgrown with grass, it is not exactly Arles, but much masonry
remains. It is still sometimes used for theatrical performances
and is so visible from the road past the hôtel de ville that one
need not ask for the key to go in. The town remained prominent
into Norman times, and William the Conqueror met his barons
here in 1066 to persuade them of the rightfulness of his proposed invasion of England. Finding one's way into the castle is
not easy – the entrance is through a small door in the Rue
Césarine on its northern side – but there is a tall, circular donjon,
another tower and walls, all of thirteenth-century date. The
municipal museum – next to the syndicat d'initiative in the Jardin Jean Rostand, which laps the castle's southern side – has
a display of art, local history and archeology, and is open in the
afternoons.

The road eastwards fringes flat land, silted up since Roman
times, on which the vast Port Jérôme complex now stands. Here
marshalling yards run alongside oil refineries and a forest of
silver smokestacks and giant alembics. Thread your way quickly
through Petiville to Vieux Port at the Seine's edge. The jetty is
rotted and *bacs inter-départmentaux* no longer call. Continue to
St-Maurice d'Etelan where beyond, hidden by trees, is one of
the least known of the châteaux of Seine-Maritime. Etelan merits
only a line in most guidebooks, possibly because it is so difficult
to get to see. It is a good example of how some planning is
required on any château-trail. It is open only for a month and a
half, not in the mornings and not Tuesdays, so the odds are
stacked against the chance traveller as he bowls along. Built in

1494 in Flamboyant Gothic by Louis Picart, its ground floor walls are stone, the first floor in striking stripes of stone and brick. It has had many owners and was long abandoned after being damaged in 1940. Restoration, begun in 1978, goes on. To see it, on one of those forty afternoons in the year, would put you distinctly one up.

From Norville an attractive road leads into Villequier. Two families and a tragedy that befell them have made this charming little town memorable. The Vacqueries, shipbuilders from Le Havre, had a fine house on the waterfront. Their son Charles married the poet Victor Hugo's daughter Léopoldine in 1843. Six months later the young couple were rowing on the Seine with two relatives when the *mascaret*, sweeping upriver, drowned them all. They are buried in the local cemetery, and the house of the writer Auguste Vacquerie is now the Victor Hugo Museum, whose family furniture, paintings, drawings and letters offer a tasteful evocation of the mid-nineteenth century. Peering into a glass case I saw that Victor Hugo in a crabbed and slanting hand had made the not really very profound but much quoted observation, 'Normandy is to Italy as an apple is to an orange.'

Caudebec-en-Caux, much bigger, is in a natural bowl overlooking the Forêt de Brotonne, and although almost entirely rebuilt after a fire in 1940 is deservedly one of the most frequently visited places in the lower Seine valley: Turner painted it from a hill to the north. The fire destroyed all but three old houses and the magnificent church of Notre-Dame. Henri IV called this church 'the most beautiful chapel in my kingdom': it is a glorious piece of Flamboyant Gothic with a priceless organ, stunning stained glass and a remarkable hanging keystone. It is not in many religious houses that I make a close inspection of all the side chapels and every window, but in the aisles and ambulatory of Notre-Dame there are nineteen chapels and all but one or two are interesting.

Caudebec would make a good base for motorist or walker. The GR211 and 211A climb up from the Seine into the Pays de Caux to the north, passing immediately through the pretty village of Ste-Gertrude with its fine, upstanding Flamboyant Gothic church, and the Forêt du Trait-Maulévrier behind. A break could be made at the restaurant – Au Rendez-vous des Chasseurs.

63

A new but harmonious addition to the landscape is the Pont de Brotonne, its slender green carriageway hung from a series of parallel golden rods like harpstrings. Just before passing the point where it leaps out from the chalk escarpment a striking stone and concrete monument flanks the road like a billboard. It is rather arcanely called 'Those of the Latham 47', which I take to be the kind of seaplane in which six men, Roald Amundsen among them, were lost in a bid to reach the North Pole in 1928. They flew off from the Seine at Caudebec to Bergen and Tromso and then just disappeared.

From Caudebec what the signs call *Le Circuit des Abbayes* is within easy reach. Just up a valley from the Seine is the fine Abbaye de St-Wandrille (see p. 100). Oddly, a local church is more prominently advertised than the abbey, but if you drive into the village you will see an enormous stone entrance gate (built by the Marquess of Stacpoole in the last century) under a thickly spreading tree. Park near here, walk down a side road, and look for a fifteenth-century doorway. Inside is the vast Porter's Lodge from which guided tours depart three times a day. Note that the cloisters are only open to men. I heard mass sung in the church, rather quaveringly, by predominantly old men. The church is a fifteenth-century tithe barn transplanted ledge, stud and batten, from La Neuville-du-Bosc in 1969. Do not forget the ancient chapel of St-Saturnin, a tenth-century oratory just outside the abbey precincts.

The Seine brings you back to the twentieth century with a jolt, for St-Wandrille today is an international port. Push on through Le Trait to Yainville, a modern little town which was interesting for me for what it does not have – that is to say, no water running through it. It is built in a dry valley bed and is a rare example of something called river capture. The Ste-Austreberthe tributary used to run into the Seine through Yainville, but the Seine captured it and it now comes in upstream at Duclair.

Turn right in Yainville for Jumièges and you will be able to follow the course of the Seine's first great meander. Here the river is truly serpentine. Indeed, the Roman name for it, Sequana, is said to stem from the Celtic *squan*, meaning to curve. The towers of Jumièges are easily seen from every approach. It is a glorious ruin (see p. 100) and for today's tourist a DIY abbey – no guided tours unless requested. It belongs to the state and has a well-stocked, not too commercial souvenir shop. The abbey church is almost entirely roofless, but much masonry survives, some of it dizzily erect and beetling. The undersides of the Romanesque arches in the nave even retain some paint. I compared it with St-Wandrille – a working abbey with occasional guided tours; somehow Jumièges evokes more of the atmosphere of monastic life. One can easily imagine monks shuffling along the triforium, now exposed and grass-grown.

There is a longer Seine-side route via Port Jumièges and Conihout, with its string of detached smallholdings each hiding in its orchard, but I prefer the D65 straight to Le Mesnil-sous-Jumièges. On the way you can see the thirteenth-century manor house where Agnes Sorel, mistress of Charles VII, died. There is a *bac* here which leaves Yville every hour on the hour, and returns from Le Mesnil on the half-hour. The crossing only takes three or four minutes, so the *bac* man has a nice life, with plenty of time to sit in his glass box and read *Paris-Normandie* between trips.

From Le Mesnil a very pretty riverside road leads north to Duclair, attractive and yet the sort of town one just passes through as there is nothing of specific interest. The most ravishing stretch of all is the D982 from Duclair to St-Martin-de-Boscherville. It is busy, however, so the driver will be able to enjoy it less than the passengers. Here is a third abbey, St-Georges (see page 100), easily found in the heart of the village. When you enter the abbey, marvellously pure white stone dazzles the eye. There are solid round pillars in orderly rows and neat box-pews in the nave. The church is almost devoid of furnishings or ornament; it would please the most Calvinist spirit. There is a fine organ built in 1627 and silent since the Revolution but now in the process of being restored. In the centre of the sanctuary an incised slate slab with the figure of a bishop is let into the flagstones. A notice announces: 'PIERRE TOMBALE, 16^{e}s'. The English girl in front of me asked her friend, 'Who was Pierre Tombale?' 'Don't be a dope,' he said, 'it means tombstone.'

Rejoin the D982 and after a climb to the plateau cross the Forêt de Roumare and drop down through Canteleu to the big city glimpsed momentarily below. The literary-minded should now go on a tiny pilgrimage before Rouen envelops them. At the traffic lights at the foot of the hill turn sharp right and take the broad docks road. After the Canteleu hôtel de ville go slowly (*pavé* and railway lines will see to this) and you will soon come to a drab grey building inside a railed garden. This is the Pavillon Flaubert at Croisset where from 1844 to 1880 he worked on *Madame Bovary, Salammbô* and other novels under the watchful eye of his mother and friends. The rather sad little shrine, surrounded by factories and racing traffic, is open at normal hours except on Thursdays. One of my perennial problems in Rouen is how to stop somewhere in it before coming out at the other end and heading for Paris. I once came swooping down the hill from the Forêt de Roumare (beautiful, fleeting panorama over the river) on the zig-zag D982, at the bottom of which the road is joined by several others heading into the city. Each time I saw a turning marked *'Centre Ville'* I was blocked off by fast-moving neighbours and could not get to it. This vital throughway now runs alongside the Seine and is doubtless a boon to the Paris-bound. At the eastern end of the city I managed to swing off into a normal road system where I map-read myself into the right area and then, more by good luck, fetched up in the ideal street – Rue Martainville – almost in the shade of the church of St-Maclou, which is a good place to start a tour.

Any exploration of a city such as Rouen will be governed by the length of time available. What follows are the bare bones only, fit for a two- or three-day visit – the minimum. Given a week – and Rouen needs and deserves the fuller treatment – a much more thorough study is possible. Victor Hugo set the pattern for a simple tour of Rouen as early as 1835: *'13 août – Cathédrale, St Ouen; 14 août – Hôtel de Bourgtheroulde, Palais de Justice, St-Maclou, maisons, fontaines.'* You must add to these the Place du Vieux Marché and the Gros Horloge to complete the most basic itinerary.

The Rue Martainville contains many fine half-timbered houses, and there are over seven hundred of them in the entire city. The bombing of 1944 blew away a lot of their wattle and daub, lath and plaster, but the timber frames generally withstood the blast and have now been carefully walled up again. Next door to an antiquarian bookshop at Nos 184–6 there is an archway, through which you will find some cloisters – the Aître St-Maclou. These are not true cloisters but a medieval charnel house built in 1526–33 to house plague dead. They were buried in the rectangular centre, and to make room for succeeding genera-

Jumièges Abbey

tions earlier skeletons were disinterred and the bones stacked in the houses around. I loved the grim wooden frieze with skulls, bones and gravediggers' tackle carved in low relief. This rare survival functioned until the 1780s, but nowadays colourfully adorned students bustle in and out with their canvases – it is the Ecole des Beaux-Arts.

The pedestrian precinct begins as you approach the church of St-Maclou along its north side. Note the fountain on the north-west corner, which outdoes Brussels – not just one Mannequin Pis, but two. Dedicated to the Welshman who preached in Brittany (St Malo, in fact), the church was built between 1437 and 1521 and is a pre-eminent example of Flamboyant Gothic. Yet, surprisingly, much of it was still being built long after Cardinal Georges d'Amboise had introduced Renaissance forms to France. The west front is amazingly decorative and the wooden panels on the doors of the central porch are examples of later Renaissance work. War damage is still being repaired forty years on, so not all the interior may yet be visited.

After admiring the west front from the Place Barthélémy proceed up the pedestrianized Rue Damiette. Running into it is the Rue Eau-de-Robec, built over a stream – the *rot-beck*, or red stream, a rare survival of a Viking placename. A plaque in this street marks the house where one of the city's lesser luminaries, Edouard Jean Adam, was born in 1768. In 1800 he invented a way of drawing spirits from wine, thus contributing marginally to our pleasure.

Looming up is St-Ouen, the second great Rouen church and often mistaken for the cathedral. This, too, has its current disturbances; a vast underground car park was being dug in front of the west doors when I saw it in 1984. Here it is the west front that is dull. You must go through the hôtel de ville into the gardens behind to see the *chevet* and flying buttresses at the east end and medieval architecture at its most magnificent. The interior is well-proportioned, early Gothic work, standing on the site of Rouen's oldest abbey (see p. 98).

From here there are many ways of passing westwards through Old Rouen. You should come to the Rue des Carmes and, leading fom it, the Rue aux Juifs. This will bring you in a short time to the marvellous late Gothic and Renaissance façade of the Palais de Justice where a twelfth-century synagogue was recently unearthed. There is more superb Renaissance work inside, flanking the main court. Roulland le Roux built it all for the Rouen Parlement in the 1520s, and much intricate restoration work has gone on since 1944.

If you continue west down the Rue Rollon you come to the Place du Vieux Marché, where you will be reminded that Joan of Arc has left her unmistakable print on the consciousness of the city. Her story is well known – saviour of France and Charles VII, captured at Compiègne by the Burgundians in 1429, sold to the English, tried for heresy, sentenced to life imprisonment, tricked into resuming male dress, and burnt at the stake on 30 May 1431. You can see the spot in the Place du Vieux Marché where Joan's pyre allegedly stood. I admired the extraordinary modern church with its slate roof in a twisted fishtail shape and some remarkable stained glass conveniently set at eye level. Also in the Place is France's reputedly oldest restaurant – the Hôtel-Restaurant La Couronne at No. 31, Salvador Dali's favourite and still serving top-class food as it has done since 1345.

Just off the south side of the Place is the tiny Rue de la Pie. At No. 9 is an astonishing survival – an early sixteenth-century shop. But the street's main interest lies at No. 4, the house – now a museum – where the great French dramatist Corneille was born in 1606 and lived for most of his life. Turn back, then south into the Rue du Vieux Palais, then left into the Place de la Pucelle. Here is a fine late Gothic and Renaissance building, the Hôtel de Bourgtheroulde. This is the finest of a number of Hôtels in Rouen – d'Etancourt and de Senneville are others – which are, of course, not places to stay but the grand town houses of the Renaissance nobility. This Hôtel was built about 1500 for Guillaume le Roux, a notable Norman financier and Lord of Bourgtheroulde in the Roumois. Appropriately, the Hôtel opens during banking hours.

Return to the Place du Vieux Marché and turn right into the Rue du Gros Horloge. Head east along the line of the main street of Roman Rotomagus and you will come to some of the oldest houses in Rouen. Those that lean storey by storey progressively towards those on the opposite side of the street must pre-date the edict of 1525 which prohibited this practice. Ahead of you is Rouen's most popular feature, the vast clock known as the Gros Horloge, once housed in the belfry that stands by its side. It is worth climbing the belfry, begun in 1389, to see the various bells, such as the Cache-Ribaut which has sounded the curfew at nine every night since 1260, and to enjoy the amazing view from the top. The Gros Horloge itself, built across the street (the better to be seen) in the mid-1520s, is worth inspection too – particularly its underside.

And so, saving the greatest until last, you approach the cathedral from the most advantageous direction. In front of you suddenly is revealed the most monumental façade, a veritable cliff face of intricate stone carving beyond which is one of France's greatest cathedrals. Peter Gunn's book *Normandy* dissects and explains at length the complex composition of this enormous façade. Monet painted it five times, catching it in different lights. Inside, the sheer height is breathtaking, and there is beautiful stained glass, much of which survived 1944.

Turn round north into the Rue St-Romain with its Booksellers' Court and the fifteenth-century Archbishop's Palace, whose wall contains a fragment of the building in which Joan of Arc was condemned to death. Ahead lie St-Maclou and the Rue Martainville where your walk began.

This tour has barely touched on Rouen's great museums – it is often called *La Ville Musée*. These are numerous, extremely important and, of course, demand more time. The tour described above could be expanded to include many of them and a number of other treasures so far unmentioned. From the hôtel de ville, by the abbey church of St-Ouen, you could head just a few yards up the Rue Louis Ricard to find the Lycée Corneille. Not too many schools can list among their Old Boys such a galaxy as Pierre Corneille himself, Robert de la Salle (discoverer of the Mississippi), Gustave Flaubert, Guy de Maupassant, Jean Corot and André Maurois.

Just a little further to the north, past the gendarmerie, is the Museum of Natural History, Ethnography and Prehistory, and next to it the Museum of Seine Maritime History. The greatest of them all, though, is the Fine Arts Museum with its adjacent Musée de Ferronnerie Le Secq des Tourelles (displays of ironwork and old household artefacts in a former Flamboyant Gothic church) which both lie south-east on the Rue Thiers. On the way there, not far from where the Rue Jeanne d'Arc runs into the railway station forecourt, is the Rue du Donjon, with the surviving tower of Philippe Auguste's castle of 1204 in which Joan was imprisoned in 1430.

Some few hundred yards further out to the north-west, up the

Rue St-Gervais, is the ancient church of St-Gervais in whose fourth-century crypt William the Conqueror lay after his death (see p. 112). South of this, and completing the outer circuit of additional sites, you will come to Flaubert's birthplace in the Rue de Lecat, now a rather gloomy house, which is a Museum of the History of Medicine, containing some macabre exhibits.

The opening times and ticket arrangements for these places (some tickets cover two places) can best be discovered by getting a leaflet from the Tourist Office in the Place de la Cathédrale, itself housed in the Hôtel des Généraux – an elegant Renaissance Hôtel (as at Caen) with stone cupids supporting medallions over the door.

Opinions of the two-thousand-year-old city vary. Victor Hugo's first journey there was a kind of pilgrimage: *'Tu sais quelle rage j'ai de voir Rouen'* he wrote to his wife the month before. For John Ruskin, too, it was very important: only three places had had a formative influence upon him, he said – Rouen, Geneva and Pisa. Others, however, have fallen much less under Rouen's spell. It is, and has long been, an industrial city. Spinning and cotton weaving made *Rouennerie* famous worldwide. Velveteen and twill were invented here in 1730. Dyeing, finishing and bleaching complete the production process and, together with the ever-enlarging port, have contributed to the spread of industrial blight – which must have been at its worst when Arthur Young came in 1788: 'This great, ugly, stinking, close and ill-built town,' he wrote, 'full of nothing but dirt and industry.' Before World War II there was a maze of murky slums between the cathedral and the Seine, in which Guy de Maupassant found Mme Tellier's establishment. But the slums have gone and it is easy to ignore the industry, if you wish, as it has tended to gather by the river – which is not attractive just here – and mainly on the south bank. On my visits I have at least been luckier than James Joyce, whose letter to Harriet Shaw Weaver in 1925 included the lines:

> Rouen is the rainiest place getting
> Inside all impermeables, wetting
> Damp marrow in drenched bones.

Although Rouen and the Seine valley and those parts of the Pays d'Auge, Lieuvin and Roumois already described will exert by far the greatest magnetic pull on visitors arriving in Le Havre, there may be some who hope to head for the Pays de Caux itself, either along the line of the N15 to Bolbec or Yvetot or northwards to Etretat and Fécamp.

The N15 to Rouen is straight and fast but, like many *routes nationales*, not a specially pleasant way of enjoying France. Bolbec and Yvetot are both bypassed and the villages between them have somehow been so pushed aside by the impact of the road and the infilling of petrol stations that they have become dull and characterless. It is what lies off the N15 that is of more interest.

Before leaving Le Havre, to the left of the Rue de Verdun, there is the old priory at Graville. This has been a religious site since the eighth century and the eleventh-century fabric, with some additions, is there still, surrounded now by industrial suburbs. A very good museum shows the priory's history, with architectural fragments, statues in stone and polychrome wood, processional crosses, documents and model houses. It is free, and open from Wednesday to Sunday during normal opening hours.

After Harfleur a right turn off the N15 leads to Gonfreville and the Château d'Orcher. An eleventh-century fortress, added to in the eighteenth, it is set in an attractive park with fine views over the estuary from the 90-m-high terrace.

Your instincts now are probably to head for the interior where another, quite different, château awaits. At St-Romain-de-Colbosc turn left at the second set of traffic lights and take the Goderville road. Just past the airport, turn right to Gommerville. Through the village, 200 yards on the left, you will see, peeping through trees at the end of the short drive, the Château de Filières. As at Etelan, you may or may not be lucky enough to find it open on the day you are along this way; the public are admitted on Wednesdays, Saturdays, Sundays and holidays, afternoons only. Its curious mixture of styles is explained by its history. First a medieval fortress, of which only the moat remains; then a modest late sixteenth-century château – the west wing. In the late eighteenth century the Marquis de Mirville planned a spectacular rebuilding. He hired Victor Louis, a celebrated architect, and the work began piecemeal – the elegant new Caen stone slowly replacing the old château from east to west. Only the east wing and the central *corps de logis* was finished when the Revolution halted everything. So now we have two-thirds of a château in the delicate style of Louis XVI and one-third a survival of the Wars of Religion. Inside there is much to savour: décor by Ingres *père*, good eighteenth-century furniture, much *chinoiserie*, and paintings by Fragonard, Nattier, Mignard and Van Loo. The park is by Le Nôtre.

The road ahead, to St-Jean-de-la-Neuville, is narrow and exciting – will you meet head-on that determined-looking, blue-overalled *paysan* at the wheel of his tractor? Soon you will be in Bolbec, a textile town rebuilt after a bad fire in the eighteenth century.

At 7 kms short of Yvetot take a right turn off the N15 for Caudebec. The first village down the D33 is Allouville-Belle-fosse, where an oak tree in the churchyard is claimed by locals to be 1,300 years old, and comes high on the list of Norman oddities. In its hollow trunk two tiny chapels have been built, one above the other. Its bole is certainly 16 m round, and it was in bright green leaf when I climbed the wooden stairs around it to visit the topmost chapel – a simple and rather moving little shrine, an octagon of linenfold panelling with a wall crucifix. I was there very early in the morning and crowds, I suspect, could dim its appeal. There is a Museum of Nature – the wildlife of Normandy – in a former barn nearby.

Yvetot is in the centre of the Caux region and yet somehow drawn more to the Seine valley. Its heart was demolished by the war. The fine white hôtel de ville reminds us of the old Yvetot, while the uncompromisingly modern cylindrical church of St-Pierre represents the new. From medieval times to the Revolution Yvetot was a kind of San Marino, an independent tax haven whose Lord was *'Roi d'Yvetot'*. Guy de Maupassant was sent to boarding school there, it may well have been a model for Gustave Flaubert's Yonville-l'Abbaye, and Victor Hugo wrote some scathing lines about its dreadful inns. But the church is the thing to see: a modern Florentine *duomo*, gasometer-shaped, ferro-concrete and with separate campanile. An elaborate frieze over the main entrance extols freedom and fine stained glass by Max Ingrand can be seen inside.

Finally, some people will wish to travel up the 'nose' of the Caux to Etretat and Fécamp. There are two routes: the first is by Montivilliers and Goderville, and the second, from Ste-Adresse, by the coast. Permutations of the two are possible – and desirable.

Montivilliers is reached from Le Havre through the rather surprising Tunnel Jenner, which is at the top of the Cours de la République and cuts under a cemetery to the Forêt de Montgeon. It is a crowded, rather scruffy, poorly signposted little town of monastic origins, offering a good Romanesque church but little other incentive to stop. At Epouville you turn right for Manéglise, where there is an interesting eleventh-century church. It was only half-past eight in the morning when I was there and the church was locked. Just as I was about to drive off a man in green wellies stopped his mowing machine and told me the key was at a farm. I had already made up my mind to move on but I could hardly ignore his helpful guidance. I was trapped. I drove up the lane to the farm and a little man, who gave the impression of being trouserless, appeared at an upper window. In a while he emerged, clipping on his brown dungarees, a slightly cross-eyed, gnome-like figure with a consumptive cough. He took me across the fresh-cut grass to the church which, though tiny, has two aisles and is quite charming – a good example of a rustic Norman church, dusty, cluttered, full of surprisingly rich features, un-selfconscious. The little sacristan was a friendly, unobtrusive guide; it was a most pleasant encounter.

Cross-country lanes brought me to St-Martin-du-Bec, where the much restored twelfth-century castle of Le Bec, stands against a dark backdrop of trees. The river Lézarde has been diverted to make a moat and two swans provided the necessary touch of class. It is not open, but is easily seen from the road and has a pleasing perfection of form.

I then headed to the coast at St-Jouin where in 1976 the Havre–Antifer oil terminal was built, to the great annoyance of the citizens of Brest who wanted it for themselves, to accommodate supertankers. Beyond St-Jouin is a belvedere from which the port installations (surprisingly few to the untrained eye) can be seen. There is a Salle d'Information for committed energy enthusiasts.

Just a little way to the north is a rather silent little village in a chine between the cliffs – Bruneval. It was the scene of a raid in 1942 when the RAF dropped paratroopers to capture a German radar station. This was the first successful, medium-scale Allied landing in occupied France, and if you climb the Escalier Charles de Gaulle you will come, half-way up the cliff, to a monument which includes a statement by Lord Mountbatten, head of Combined Operations. Notice also, let into the steps, the Mauthausen stone, a piece of granite from the concentration camp to which so many French Resistance fighters were deported.

Now you are on the edge of Etretat – a delightful town which serves as the terminus of routes northwards from Le Havre. The fields here run lush and green right up to the edge of the vertical chalk cliffs that have made the area so famous. This is good country for walkers and, like Britain's long-distance coastal paths in the west of England, the GR21 follows the attractive Lézarde valley north out of Le Havre to the cliff edge at Etretat and along it, just above the much-photographed Manneporte natural arch and the Falaise d'Aval, with its more slender 'flying buttress' and isolated sugarloaf. Leave the D940 at Le Tilleul, at the decaying gates of the imposing-looking eighteenth-century Château de Fréfossé, now a holiday home for British children which advertises 'French without tears', and follow the path, marked with the usual red and white flashes, to the cliffs. You will then pass between a vertiginous edge and Etretat's beautiful and once fashionable eighteen-hole golfcourse, and come slowly down into the town.

Etretat has a charm which has long attracted visitors. Like almost all resorts between here and Le Tréport it occupies a natural gap in the otherwise continuous chalk cliffs and fills all the vacant space behind the shingle beach. It is the pearl of the Alabaster Coast – if that is not a biological impossibility. Almost everywhere from here to Le Tréport is shingle, so other factors may govern your choice of resort. By all counts Etretat should rate high. It is relatively quiet, yet bright, cheerful and friendly, with good restaurants and hotels. In World War II Etretat was liberated by the 51st Highland Division in September 1944, and the town expresses its gratitude in a plaque on the fine old (reconstructed) Market Hall in the centre. On a cliff top to the east, near another natural arch cut by the sea, the Porte d'Amont, stands an interesting monument to a brave attempt on the transatlantic air crossing in May 1927. Charles Nungesser and François Coli might have been the first to fly east to west in their *Oiseau Blanc*, but disappeared without trace. For lovers of aviation history there is also a museum nearby, open June to mid-September.

Guy de Maupassant spent his childhood in Etretat, Offenbach composed *The Tales of Hoffmann* there, the novelist Alphonse Karr wrote and Victor Hugo sketched. Since A.-J. Noël in 1778 many painters have come here, among them Isabey, Boudin, Monet, Jongkind, Courbet and Matisse. Before you leave Etretat spare some time for the powerful church of Notre-Dame, just off the coast road to Fécamp. It has a fine twelfth-century doorway and in the darkness of its nave, accentuated by the bright sunlight from which I had stepped, I noted the stubby pillars and the Romanesque arches, each in different style. In the centre is an octagonal lantern with eight lancet windows in it. On a calvary back on the sunlit road it said: *'Aime Dieu et va ton chemin'*, and so I did.

3 The Cotentin

Cherbourg and Beyond

Cherbourg can be reached in four and a half hours from Southampton, or in rather less than four from Weymouth. Night sailings take longer, but are of course more comfortable. Yachtsmen, who understand the fickleness of the wind, will resist such notions as an average time, but for the sixty-mile crossing under sail from the Needles or the Nab Tower to Cherbourg, generally blessed with a wind with some north in it, mine has been thirteen hours (based on perhaps a dozen trips).

The crossings have usually been made at night, guided in by the French lighthouses at Cap de la Hague and Barfleur and radio beacons. There was one heart-stopping occasion when a thick fog descended as a friend and I approached the French coast in an old converted lifeboat. The expected sighting of the Cap de la Hague light didn't occur, but we picked up its foghorn and aimed for that instead. Quite suddenly we were right under it, held in the grip of the dreaded Alderney race which runs tight round the Cap de la Hague at up to eight or nine knots. The highly manoeuvrable lifeboat responded, however, and we slid past the black rocks of the Gros du Raz with feet to spare. Terrified, we continued cautiously in a north-easterly direction, hoping to find a harbour before Cherbourg. I knelt at the bows peering into the fog, periodically shouting, 'Rocks! Rocks!' as they loomed up on all sides. Then I distinctly heard the crack of gunfire. We were being shot at! We must have entered a no-go naval zone. It was by the sheerest good fortune that we came upon a ghostly fisherman, alone in his boat, who indicated that there was a harbour just round the next rocky promontory. There was – the smallest one in France, at Port Racine, so small we could not get the lifeboat in it. Thankful to have made landfall without ripping the bottom out of the boat or being picked off by naval marksmen we rowed ashore for a lobster celebration at the Hostellerie L'Orguillère overlooking the harbour. I later learned the shots were a regular form of warning for inshore navigators, alarmingly distorted by the exceptionally thick fog.

The Channel is always busy and one of the constant excitements of the sea approach to Cherbourg is navigating across the path of the shipping lanes. White, green and red lights move eerily across the horizon and in fog engines thrum and horns blare from unseen cargo vessels and tankers. One of the oddest phenomena at night is the light that does not move – most often, a fishing boat hauling in its nets. Sometimes you see what looks like a floating resort hotel with all its lights ablaze drifting silently like a ghost-ship. This will be the night ferry for Cherbourg which, rather than arrive before the dawn, switches off its engines and waits in mid Channel for two or three hours.

The town of Cherbourg gets a universal hard time from the guidebooks; few argue with Baedeker's judgment: 'Comparatively uninteresting'. Nonetheless it is one of the ports at which the British arrive in great numbers, and for those coming in by yacht and intending to sail shortly for the Channel Islands or England, Cherbourg is fun simply because it is France. As it has all the necessary port facilities and offers good value for money it is justifiably one of the most popular harbours. There is an excellent marina with over seven hundred berths, a yacht club and Joseph Ryst's well-known establishment which supplies vessels with duty-free goods. Cheap but sustaining restaurants can be sought out in the narrow streets behind the hôtel de ville, their proprietors quite accustomed to half-starved crews poring over long, hand-written menus, ordering noisily in Franglais and consuming vast quantities of raw plonk with apparent relish. For the longer-term visitor, unless interested in World War II (there is a good war museum) or the painter Jean-François Millet (born 16 kms away at Gruchy in 1814 and well represented in the Musée Thomas Henry), it is difficult to revalue Cherbourg appreciably. Even a merchant-ship enthusiast cannot get very excited now that the transatlantic trade has dwindled with the increase of air traffic; the commercial installations and great terminal buildings stand empty.

It is still a busy cross-Channel port, however, and most visitors arriving by ferry pass through what is perhaps Cherbourg's most astonishing feature without realizing it: the extensive *digue* or breakwater – over 3 kms long – which protects the Great Harbour. Although the town is well sheltered its anchorage is not, and yet the site has a clear strategic value. It was Vauban (Louis XIV's military architect) who in 1686 first saw the importance of the formidable sea defence which now exists. Work did not begin, however, for another hundred years. In 1784 a series of enormous, circular wooden tubs filled with boulders and rubble were sunk, but a storm carried everything away. In the 1830s concrete was used successfully, and Napoléon III's engineers topped the *digue* with forts in 1853. A vast armada could now be marshalled here and Queen Victoria and Prince Albert were the first to see it for themselves. Napoléon III visited the port in August 1858 and inaugurated the new Paris–Cherbourg single-track railway, a considerable work involving almost four hundred bridges and largely carried out by British engineers; he opened the deep-water dock in what is now the military port; he unveiled a statue to his uncle, Napoléon I, whose idea it had been 'to renew at Cherbourg the marvels of Egypt' and finally he received Victoria and Albert on their state visit. A dramatic portrayal of the scene by Jules Noël, a notable Norman painter of seascapes (1815–81), shows Napoléon on board the French flagship *Bretagne* watching the approach of Victoria and Albert in a state barge. The royal party drove up to the Fort du Roule for its panorama – still worth seeing – and there were gun salutes, banquets and speeches. But it did not pass unnoticed that the French navy was there in strength and the two years that followed saw British government defence spending shoot up. Today vessels slipping down the Solent bound for Cherbourg may not know that they are sailing between Palmerston's response to the supposed French threat to Portsmouth naval base – the great drum-shaped forts at Gilkicker and Horse Sand.

For most people arriving in Cherbourg, the open road calls. The hinterland of an arrival port is often a much disregarded area, but the Cotentin has a great deal to offer, and it is anyway more than a manageable day's drive from Paris.

You can head west, east or south. The roads west, the D901 and D45, take you into country more typical of Brittany than of Normandy – the small walled fields of the de la Hague peninsula and the massive west-facing cliffs of the Nez de Jobourg. You can look down on Port Racine in the Anse-St-Martin, its tiny stone arm encircling a tiny corner of the bay. Port Racine, Goury and Omonville-la-Rogue are all within a small enclave that the early invading Vikings captured and walled off. An earthwork called the Hague-Dicke runs across this finger of land, and the whole area behind the Dicke, or dyke, still has a rather ghostly feel. St-Germain, at Querqueville, is one of France's oldest churches. It was built in the tenth century. You will see two towers on a hill overlooking the village, but do not be put off if, when you enter the churchyard, a dull nineteenth-century edifice confronts you. The Chapelle de St-Germain is hidden behind it. Here we are in *'-ville'* country: almost every village has this suffix – Urville, where a British raiding party landed in 1758, and Nacqueville and Vauville with their interesting châteaux.

I can never drive past Omonville without remembering a trip I made from Poole to its little harbour in an old eleven-ton Morecambe Bay prawner. Omonville's stout breakwater protects it well from westerly or northerly weather but leaves it exposed to storms from the east. We dropped anchor and waved to our neighbours, a husband and wife on their yacht *Mousetrap*, then rowed ashore for a meal in the tiny fishing village. It was here that I first tasted the salty subtleties of *moules marinières*, mountains of them, served from a bucket. That night the wind freshened and veered round to the east, and big seas began to pour over the breakwater. It looked bad, but the *Mousetrap* decided to run to Cherbourg, only seven miles away but due east, which meant tacking into the teeth of a Force 6. As the storm increased we began to think we were moving slowly towards an exposed reef in the harbour. Was it our imagination or were we dragging our anchor? And would our single anchor hold, attached to the chain by its ridiculously small shackle? We were the only remaining occupied boat in the harbour.

We maintained an anchor watch, and from time to time fishermen gathered in the brightly lit doorways of the cottages would look over at us. If the anchor lifted, the surge of the waves would have carried us on to the rocks sooner than I could rouse someone to start the engine. The anchor still held at dawn, but during the morning we noticed some fishermen heaving a rowing boat into the huge breakers. Six of them jumped in and frantically dug in the sea with their stubby oars. They painstakingly made for a large mooring buoy, fastened a thick rope round it and then pulled across to us, coming alongside with great skill. Their leader boarded us and made the other end of the

Routes from Cherbourg: The Cotentin

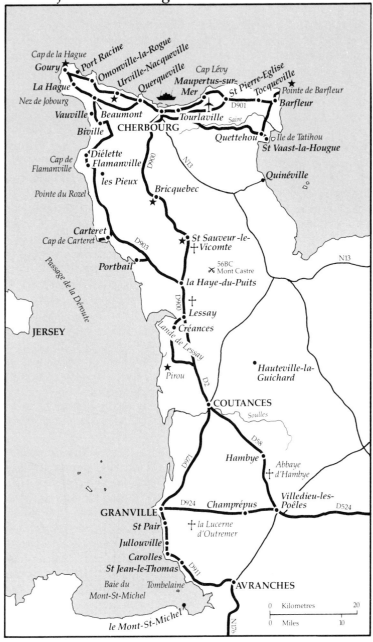

hawser fast round our mainmast. Doubly tethered we could sit out the storm safely. We had experienced one of the finest expressions of the camaraderie of the sea; those fishermen had taken great risks for us. When the storm abated, we went to make our thanks, and there was much backslapping, handshaking and many nips of Calvados. When we moved on to Cherbourg we passed on the way the wreck of the *Mousetrap*, driven up on some rocks. We later heard that her crew of two had perished.

East of Cherbourg the countryside is gentler and by contrast with the west distinctly cheerful. A pleasant route south out of the Cotentin would be via St-Pierre-Eglise, Barfleur, Quettehou and Utah Beach. After Tourlaville, where there is a château now owned by the town of Cherbourg, the road climbs to the airport at Maupertus. Driving east along the D901 towards Barfleur a few wry memories were stirred when I first came to a village called Tocqueville. The château here was bought in later life by Alexis de Tocqueville, the nineteenth-century political scientist and writer, and he is buried in the cemetery. His *L'Ancien régime et la révolution* had once been a set book of mine at Oxford. I did not much love Alexis de Tocqueville, but I certainly admire his château.

Barfleur is a most attractive little port, but not much good for boats with keels because it dries out. Though less forbidding for seafarers than the western tip, this eastern end of the Cotentin still has it dangers. The powerful lights at Cap Lévy and the Pointe de Barfleur keep ships clear of some of them, but when the wind is against the tide the Barfleur race is as nasty as the notorious Alderney one.

In 1692 the exiled James II, anxious to regain the throne of England, was waiting in the Cotentin to be carried back to Britain by Admiral de Tourville (a local man) on Louis XIV's orders. Out in the Channel lay Admiral Russell with ninety ships of William and Mary's navy. Tourville only had half as many but nevertheless attacked, only to be mauled and forced to flee. As with the Spanish Armada of a century before, contrary winds drove many of his ships on to reefs. Fifteen survived and ran for shelter to St-Vaast-la-Hougue, just south of Barfleur, where Russell sent in fireships to complete their destruction. Russell was subsequently ennobled and took Viscount Barfleur as one of his family titles. This was the first of many such titles to use the name of an overseas British victory. Tourville later had his revenge on English and Dutch fleets and was made Marshal of France. His vast statue – worth seeing – still overawes the little village of Tourville-sur-Sienne, north of Coutances.

From St-Vaast-la-Hougue (pronounced 'St Var' and famous for its oysters) historians take the name of the battle – La Hougue or La Hogue. The disaster has left its mark here in the shape of Vauban's defence works on the Ile de Tatihou and the Fort de la Hougue, built, like so many such works, rather superfluously after the defeat they might have averted.

From here on southwards the coastlands are flat and dull. They form part of the story of the Allied invasion of 1944, for this is where the Americans came in, planning to break through to the north and liberate Cherbourg. Return to Cherbourg, then, through Quettehou and up the pretty valley of the Saire, blessed by Michelin maps with a green line along almost its whole length, indicating that it is a *Parcours pittoresque*.

So far I have suggested detours to the north-west and north-east tips of the Cotentin. You could take a day trip from Cherbourg to either one before using the other as a route to the south, thus avoiding the crowded *routes nationales*.

If you are in a hurry take the N13 direct to Valognes, Montebourg and Carentan, all of them almost wholly destroyed in World War II and since rebuilt. The road is Roman and dead straight (see pp. 126–7). Cherbourg was a Roman station called Corallum, and probably not, as the Victorians claimed, Caesaris Burgus, 'Caesar's Fort'.

The other interesting way out of the Cotentin peninsula to the south would be by the Atlantic-facing west coast on the D904 – through Carteret, Coutances, Granville and Avranches. If this roll-call has the ring of English eighteenth-century politics about it, it is because John, Lord Carteret, who succeeded Walpole in the 1740s, became 1st Earl Granville. Many Cotentin families came across with the Conqueror and their names, often (like Percy) the names of the places they sprang from, have become embedded in English life. Although Percy, between St-Lô and Avranches, is the ancient home of the present Dukes of Northumberland, sadly it is also a modern-looking, rather ugly town with a plain nineteenth-century church.

Almost all these places, however, have something of interest to offer visitors but get few of them, probably because they lie fractionally off the mainstream of the rush southwards. After having a look at the magical, almost Cornish, de la Hague peninsula, you could leave the Nez de Jobourg (from which on a breezy August afternoon I once counted fifty sail out at sea) and pass through Beaumont-Hague with its vast, unlovely nuclear power station on your way to Biville and Diélette. If you have an eye for history, though, take the quieter D900 via Bricquebec and St-Sauveur-le-Vicomte. In Bricquebec – and here is a name with associations as Norse as Troutbeck – is one of Normandy's two Trappist monasteries, and a fourteenth-century castle ruin, part of which is now a hotel beloved by British visitors on their way to or from Cherbourg. The castle is open at the usual hours except on Tuesdays. St-Sauveur-le-Vicomte also has a *château-fort*, the gift of Edward III to Sir John Chandos and now housing a museum to Barbey d'Aurevilly, a notable local writer born in the town in 1808. There is an interesting abbey church, too, but no decent, reasonably-priced place to eat. Continue south via the twelfth-century Premonstratensian abbey of Blanchelande at Neufmesnil to join the main route at La-Haye-du-Puits.

At Diélette some years ago I underwent another minor maritime disaster, once again averted by the exceptional helpfulness of the sailing community on this rugged coastline. I was in the old lifeboat again, and having moored in the harbour at Diélette, and knowing that the low tide leaves the harbour completely dry, we began the awkward process of 'putting on her legs'. There is a difference between high and low of as much as 12 metres, and the water-level changes very quickly. The lifeboat carried two stout wooden legs that can be screwed on to the outside of the hull to keep her upright when beached. As we were bolting on the starboard leg there was an ominous bump as the keel struck the harbour bottom. We rushed below to get the other leg, and when we emerged on deck saw that most of the boats in the harbour were already aground and the cyclopean rocks which made up the breakwater towered above. As we struggled to fit the port leg the waves surged and sucked around us. Suddenly there was a sickening lurch, the sound of splintering timber, and the boat keeled over, smashing the unsecured leg against the breakwater.

It was a Sunday, and Diélette has only a hotel, a restaurant and a few tiny shops. But we found a *menuisier* who was prepared to make a replica of the broken leg that very afternoon.

A little south of Diélette is Flamanville, with a seventeenth-century château built on earlier foundations. Carteret, the next port of call by land or sea, is a quiet holiday resort and fishing harbour from which it is just 27 kms or an hour's trip in the summer to Gorey in Jersey. There is a daily boat. This whole coast from Vauville to Mont-St-Michel is a broad, sandy 110-km-long beach interrupted by the odd extrusion of rock, as at the Cap de Flamanville, the Pointe de Rozel or Carteret. In bad weather it catches the Atlantic gales, but it is Gulf Stream water and there are good semi-tropical parks and gardens at Flamanville, Coutances and Avranches.

South again to Portbail, lately discovered to be an ancient Christian centre with traces of a sixth-century baptistery, and which is now an attractive little port on a muddy estuary. The road cuts inland here to La-Haye-du-Puits with its Norman donjon, and then flat and straight to Lessay and its famous abbey (see page 104).

After Lessay, Coutances. What a marvellous progression can be enjoyed here: the sandy Romanesque severity of Lessay is followed by the soaring Gothic purity of Coutances. But on the way — and it should not cause architectural indigestion — you could take the quieter D72 via Créances to Pirou where, behind the sand dunes, a 12-metre-high watchtower overshadows the ruins of what is perhaps Normandy's oldest *château-fort*. It is difficult to find, not being exactly at Pirou but at La Barberie, near Pirou-Plage. Approach it via the D650. It is privately owned, open all the year round and has ducks on an algae-covered moat.

Coutances Cathedral, standing on a hill and visible from all directions, is worth a long pilgrimage. Some people believe it is the most beautiful building in Normandy, if not in all France. I first came upon it from the south in a French army bus. There is a fine view of it across the steep valley of the Soulles, and even some of the tough French soldiers who were with me turned to give it an appreciative glance. The history of Coutances mirrors that of, say, Lincoln or Norwich: first a Celtic settlement, Cosedic; then a Roman one, Constantia; Christianized in Gallo-Roman times, becoming one of Normandy's seven dioceses in 571 or earlier; attacked by Vikings in the ninth century; the basilica abandoned and in 900 levelled. Over a century later, with the Norsemen now Christian and the recognized rulers of the duchy, a new church was built by Geoffrey de Montbray. He raised the necessary money in southern Italy from wealthy Normans, themselves originally from Hauteville (between Coutances and St-Lô), who had lately seized Calabria and Apulia from the Saracens.

But Bishop Geoffrey's church is not the one we now admire, for that was damaged by fire in 1218 and its shell is now incorporated in the beautiful early Gothic building which replaced it. Fortunately the cathedral survived the summer of 1944, though sadly the town did not, and it is not as noteworthy an example of sensitive urban rebuilding as, say, Caen or St-Malo.

Those pressed for time will bowl off down the D971 (once the N171). Meanderers should take the D7, D27 and D58 past little fields, lush and deep green, south-east to Hambye. Beyond the village, sheltered by a steep escarpment, is the well-preserved ruin of the Abbaye de Hambye (see p. 104). Contented Norman cows munch in the rich meadows round about, and for visitors there is the Restaurant de l'Abbaye across the road from the Auberge de l'Abbaye – the monastic obligation of hospitality in its more secular, commercial form.

Abbey, cathedral, abbey. You may have noticed (perhaps with some relief) that I have not mentioned a château since Flamanville, far to the north. That is not to say that they do not exist in this corner of the department of Manche, but they are fewer and less noteworthy. The architectural emphasis is on ecclesiastical buildings, with which the region is well endowed.

For a change and while out in the sticks, head south for the short distance to Villedieu-les-Poêles (God's-town-of-the-pans). Here for centuries they have cast bells and beaten copper milk churns. If you enjoy cooking, ignore the tatty copper souvenirs and invest in a traditional thick copper saucepan or two – not easy to find in England. You could do this after seeing them being made in the Atelier du Cuivre at 54 Rue Général Huard (the road out to Caen). It is open at the usual times from 1 June to 30 September. There is a Musée de la Poëslerie across the road and a bell-foundry (Fonderie de Cloches) not far from the church and open all year round at normal hours. It is an attractive town, and the Villedieu part derives from Henry I's establishment here of a *commanderie* of Knights Hospitaller of St

Coutances Cathedral (Victoria Southwell)

John, whose houses were all called Villedieu; every four years since 1655 a commemorative procession takes place on the third Sunday after Whitsun. The next is in 1987.

I quite like the somewhat unregarded St-Sever-Calvados. Set in a forest, it has a very old abbey church, a sombrely slated clock-tower and other former ecclesiastical buildings of some style. But this involves straying too far west – into Calvados, in fact – and the route must head back to Manche and the sea at Granville.

All roads to Granville are interminably straight, roller-coasting across the green, hedged countryside to the sea. (If you find this tedious and feel like a break on the way from Villedieu, and the rather incongruous idea of a wander round a zoo appeals to you, then pause at Champrépus.) In historical terms Granville is a relatively new town – it was founded by the English in 1439; most of the great centres of Normandy are of earlier date. Brittany has more obvious Celtic origins, but they exist too in Normandy. The Celts – and those who settled in what is now France were also termed Gauls – were settled here long before the Romans, though there is not much visible trace of them left today. They were divided into 'nations' whose names, long overlaid by Roman, Norse and French variants and additions, are sometimes still just discernible: the Abrincatui lived around Avranches, the Lexovii in the Lisieux area, and Bayeux was in the land of the Baiocassi. They imported tin from Cornwall up the Seine and traded with Ireland. But the Romans overran them all between 58 and 51 BC. The Gauls of the Cotentin rose in revolt in 56 BC but one of Caesar's deputies, Sabinius, subdued them at Mont Castre, a 130-metre hill just east of La-Haye-du-Puits (where, incidentally, the Germans put up fierce resistance to the advancing Americans in July 1944).

At Granville a considerable granite headland protects vessels sheltering from the north wind, so there may have been a small port and some habitation here before the English came. In a final effort to complete the recovery of Normandy during the Hundred Years' War, eight thousand English in 1434 invested Mont-St-Michel, but were thwarted by just 119 French soldiers under Louis d'Estouteville. A few years later, therefore, they took the nearby Granville promontory and fortified it. It was not for long, however, for in 1442 d'Estouteville flushed them out. Gradually a large commercial and fishing community grew up around the bay below, and in due course hotels and a casino were built and a railway line from Paris brought in holiday-makers (it is four hours by through train to Granville from the Gare Montparnasse). So developed the curious arrangement of the *haute ville*, more ancient and sternly fortified, looking down on the more modern sprawl of the *basse ville* behind it.

The *haute ville* itself is fascinating – a narrow grid-iron pattern of streets with trim eighteenth-century houses and a Cornish air. The church of Notre-Dame and the museum are well worth a visit. From a *table d'orientation* at the eastern, upper end of the *haute ville* you can see sands stretching away to north and south, and in good visibility the French Iles Chausey, Jersey and the Breton coast. Inland, you peer down into the *Tranchée aux Anglais*, dug out across the isthmus of the promontory in 1439. The walls, stormed unavailingly by an ill-armed force of twenty thousand Royalists and Catholics from La Vendée in November 1793, look impregnable today, and as you follow the one-way system out of the *haute ville* you pass through a postern and over a narrow dawbridge that still looks serviceable.

In the harbour a busy fleet of fishing boats brings in catches apparently exclusively of cockles. There is an enormous tidal rise and fall, which is why Granville is said to have the largest lock gates in Europe. In season there are ferries to Jersey and the Iles Chausey, and on the last Sunday of July a statue of the Virgin is carried in procession through the streets. So there is plenty of life in Granville all the year round, but 'the Monaco of the north'? That sounds more like the hopeful effusion of a syndicat d'initiative public relations officer.

South of Granville runs one of those stretches of coast to which it is surprising that the French have not given one of the sobriquets that they so love – Côte Fleurie, Côte d'Eméraude, and so on. It has a distinct character of its own and is full of quiet, relatively inexpensive villages with good sand and plenty of interest, such as St-Pair, Quéron, Jullouville, Carolles, St-Jean-le-Thomas and Genêts. At St-Jean-le-Thomas you have to time your swims carefully or be a keen jogger, for at low water the sea recedes some 6 kms. South of Carolles the dominant prospect is an apparently limitless expanse of sea or sand, with the rock of Tombelaine rising from it and behind that the familiar but still breathtaking outline of Mont-St-Michel.

The best view of this 'miracle of the west' is had, it is said, from the hill-top town of Avranches. On the four occasions on which I have visited this town it has been raining. Perhaps this is why it used to be a favourite of the English. In the nineteenth century it had, as did Dieppe and Dinard, a flourishing English colony. An early visitor – though as Duke of Normandy as well as King of England he was essentially on home ground – was Henry II: the stone flag on which he knelt and did penance for his complicity in the murder of Thomas à Becket at Canterbury in 1170 can still be seen. But in recent times Avranches has drawn more Americans than English. General Patton liberated the place in July 1944; a massive monument to his achievement is ringed by trees brought over from the USA which surround a piece of ground, now a roundabout, regarded still as American territory.

There is, finally, the mysterious affair of the cathedral. Avranches is said to be 'a cathedral city without a cathedral'. No one seems to know whether it was destroyed in the Revolution, or just fell down by itself. But the odd fact remains that on my 1983 visit I bought a modern postcard showing a Gothic-looking building with two large towers at its west end, captioned *'Avranches – La Cathédrale'*. It turns out that they have recently upgraded the nineteenth-century granite church of Notre-Dame-les-Champs. Opposite its west front is the extremely fine Jardin des Plantes, ablaze with colour in summer and a paradise indeed for horticulturists. There are superb hummocks of flowers and succulents crowned by clusters of gladioli, fuchsia and false bananas. At the garden's tree-covered lower end is the famous view over the estuaries of the Sée and the Sélune to Mont-St-Michel.

On a wet day Avranches has much to offer indoors: a museum and library with a collection of ancient manuscripts and early printed books unrivalled in France. Here are works by Cicero, Boethius, and Peter Abelard. And on a good day visitors can explore some characteristic medieval streets – still in existence despite the pasting the town got in 1944 – the ramparts, a donjon and a fine *lycée*. While in this area do not fail to sample the excellent mussels which thrive on a special plankton living in the bay of Mont-St-Michel. The saltmarsh lamb is also delicious. Not far south of Avranches, at Céaux near Pontaubault, is a small hotel called Au P'tit Quinquin, which has a good restaurant.

For walkers Avranches (which has a working railway station)

Stacking cockles in Granville harbour (Sally-Anne Greville-Heygate)

Granville, with the church of Notre-Dame in the distance

could be a good starting point. It lies near one end of a 160-km track to Bagnoles-de-l'Orne (see page 161). This is part of one of France's many *Sentiers de Grande Randonnée* which lace their way across the country and are all properly waymarked and written up in guides. For the motorist, heading south to Fougères and the Loire valley, the N176 beckons.

The Jardin des Plantes, a horticulturist's paradise

4 Norman Normandy

Castles, Abbeys and Cathedrals

The Vikings came into northern France at the same time and in the same way that they came into Anglo-Saxon England. Throughout the ninth century they made seasonal raids, liked the look of what they saw, built permanent camps and were eventually bought off with a large grant of land. From these Norsemen, or Nordmanni, the northern territory of the Franks, then called Neustria, acquired the name of Normandy.

Surprisingly little remains of their early presence. The great Norman castles, abbeys and cathedrals did not appear until the Norsemen had, by assimilation with the native Franks and other immigrants, become transmuted into Normans in the tenth and eleventh centuries. The true Viking civilization, evident from Greenland to Novgorod, did not leave much of a mark on Normandy – no spectacular excavations of wharves and warehouses as at Coppergate in York, no ship burials like those at Gokstad or Oseberg in Norway, no military camps like Trelleborg in Denmark, no Swedish runes. Normandy possesses the dike built as a defensive wall across the furthest tip of the Cotentin; just one Scandinavian burial, at Pitres; a Viking sword fished from the Seine; a coin hoard found at Fécamp; but little else except placenames. So to get the feel of the Viking invasions requires imagination.

Seaborne marauders from Norway and Denmark penetrated up the Seine, the Loire and the Garonne, and of these rivers the Seine was their first target. It was nearest and, after the passage of its troublesome estuary, there was an easy run to rich pickings. They first came in 820 in thirteen ships, but were seen off with some loss of life. Upstream, however, the abbeys of St-Wandrille and Jumièges and the small cathedral city of Rouen lay defenceless. So in 841 Osker sacked them, and in 845 Ragnar

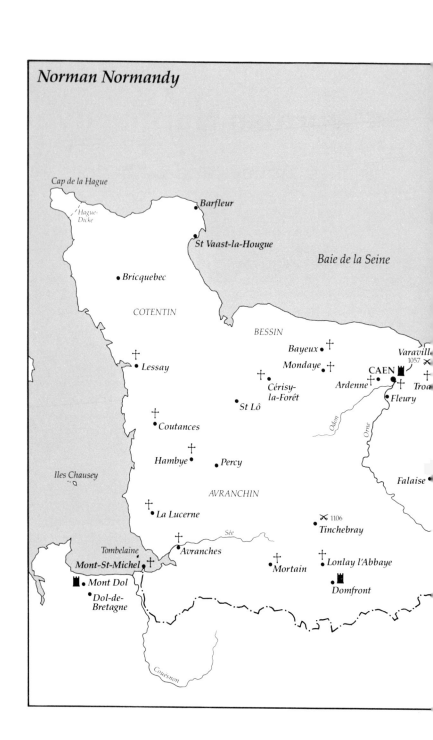

Norman Normandy

Cap de la Hague

Hague-
Dicke

Barfleur

St Vaast-la-Hougue

Baie de la Seine

Bricquebec

COTENTIN

BESSIN

Bayeux

Mondaye

Varavill

1057

✠ Lessay

✠

Cérisy-
la-Forêt

St Lô

CAEN ▮

Ardenne ✠ Troa

Fleury ✠

Coutances

Hambye

Percy

Iles Chausey

AVRANCHIN

Falaise

La Lucerne

✗ 1106
Tinchebray

Sée

✠ Tombelaine
Mont-St-Michel ✠

Avranches

Mortain

✠ Lonlay l'Abbaye

Domfront

▮ Mont Dol
Dol-de-
Bretagne

Couesnon

Odon

Orne

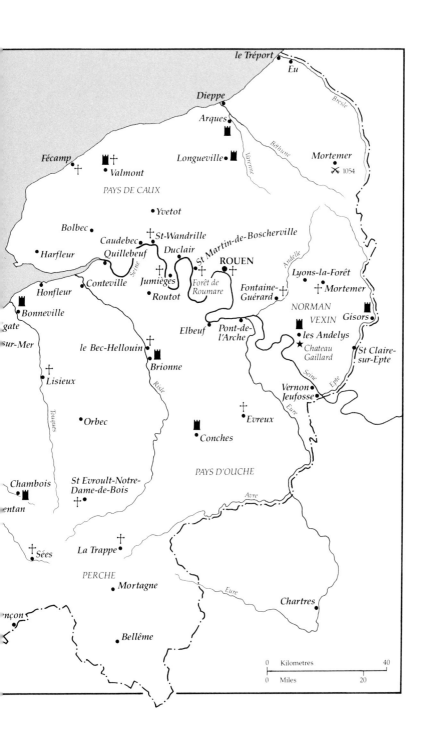

le Tréport

Eu

Dieppe

Arques

Fécamp

Longueville

Mortemer

⚔ 1054

Valmont

PAYS DE CAUX

Yvetot

Bolbec

St-Martin-de-Boscherville

Caudebec

St-Wandrille

Duclair

ROUEN

Harfleur

Quillebeuf

Andelle

Lyons-la-Forêt

Conteville

Jumièges

Seine

Forêt de
Roumare

Fontaine-
Guérard

Mortemer

Honfleur

Routot

NORMAN

Bonneville

VEXIN

Gisors

gate

Elbeuf

Pont-de-
l'Arche

les Andelys

sur-Mer

le Bec-Hellouin

★ Chateau
Gaillard

St Claire-
sur-Epte

Brionne

Seine

Epte

Lisieux

Risle

Vernon
Jeufosse

Touques

Orbec

Evreux

Eure

Conches

Chambois

PAYS D'OUCHE

St Evroult-Notre-
Dame-de-Bois

Avre

entan

Sées

La Trappe

Eure

PERCHE

Mortagne

Chartres

nçon

Bellême

| 0 | Kilometres | 40 |
| 0 | Miles | 20 |

Lodbrok over-ran Paris itself – the first of four such humiliations for its Carolingian rulers.

The Viking past has readily come to life for me at places such as Lerwick, Lindisfarne and Tynwald Hill in the Isle of Man. In Normandy the best evocation I have found is to overlook the Seine from the village of Jeufosse (itself a Viking name), south of Vernon. The Vikings grew more and more brazen, and after lurking in the lower reaches of the river all through the winter of 851 they sailed past Rouen and established an advanced base on the island of Jeufosse. From here they could harry the country around on stolen horses, seize slaves and pillage the now abandoned monasteries. Charles the Bald, Charlemagne's grandson, tried in 864 to defend the river route to Paris at Pont-de-l'Arche, but the raids went on and little by little the Franks became as demoralized as the Angles of Northumbria and Mercia in the face of the same enemy.

The only respite came in 866–85, when the Norsemen turned their attentions to the Saxons of Wessex. During those years Alfred the Great organized a resistance movement and finally checked Guthrum's Vikings at the battle of Ethandune in 878. The Treaty of Wedmore acknowledged Norse control of all the lands north-east of Watling Street, to become known as the Danelaw. In France Charles the Simple later tried a similar solution – in 911 he came to terms with the Norseman Hrôlfr, or Rollo, at St-Clair-sur-Epte. Rollo, like Guthrum, accepted Christianity, and swore allegiance to Charles, agreeing to hold what we now call Normandy as a buffer state against attacks from other Vikings. Rollo had been occupying the lower Seine valley for ten years and now became the duke of territories north-west of the Epte (which flows into the Seine near Vernon), the Eure and the Avre. St-Clair-sur-Epte, now on the N14 between Paris and Rouen, is still a sleepy village on the Normandy–Ile de France border. Whereas Alfred the Great's successors gradually drove the Vikings from the Danelaw and reasserted their rule over all England, the reverse happened in France: Rollo's successors slowly extended Norman control westwards over the native Franks to cover all of present-day Normandy. But of course the Normans had the last laugh over the English in 1066.

In the absence of visual Viking excitements we have to fall back on placenames. Elements of Old Norse are thickest in the Pays de Caux (inland from Fécamp), the Seine valley and the

Cotentin. But they are never so evident as in Yorkshire or Lincolnshire, which are sprinkled with placenames ending in -by, -wick, -toft, -thorpe, -thwaite and -beck and whose prefix is probably of Viking origin too. In Normandy the Norse suffix is likely to be grafted on to a persisting Gallo-Roman survival. This says something about the nature of the Norse settlement; it was never so dense or so complete as that in Northumbria or Mercia. A Viking lord might replace a Frankish one, but the Frankish peasants would not be displaced nor would they be swamped by Viking incomers.

As you bowl along through Normandy ask your children to make a list of all the village names ending in -ville. Apart from any scholarly result it may have, it will keep them wholly absorbed for many miles, for inland of Dieppe, Le Havre and Cherbourg these names are everywhere and they mark the site of a Gallo-Roman villa or farm. Often the prefix will preserve the name of the new Norse landowner: Grimonville – Grim's farm; Tourville – Thor's farm; Herouville – Harald's farm; and so on, with Borne- for Björn, Godar- for Guddar and Hacque- for Haco. But be careful – not all Viking names are exclusive to Scandinavia. Some are, like Ragnar and Haakon, but others can be found in very similar form in Germanic (and that includes Frankish) genealogies. So although Gunnar, Harald, Ketel, Osmund, Thorkill and others may seem quintessentially Viking – Ketel the Flat-nosed was the first Norseman to establish himself in the Outer Hebrides – the same sort of names occur among Germanic peoples. There were settlements of Saxons in the Bayeux area before the Norman conquest of it, quite aside from the Franks who had already lived in Normandy for four hundred years.

Your children could also be asked to look for the rarer animal, the Old Norse element: our -beck is -bec, our -toft is -tot, and there are quite a few of those, such as Yvetot, Routot, Bolbec and Orbec. There are other Norse elements dotted about: -fleur has nothing to do with flowers but indicates a place where the tide flows; many sea ports, such as Barfleur, Harfleur and Honfleur, carry this suffix; -haugr (headland) occurs at either corner of the Cotentin in La Hague and La Hougue; -gate indicates a road – Oslo's main street today is Karl Johans Gate – and gives us Houlgate; -beuf is common (Cricquebeuf, Quittebeuf) and means that a *buth* or booth stood there; -mare is a mere and appears in Hectomare and Roumare. And so one could go on, although perhaps on increasingly contentious ground.

The Forêt de Roumare, just west of Rouen, is a good place to begin a search for Norman Normandy. There is legendary evidence here of the good order that Rollo, first Duke of Normandy, was able to enforce among his people. Rollo, once called The Ganger because his great height made the small horses of the time useless to him and he chose to 'gang' to war on foot, was now renamed Robert and settled in a ducal palace in the Gallo-Roman town of Rouen.

The Romans had built Rotomagus on a Celtic site where the Seine is split into two narrow arms by the Ile Lacroix and could therefore be bridged. Robert improved and drained the town, set up a mint and built quays, deepening the riverbed, but there is little or no sign at Rouen today of his work or that of his immediate successors. It is true that you do not get much sense of all this as you stand at Grand Couronne and look across at the port and the industrial blight that now surrounds it, but this is how the city began.

There is much to be said for pacifying a region by recognizing and legitimizing its chief bandit. Under Robert, the ex-pirate, the slow business of reconstruction could begin, and before his death in 933 it was claimed that he proved the measure of his success by hanging his gold necklace on an oak tree in the Forêt de Roumare and finding it still there three years later. A lingering Celtic religious practice may partly account for this, if the story is at all true, for it was their long-established custom to hang gold votive objects in trees.

Rouen, however, had been a Christian centre since 260, according to some accounts, when St-Mellon had converted the Gallo-Romans there. From its first cathedral an archbishop ruled the province with its six bishoprics of Avranches, Coutances, Bayeux, Lisieux, Evreux and Sées. In Robert's time Rouen was full of exiled bishops and monastic heads still too afraid to return to their dioceses or their abbeys, and with some reason – Bishops Baltfridus of Bayeux and Lista of Coutances had been murdered by Vikings in 858 and 889, while Adalhelmus of Sées had been enslaved. In 867 the Frankish king, Charles the Bald, handed over the lands of the three westernmost bishoprics to the Bretons. All the dioceses either have gaps in their lists of bishops, Lisieux from 832 to 990 and Avranches, Bayeux and

Sées for slightly shorter periods within those years, or they had absentees – five successive bishops of Coutances, from 913 to 1024, found it safer to shelter in Rouen.

Robert's Duchy of Normandy had the same shape and extent as the Archbishop of Rouen's province, which was itself based on the frontiers of an old Roman province. Robert and his son William Longsword (933–42) secured the dioceses of Bayeux and Sées in 924 and drove the Bretons from the Cotentin and the Avranchin in 933. In 911 Rouen itself had been the only cathedral town and Mont-St-Michel the only monastic house still – just – functioning. Under the early dukes the church made its slow climb back.

But the 'Jarls of Rouen', Robert, William and their three successors – all called Richard – were hardly saints; their chests were full of white shirts – the garment worn by penitents at baptism, which in the case of these arch-lapsers was a recurring sacrament. They married 'in the Danish fashion', and most of the dukes were born illegitimately of Breton concubines, foresters' daughters and the like. In 1013 and 1014 Richard II (996–1026) entertained at Rouen his barbaric kinsman King Olaf of Norway, who was in the course of enjoying an eighteen-month season of rape and pillage up the rivers of south-west France. Despite the foundation of monasteries and abbeys it was a rough, unchristian time.

The Normans were always great assimilators and adapters and they quickly fell in with Frankish ways and took up their language. A contemporary, Dudo of St-Quentin, says that by 1025 Norse was no longer heard in Rouen, though it lingered in Bayeux. None of the six dukes married a kinswoman from Scandinavia or England – their womenfolk were all Breton or Frankish. Normandy became something of a melting pot of peoples in the eleventh century: the old Frankish nobility had long gone, but Richard II and his successors brought in Frenchmen, Angevins, Germans and Bretons to act as *comtes* and *vicomtes* in the duchy and collect taxes, dispense the duke's justice and keep custody of his castles.

Cosmopolitan though Normandy may have been, its fortunes were determined personally by this tough, autocratic line of dukes, who stood on the triple pillars of church, law and army. Their relatives and descendants were known from their progenitor as the Rollonides, and they filled all the important jobs in the duchy.

Today the church offers visitors one of the best glimpses into these distant years. With Rouen as a starting point you can set off, charged with the necessary spiritual zeal, on a fascinating mini-pilgrimage: to St-Martin-de-Boscherville, Jumièges, St-Wandrille, Fécamp and Le Bec-Hellouin. Here, in the Seine valley, is the crucible in which the Benedictine revival of the Norman church was forged, and much evidence of it can still be seen.

Begin at the church of St-Ouen in Rouen, built in 1318 on the site of the old abbey church, of which unfortunately nothing now remains. But the old abbey was the first to be rebuilt, about 930, in Robert's time. This site, in Old Rouen, is where the regenerative impulses were first felt.

Take the D982 west out of the city, through the dense Forêt de Roumare. Here the Seine makes one of its spectacular southern loops, and you will quickly rejoin the river at St-Martin-de-Boscherville. The abbey (see page 65) was founded in 1050 by William the Conqueror's Great Chamberlain, Raoul de Tancarville. It was soon taken over by the Benedictines and much later was saved from the attentions of the Black Band, who destroyed monastic foundations after the French Revolution, by becoming the town's parish church.

Follow the Seine to Duclair, then resist your impatience and cling to the D65, which is the prettier route along the river, all the way until you reach Jumièges. St-Philibert's Benedictine abbey was founded about 654, and some stonework of the pre-Viking house can still be seen. After the ninth-century depredations the monks returned from their refuge at Haspres, and by 940 were resettled on lands restored to them by Duke William Longsword. This is one of the jewels of France and there is much to see, a lot of it post-Norman. Duke Robert II's eleventh-century nave, dedicated in the presence of William the Conqueror in 1067, still stands, though roofless.

Sixteen kilometres downstream, just short of Caudebec, is the Abbaye de St-Wandrille, or Fontenelle as it was first called (see also page 64). It was founded in 649 by St-Wandrille himself, and the nearby oratory of St-Saturnin, tiny, clover-leafed in plan and rebuilt in the 900s, is a rare reminder of those times. The main abbey was also rebuilt and renamed, after the return of its monks in 961 from exile in Chartres, Boulogne and Ghent. Like Jumièges it became a great centre of Benedictine learning and

The Abbaye de St-Wandrille

education; Einhard, author of the *Life of Charlemagne*, was one of its many distinguished abbots. After the Revolution it became a textile factory, then the home of the Belgian playwright Maurice Maeterlinck and, since 1931, a Benedictine house once more. It is a memorable experience to hear Gregorian chant in the abbey church, which is a fifteenth-century tithe barn dismantled at La Neuville-du-Bosc and carried 90 kms to be re-erected here in 1969. Mass is sung at half-past nine on weekdays and ten o'clock on Sundays; vespers can be heard in the evening. From St-Wandrille thread north and get on to the D926. From here it is just short of 50 kms across the Pays de Caux to the seaside town and fishing port of Fécamp.

If you look closely at a bottle of Benedictine you will see on the label round its neck '*Antiquorum Monachorum Benedictinorum Abbatiae Fiscanensis*' – 'From the old Benedictine monks of the abbey of Fécamp'. Since 1510 the famous golden liqueur has been distilled from the aromatic herbs that grow on the cliffs nearby, but the abbey's history is much older.

Fécamp is geographically like Dover, wedged between chalk hills, and historically like Glastonbury, with which it shares a legend: both are supposed sites of the Holy Grail, receiving by well-nigh miraculous means relics of Christ's blood. In the case of Fécamp, the story goes that a nephew of Nicodemus (who helped to bury Jesus), fearing that the Romans might seize a casket containing *le Saint-Sang*, consigned it to the waters of the Mediterranean in a hollowed out fig tree. Here credulity is stretched. Sea currents are supposed to have borne the tree all the way to Fécamp (Fécamp=*fici campus* or 'the field of the fig tree'. But there is an inconvenient 's' in *Fiscanensis* which gives the lie to this hopeful attribution. Fécamp is in fact derived from the Gallo-Roman Fiscamnum.) At all events, pilgrims came. A spring, the Fountain of the Precious Blood, produced, and still produces, water. In 658 some nuns built a convent to house the casket in a shrine. Vikings destroyed the convent, but the relic survived and Duke Richard I built a sanctuary there. His son, Richard II, founded an abbey and William of Volpiano, eminent leader of the Cluniac revival, was lured from Burgundy to run it in 1003. Succeeding Norman dukes, including William the Conqueror, habitually spent Easter there. The church of the Trinity which can be seen today is the fourth on the site, and was built between 1175 and 1220. It hides behind an eighteenth-century façade and over the years has been a point of pilgrimage in Normandy second only to Mont-St-Michel.

The last of the great religious houses of the Seine valley is Le Bec-Hellouin, which lies among wooded hills hemming in the Risle, just north of Brionne. If Fécamp was a devotional centre, where believers could worship in the presence of the blood of Christ, Le Bec-Hellouin was the university of the Norman church, attracting international teachers and acting as a repository of Christian scholarship more famous even than Jumièges or St-Wandrille.

It was named after Herluin, a Norman soldier turned contemplative, who set up a hermitage near Bec in 1034. He and his companions were devout but impractical and had to move twice: the first site had no water, while the second was subject to flooding. In 1042 the Lombard scholar Lanfranc joined them and the abbey's brief but glorious hour as a centre of learning began. There is an impressive honours board of Old Boys on the wall of St-Nicholas' tower, which includes a pope, Alexander II; three archbishops of Canterbury, among them Anselm of Aosta, possibly a greater intellectual even than Lanfranc, whose genius lay perhaps more in administration; three bishops of Rochester; and numerous abbots.

Much of what is visible today is of seventeenth-century date and the last abbot, when the house was in obvious decline, was, astonishingly, Talleyrand, Bishop of Autun and later President of the National Assembly. A Vicar of Bray on the grand scale, Talleyrand served Napoléon during Directory, Consulate and Empire and was a statesman under the restored Bourbons. The abbey meanwhile became a stud farm, a military remount depot and in 1944 a temporary barracks for British soldiers, before its restoration as an active Benedictine house, could begin in 1947. A 1938 photograph in its guidebook shows the refectory being used as stabling for horses, with fodder racks lining the wall, and another shows it today, a recognizable refectory again.

The only substantial survival of the old abbey is the tower of St-Nicholas, built in 1475. This structure, and others of similar dedication, are a standing reminder of a widespread practice in the Christian world for which the Normans are partly responsible. When at Christmas we sing 'I saw three ships come sailing in' and fathers dress up in red cloaks and white beards to play Santa Claus we should acknowledge some indebtedness to the

Normans. 'Santa Claus' is the St-Nicholas who, if he existed at all – and Pope John Paul II recently struck him from the approved list – was a fourth-century Bishop of Myra in Asia Minor whose tomb there became a popular shrine when his bones were found to exude a watery liquid with therapeutic qualities. When the Saracens over-ran Turkey in 1087 the Normans, then colonizing Apulia under Roger I, sent an expedition from Bari to Myra to secure the bones. The carol commemorates the return of this Norman flotilla with the sacred relics. The citizens of modern Bari symbolically re-enact this event each May by bringing ashore a portrait of St-Nicholas to the supposed landing place. In Norman days pilgrims thronged to the basilica dedicated to the saint, and they would often wear simple hooded cloaks in Bari's colours of red and white.

Outside the Seine valley there are still more than a dozen religious houses scattered across Normandy which have Norman origins. In the Cotentin there are Hambye, founded by Guillaume Paynel in 1145 and one of the finest, and Lessay. At the former, the nave, choir, transept, chapter house, scriptorium, library and kitchen all survive, though mostly open to the sky. It is strongly atmospheric, however. The abbey church at Lessay looks a Romanesque gem, and what could be more evocative of Normandy's Viking past than the name of its founder, Turstin Haldup. The work was begun ten years before the conquest of England but in some ways the most remarkable moment in its history was very recent. In 1944 it was flattened in the course of General Patton's expulsion of the Germans from the Cotentin and in the ensuing thirteen years it was lovingly rebuilt to re-create the original structure without the additions and adaptations of the intervening centuries. La Lucerne d'Outremer, 12 kms south-east of Granville, was founded in 1143 in a particularly peaceful setting in the valley of the Thar. The choir and transept of the abbey church are still in use. The rest is a pleasant muddle of ruins and farm buildings with an enormous cylindrical dovecote open to the sky. In those pious times an abbey might spawn daughter houses, as today a prosperous shopkeeper might open sub-branches, and La Lucerne gave birth to four, including Ardenne (see below).

In the *bocage Normand* are the White Abbey at Mortain and Lonlay l'Abbaye, north-west of Domfront. Mortain, a twelfth-century foundation, is still a seminary. Barrack-like and dark from the outside, it got its name from the white habits of the Cistercians. Lonlay-l'Abbaye stands in a pleasantly watered valley, and its stern, upright abbey church of Notre-Dame was founded in about 1020 by William of Bellême. St-Evroult-Notre-Dame-du-Bois, in the Perche Normand, is a Benedictine house. Founded in the eleventh century, it was developed by Lanfranc into an early seat of learning from which five monks went out to teach at Cottenham in the Cambridgeshire fens. They are thought to have influenced the foundation of the university on the nearby river Cam. From the Abbaye de Breuil-Benoit near Pacy-sur-Eure, now ruined, a group of monks set out in 1140 to found the Abbaye de la Grande Trappe, half-way between L'Aigle and Mortagne. It was in this latter house, in the seventeenth century, that the silent reformed Cistercian or Trappist order evolved.

Ardenne, a twelfth-century Premonstratensian house, and Troarn, of slightly later date, are respectively 7 kms west and 12 kms east of Caen. Mondaye, south of Bayeux, dates from 1200 but is entirely an eighteenth-century structure. There is yet another remarkable abbey between Bayeux and St-Lô at Cerisy-la-Forêt. Its story is the familiar one – founded in the sixth century by Bishop Vigor of Bayeux, it was wrecked by Vikings and re-established in 1032 by Duke Robert II. The present buildings, including the superb choir, are twelfth- and thirteenth-century. In July and August you can see a *Spectacle Lumineux et Sonore* which recreates, the blurb says, a true fairyland in the framework of the Middle Ages.

For those not sated by the glories of the church of the Trinity at Fécamp there is a fine abbey, rebuilt in the fourteenth century, at Valmont, 14 kms to the west. It was founded by Nicholas d'Estouteville in 1169 and what remains is in good order.

This leaves the region of Rouen, convenient for those en route between Dieppe and Paris. In the same small area, the valley of the Andelle which runs into the Seine almost opposite its confluence with the Eure, are two interesting abbeys. Fontaine-Guérard was a Cistercian nunnery founded by Robert, Earl of Leicester in 1198. The church, chapter house and a dormitory survive in quite a good state. Mortemer, a Cistercian monastery 14 kms east – decently far away from the nuns – lies in the Forêt de Lyons, in border country known as the Norman Vexin. Here in a valley in thick woods are the ruins of a twelfth-century house which flourished so spectacularly that French and English kings lodged there. Fish from its monastic stews (still a pleasant feature of the valley) may have played their tiny part in history, for it was at Mortemer that Henry I ate the surfeit of lampreys of which he died at nearby Lyons-la-Forêt the day after.

Normandy's proud jewel, though but for an accident of geography it could be Brittany's, is the Abbaye de Mont-St-Michel. At the furthest end of the province, it is lapped close on its western side by the sluggish outflow of the river Couësnon, the traditional border. So much has been written about 'La Merveille', as the French call it, that it is a goal as keenly sought by tourist pilgrims now as it was by religious ones in times past – it is France's second-biggest tourist attraction, after Versailles. Its familiar profile, a hummock of rock, high, beetling structures of stone and slate, intricate finials, soaring, slender spire, all rising from the fiercely tidal waters of the bay of Mont-St-Michel, beckons sightseers by the coachload. So try and visit it early in the day, and if you can go out of season so much the better. Although the stupendous building we see today is not predominantly Norman – its construction spanned the centuries between the tenth and the fifteenth and the principal achievement is in fact thirteenth-century Gothic – it was in the Norman era that the abbey was set fairly on its way.

Mont-St-Michel's antecedents are steeped in legend, like those of most structures built on rocky eminences that rise out of flat plains. Celtic druids and druidesses are said to have worshipped the sun there. The Romans drove them out as they did elsewhere in Gaul and built a temple to Jupiter. Mithraism flourished briefly. Then, Sir Thomas Malory claims, King Arthur came with two knights, struggled with a rather unpleasant giant, and ordered a church to be built.

We are not yet in the realms of reliably recorded history, but two things happened about 708–9 of which we can be fairly sure: Bishop Aubert of Avranches built an oratory for a college of twelve canons, and the sea flooded the surrounding forest, making Mont-St-Michel an occasional island. Myth colours even these bald facts. The church of St-Gervais and St-Protais in Avranches contains Bishop Aubert's skull, which has a hole in it. Whatever the physiological reason for this, the story runs that he was bidden in a dream to build a religious house on the rock, then called Mont-Tombe, that daily he could see protruding from the forest below Avranches. Was this the voice of the Archangel Michael, or just an ordinary dream? Twice he doubted, and the dream recurred. Eventually the Archangel struck Aubert on the head with his finger by way of reassurance. Message and finger sunk in and the college was founded. We do know that Aubert sent monks to Monte Gargano in southern Italy where a sanctuary of the Archangel Michael, patron saint of the dukes of Normandy, had, as at Mont-St-Michel, replaced a temple to Mithras. In 709 they returned, bringing two relics of the Archangel which became prized possessions of the abbey.

As the monks cleared the last hilltop to overlook Avranches and the valley of the Sée the expression on their faces would have been wonderful to behold, for something extraordinary had happened to the landscape. Mont-St-Michel bay had been, as far out as the Iles Chausey, flat, marshy woodland – the Forêt de Scissy, medieval chroniclers called it. Possibly as the result of exceptionally high equinoctial tides, the sea had flooded in, leaving Chausey, Mont-St-Michel, the smaller rock of Tombelaine and Mont Dol all as islands.

Mont-St-Michel became a safe haven for refugees from Viking attacks and a small town grew up on the southern flanks of the hill. Pilgrims came in increasing numbers and this is perhaps why the cockle shell, found everywhere in the bay, became the recognized symbol of pilgrims throughout Christendom.

In 950 a square Carolingian church was built on the site of Aubert's oratory and in 966 Duke Richard I replaced the incumbents, who had become lax, by a party of fifty Benedictines from St-Wandrille. Duke Richard II married Judith of Brittany in the church in 1023, but it was so small that many of the guests were unable to get in. Perhaps this encouraged him to contribute to the costs of the big new building programme being proposed by Abbot Hildebert.

This was a crucial moment in the abbey's development. Instead of levelling the top of the hill and those buildings that remained from a fire in 992, Hildebert insisted on an unprecedentedly bold plan: to incorporate what was already there in strong curtain walls, roof them over and then build a second storey on top. In this way the old Carolingian church became a crypt – Notre-Dame-sous-Terre – under the west end of the new Romanesque basilica. This is why you enter the abbey at a lower level and climb from the Salle des Gardes up the ninety steps of the Grand-Degré Intérieur before emerging on to the terrace of the basilica itself. And it explains one of the minor but memorable features of Mont-St-Michel, particularly pleasing to the child in all of us – the giant tread-wheel by means of which first monks, and later, after the Revolution, when the abbey was used as a jail, prisoners would haul up provisions and other goods.

Throughout the reign of William the Conqueror the building of the abbey church proceeded, and it was finished in 1060. The arches of the nave can be seen in the Bayeux Tapestry. But the builders were working by trial and error, and poor weight distribution caused the western end of the nave to spill down the hillside on Good Friday, 1103. They built it up again and this time got it right. When Abbot Ranulphe built the Salle des Chevaliers over the Cellier in the early thirteenth century he made sure, asymmetrical though it may have been, that the pillars above matched the pillars below.

Indeed, what they call 'La Merveille' proper – the range of Gothic buildings on the north side – has three storeys: on the east end, built between 1211 and 1218, the Aumônerie at the lowest level, the Salle des Hôtes above, then the Refectory; to the west, built over the following ten years, the Cellier, the Salle des Chevaliers and on top the tiny but perfect Cloisters. The whole concept was planned and achieved by three successive abbots in twenty-five years – amazing rapidity for the time. And these are not just any old Gothic buildings, but the finest of their kind in France.

Mont-St-Michel today is show business. On a good day in summer as many as seven thousand sightseers are funnelled through. So the experience it offers is bound to suffer aesthetically. Waiting crowds are shunted, like needy pilgrims, from the Salle des Gardes into the Aumônerie and then guided groups, with escorts welcoming them in a variety of languages (the English-speaking one is a much better obligatory guided tour than most in France), take off with the regularity of jumbos from an international airport – every fifteen minutes. But people seem to be prepared for this. Like the Uffizi in Florence or the Great Wall of China, everyone knows it will be thronged but it will still be worth it. As in a tropical rain forest the glories are mostly high above – instead of sunlight beaming through the jungle canopy there are the pure lines of moulded ogival arches, barrel-vaulted ceilings or light shafting through high, lancet windows. And you can always escape on to the windy platform terrace at the west end (created in 1780 when that part of the nave was thought too unsafe to leave standing), where 16 kms out you may see the white line of the incoming tide creaming over the muddy sand faster than a man could run from it.

In the Norman period Mont-St-Michel was a place for worship, study and consolidation. After 1154 Abbot Robert de Torigny brought in a library and scholars. The abbey was wealthy now, with many dependent houses, like the former Abbaye de St-Michel at Le Tréport. Endowments were showered upon it by many royal houses – in 1044 Edward the Confessor founded a priory on St-Michael's Mount, a miniature Mont-St-Michel in Cornwall, and handed it over to its Norman namesake, which, ironically, helped to provide ships for the invasion of England after Edward's death.

Mont-St-Michel had its own defence needs too. In 1203 the Bretons fired the town and damaged the abbey, so Abbot Richard Turstin built the Belle Chaise – an entrance complex including redoubt, guardroom and barbican. He also built the Tour du Nord, but it was a century before the real threat came, in the shape of the English in the Hundred Years' War, and it was a further half century later, early in the 1420s, that the long line of ramparts which guard the town on its vulnerable eastern and southern sides were completed from the Tour du Nord to the Tour du Roi by today's entrance. These defences and the intricate network of steps that lead down to them are an intriguing example of Norman military architecture which for many has greater appeal than the less robust charms of abbey and monastery.

Whether or not you wish to eat on crowded Mont-St-Michel, spare a moment to look in through the door of Mère Poularde's restaurant at the bottom of the hill, where chefs will be rhythmically beating eggs to make the famous but pricey omelettes.

There would probably be nowhere better to begin a look at Norman castles or *châteaux-forts* (to distinguish them from the châteaux of Renaissance or later date) than Falaise. Its castle is the most famous in Normandy, not only on account of its size and its good state of preservation but also because of its associations with William the Conqueror.

Falaise is a pleasant little town roughly halfway between Caen and Argentan, two-thirds of which had to be rebuilt after it was caught up in some of the fiercest fighting after D-Day. The Place Guillaume le Conquérant contains a fine bronze equestrian statue marking William's victory at Hastings. Falaise, quite naturally, capitalizes on the strong tradition that he was born here in or around 1028.

You enter the outer bailey of the castle through the curtain wall with its twelve towers. Ahead, on a sandstone outcrop, is the massively impressive rectangular keep, with a smaller adjoining donjon and the lofty, circular Talbot tower on an otherwise vulnerable shoulder of the outcrop to the west. The keep is floorless and roofless but has the thickest walls of any in Normandy at 3·5 metres and measures internally 19·5 × 16·5 metres. Two storeys remain and up a staircase in the thickness of a wall you will arrive in a small room, also within the wall, where the story of William's birth unfolds. You will be told that his father was Robert, Vicomte of Exmes, later to become Duke Robert II the Magnificent (or the Devil, if you prefer), who lived in the castle in the late 1020s. The seventeen-year-old William was up in this room when through the window he saw a young girl down below hoist her skirts and bend to do the family washing in a fountain by the banks of the Ante. Tradition has it that he watched her often from this vantage point – *'guettant'*, the castle guide told me, which just means 'keeping an eye on', but which was made to suggest that he was something of a Peeping Robert.

The girl was Herleve, often mistakenly rendered as Arlette, reputedly the daughter of a tanner called Fulbert. The young Vicomte summoned her and the story goes that she came into the castle by daylight for all to see and in her best dress. In due course an illegitimate boy, William, was born to her. Quite soon after she was married off to Herluin, not the founder of Le Bec-Hellouin but a Vicomte of Conteville, and had at least three more children, all of whom, together with her brothers and sisters, did very well. Even her father was given a modest job in the castle. Little William, after a nightmarish childhood, did not do too badly either, though his lowly origins dogged him: in

1051 he was besieging Alençon when the townsfolk hung hides and skins over the top of the walls and beat them, shouting 'Skins for the tanner!' in a taunting allusion to his grandfather's trade, which has always been widely regarded as unclean and demeaning. With a characteristic show of brutality, William replied by having the hands and feet of thirty prisoners lopped off and catapulted into the town.

I was standing at this window looking down at the stream and passers by below, as Peeping Robert must have, when it occurred to me that there was an anachronistic flaw in this delightful tale: the room I was standing in, indeed the whole keep, was not built until 1123 – almost a century after William was a twinkle in his father's eye. The walls and buttresses the visitor now sees are of a sophisticated design and the work of that great castle builder Henry I who, after defeating his brother Robert Curthose at Tinchebray in 1106, rebuilt Falaise and other fortresses in eastern Normandy to protect his domains from the King of France.

Although William or his wife Mathilda ruled the duchy from Rouen, where he died, his powerful presence is most felt, after Falaise, in Caen, which he loved and where he was brought, down the Seine and then overland, for burial. In Caen, despite its cruel battrering in 1944, there remain three great monuments of Norman date: the castle, the Abbaye aux Hommes and the Abbaye aux Dames. Other aspects of the city are described on p. 147.

Caen owes its present prominence to Duke William. At nearby Val-ès-Dunes in 1047 he defeated the rebellious barons of the Bessin and the Cotentin. After that he developed an otherwise unremarkable settlement at the confluence of the Orne and the Odon into a flourishing township and his favourite seat. In 1060, on a gentle outcrop a little north of this confluence he built a castle of which no trace remains today. The shorn-off walls of the donjon that can be seen in the castle precinct today are the work of William's son, Henry I, in 1123.

It was in the 1060s that Caen was really born, and it all resulted from William's marriage to Mathilda of Flanders. William and his prospective father-in-law, Count Baldwin V, wanted it, for their separate political reasons. Mathilda and Pope Leo IX were among those who did not. The potential bride swore that she would rather take the veil than marry a bastard. William slipped off to Bruges and made his way to Mathilda's room where he beat her up pretty comprehensively, dragging her round and round by her plaits. He then galloped back to Normandy and the girl took to her bed, so impressed by his behaviour that she averred she would never marry anyone else. William and Mathilda married at Eu in or about 1052, whereupon the Pope, who had prohibited the match in 1049 on doubtful grounds of consanguinity, excommunicated them and placed Normandy under a papal interdict.

You may be wondering what all this has to do with Caen. Lanfranc, Abbot of Le Bec-Hellouin and William's leading counsellor, was sent to Pope Nicholas II to get the interdict lifted. The Pope's conditions were that the sinning couple must each endow and build an abbey in the town where they had chosen to live – Caen. The severely beautiful western façade of William's church of St-Etienne, part of his Abbaye aux Hommes, was begun in 1062. Lanfranc, its first Abbot, had a hand in the design, hence the strong hints of Lombardy and Ravenna. Its coolly harmonious lines, inside and out, should not be missed. Mathilda's church of the Holy Trinity at the Abbaye aux Dames was dedicated in 1066 and is less astonishing but nonetheless worth seeing. Her own daughter Cecilia was the second Abbess. The two abbeys stand on a roughly east–west axis, about $1\frac{1}{2}$ kms apart and equidistant from the castle. They are the last resting places of their two great founders. Mathilda died in 1083 and lies in the choir in her original black marble tomb, disturbed twice over the centuries but still intact. William has, by contrast, fared miserably.

Things went wrong from the moment of his expiry in 1087 at the Abbaye de St-Gervais in Rouen. Important men, fearful of a disputed succession, fled to their estates. The lesser courtiers, seeing their master dead and unregarded, plundered his property and left him half naked on the floor. Several warm September days passed before means were found to convey his body down the Seine to Caen. Then a fire disturbed his funeral procession. During the requiem mass there was a fracas when shouts of 'Haro! Haro!' interrupted Gilbert, Bishop of Lisieux, in his sermon. This was the cry traditionally heard when petitioners came with grievances to their Norman lord (it is a custom still understood, if not practised, in the Channel Islands). A man called

Ascelin claimed that the very burial ground had belonged to his father before St-Etienne had been built. He was summarily silenced with a few sous. Then William's body, now bloated and putrefying, would not fit into his coffin and the attendants split it while trying to force it in. The stench was overwhelming. The notables fled while a few priests hurriedly concluded the obsequies.

Even after interment he could not rest. Protestants broke open the tomb in 1562, and the dismembered corpse was consigned to the Orne. Only a thighbone survived. There were more reburials before the Revolution, when in 1793 even that relic disappeared, to be recovered in 1984 in time to feature in a BBC television programme on the Normans. The slab in front of the high altar commemorates 'the invincible William the Conqueror, Duke of Normandy, King of England, founder of this house'.

Nine centuries on, he would not understand today's Caen – university city, port, seat of the prefecture of the department of Calvados, industrial centre, motorway terminal and airport. But he would admire the way it has overcome the vicissitudes of the centuries and been rebuilt, still using the familiar Caen stone from Fleury, after three-quarters of it was destroyed during the Liberation. And he would immediately remember the Romanesque lines of the church of St-Nicholas, just north of his abbey, built in 1083 by the monks of St-Etienne. Though they are twelfth-century buildings he would recognize in the castle the style of St-George, the garrison chapel, and the so-called Exchequer House, in fact part of the great hall of the ducal palace, with its dogtooth carving round the door. Of course, such architecture would be just as familiar to eleventh-century English eyes, and there is often a direct connection with Caen, because one of the town's greatest exports in those days was its matchless white oolitic limestone from Fleury, just to the south. When Herbert de Losinga proposed to build a cathedral at Norwich in 1096, for example, he ordered quantities of stone from Caen which was dressed in the quarries at Fleury and floated down the Orne in barges. Eventually their heavy load floated up the river Wensum to Norwich. Pull's Ferry now marks the place where a narrow creek was cut to carry the barges right into the cathedral close where they were unloaded.

Caen is a pleasant city to walk in, but to cover Norman Caen by foot would be tiring. I recommend driving to Mathilda's Abbaye aux Dames, which is the less exciting of the two but where parking is easy. The church of the Trinity is a good example of Romanesque, but the abbey itself, founded in 1042, was much rebuilt in the seventeenth century and again after World War II. Drive then north-west between castle and university up the Rue de la Pigacière (the one-way system will force you into this), swing round the top of the castle and down the Promenade St-Julien to the general area of the Abbaye aux Hommes. There are car parks in the Promenade or Place St-Sauveur to the south. This abbey is Caen's pride, and mercifully undamaged in 1944. The best outside view is still from a cul-de-sac at the west end, the Impasse Lebailly, but the abbey church of St-Etienne, consecrated in 1077, and the eighteenth-century convent buildings (now a school) look very good from across the Esplanade Louvel. After leaving the abbey I recommend you to leave your car and walk to the castle, as parking is difficult in the centre.

If the skill and sweat of hundreds of Norman quarrymen and masons contributed so much to English architecture, there is one unparalleled work involving many hands and many hours of delicate toil which went in the reverse direction – from, probably, Canterbury to Bayeux. I mean, of course, the Bayeux Tapestry. This amazing survival, still on show in the city for which it was first made in the ten years or so after the Conquest, tells the visitor more in an hour or two about the political, military and social scene on both sides of the Channel in the middle 1060s than could a shelf-full of books. It is really an enormous, intricate strip cartoon, full of vivid, telling images and is to be found in the Centre Guillaume le Conquérant (normal opening hours from June to September, slightly shorter hours at other times) in the Rue de Nesmond, a one-way street running towards the cathedral from the east. The easiest approach is from the adjacent Rue aux Coqs.

Much guesswork surrounds it, but few facts are known. First, the facts: it is not a tapestry at all, but a long piece of elaborately embroidered linen. The embroidery uses eight colours deployed haphazardly and now much faded. There is a broad central band with a text above it, and borders with often quite lively figures at top and bottom. It is 70·34 m long and 0·5 m deep. It covers the years 1063–6, and the central strip tells parts of the story of William's claim to the English throne and the seaborne invasion and battle at Hastings by which he secured it. It portrays 626 human figures of whom only four are women, 190 horses and mules, 506 other creatures – dogs, birds, deer and the like, thirty-seven ships, thirty-three buildings – palace, cathedral, motte and bailey castle, peasant's cabin – and thirty-seven trees, singly or in groups. The English have moustaches, while the Normans are clean-shaven. It is unique, though there are some similar surviving pieces of Scandinavian embroidery from the same period. It was made to hang on the walls of Bayeux Cathedral but is not mentioned in the diocesan records until 1476. Luckily it escaped the mindless destruction of the Wars of Religion and the Revolution and was used by Napoléon to boost French national fervour against the English. It was rather clumsily repaired in 1842 and since then has only left Bayeux during years of war and for a short spell after 1945 when it hung in the Louvre.

Now for some conjecture. The French call it the *Tapisserie de la Reine Mathilde*, but it is unlikely to have anything to do with Queen Mathilda. William's half-brother, Bishop Odo of Bayeux, features in it quite prominently, as do Wadard and Vital, two of his subsequent tenants, which has led to speculation that it was Odo who caused it to be made, most probably between 1066 and 1077, when Bayeux Cathedral was consecrated. It was almost certainly designed by a Norman artist who sketched an outline drawing on the linen for, perhaps, Kentish seamstresses to pick out with hand-woven woollen thread. They then filled in the figures with line upon line of stitchwork, leaving a background of bare linen. Its English workmanship is suggested by the appearance of an Anglo-Saxon letter among the rustic, semi-uncial capitals of the Latin text, various rather loose renderings of William's name, and repeated stress on the kingship of Harold. Some have read further meaning into the Aesop's Fables which are recalled here and there in the borders until scenes of carnage spill over towards the end.

Subjectively speaking, it is a sheer delight. I look for Harold's huntsmen, their skirts pulled up, carrying hounds and falcons through the Channel waves; the hair of William's mounted messengers streaming in the wind; a delightfully naturalistic Adam and Eve scene in the lower border; the dwarf groom Turold with his neat little trousers; Edward the Confessor looking decidedly

seedy and then being buried before he dies; Halley's comet blaz-
ing along in the upper border (quite authentically – it did appear
in 1066); and at the end the victors on Hastings field stripping
the chain mail shirts from the mangled corpses of the dead.

The supreme qualities of the embroidery might cause visitors
to undervalue the cathedral for which it was designed. The important date that older citizens of Bayeux will remember is 7
June 1944, for it was the first French city to be liberated by the
Allies – and with minimal damage, too. The great French
national day, 14 July, is also important for Bayeux not only as
Bastille day, but also as the anniversary of the dedication of
Bishop Odo's cathedral in 1077. Bayeux had already had a long
history: the Gallo-Roman Baiocassi were settled there and it
became a diocese in the late fourth century. Rollo the Ganger
took the town in the late ninth century and married Popa, the
governor's daughter. Their first son, to become the second duke,
William Longsword, was born here. The cathedral had been
under construction since the 1050s but only lasted until 1105,
when Henry I's soldiers burnt most of it. The crypt and the two
great west towers are the only Romanesque survivals, but the
rebuilding in Gothic style, as at Coutances, neatly encased the
earlier work. The cathedral is open during normal hours, and
from July to mid-September there is an audio-visual presenta-
tion every evening. If you are pressed for time note that the
cathedral usually opens an hour earlier than the embroidery, and
the two buildings are not far apart. Information on the other
aspects of Bayeux will be found on p. 135.

Just as a footnote, some twenty years ago, when I was a
schoolmaster, I was driving through Normandy with a minibus
full of boys on a holiday trip. It was a hot summer afternoon and
as I bowled south out of Bayeux down the D6 we had the off-
side door pulled back. Suddenly one of the boys dropped his
camera and it bounced out into the road. At 80 kph with eleven
up and a loaded roof-rack it took me quite a while to stop. As
the boys looked back they saw an old crone in black stop her
bicycle, grab the camera and pedal furiously back up the road
to some houses. By the time I had turned and driven up to the
small hamlet it was deserted. Dogs lay dozing in dusty drive-
ways. Behind lace-covered windows nothing seemed to move.

'Push on, sir,' the camera's owner gallantly said. But I refused
to let this thieving old baggage get away with it, and drove back

to Bayeux. In the neat, modern police station I told the gendarme what had happened. He motioned us to a nearby waiting room and picked up the telephone. *'Attendez!'* he said when he had finished, and so I sat quietly, chafing, thinking of the miles we still had to cover before night.

Presently the telephone rang. 'You will have your camera in a quarter of an hour,' the gendarme said. I asked how he had done it. *'Monsieur le curé!'* he said with a twinkle in his eye.

The tentacles of the Catholic church still reach everywhere in a Norman village. Apparently the local priest had guessed that it must be one of three or four old ladies whom he knew, had called round to see them, and one had cracked. . . .

Castles at Falaise and Caen and the embroidery at Bayeux are not the only evidence of Norman military prowess that can still be seen, and no architectural tour should omit the castles of Upper Normandy: Chambois, Brionne, Valmont, Arques, Gisors and, gem of the collection, Château Gaillard.

For castle buffs Chambois is a bit special. It was built by William de Mandeville in Henry II's reign on the upper waters of the Dives, north-east of Argentan, and despite being precisely where Canadian and American units met in August 1944 to close the Falaise pocket and surround the German 7th Army, the castle is perhaps the best preserved of its period in all Normandy. Four intact rectangular walls stand 25·7 m high. There are no floors or roof inside but the square towers at each corner are unusual and possibly derived from similar examples that the Normans were building in England at the time. The local town owns it, maintains the gardens and lets you in free.

Further north-east, south of the lower Seine valley and guarding the Risle, is the ruined Norman castle at Brionne. This is perhaps for enthusiasts only, for there is really only half a donjon left and even this is in a pretty poor, overgrown state. I was in Brionne on a busy Saturday morning when the streets were choked with vans unloading and baguette-clutching ladies streaming over the numerous pedestrian crossings. I tried to drive to the castle, but since the route is unsignposted and you cannot get there by car anyway I got into an awful tangle. Park in the square and stump up the hill – but unless you need an after-lunch walk for a view over the town you may not find it worthwhile.

Just east of Fécamp another Norman keep can be found, up the hill from the old Abbaye de Valmont. Built by Robert d'Estouteville, ancestor of the defender of Mont-St-Michel, the stone and brick structure has been much added to in later centuries and has newly been opened to the public.

In the hinterland behind Dieppe, and an excellent short excursion from there (see p. 21), is the fine castle at Arques-la-Bataille. Like a sleeping stone animal it lies on an isolated ridge between the rivers Béthune and Varenne before they join to form the Arques. At its higher, southern end is a square Norman keep built by Henry I around 1123 to replace an earlier fortification by William the Conqueror's uncle. The remaining curtain walls, running down the ridge and romantically overgrown and decaying, are later. It is at its most photogenic from the D100 coming from Beaumais, or from a bend on the D23 as it zigzags up from Arques towards Miromesnil.

Arques was very much a part of the struggle between the Anglo-Normans and the French in the times of Henry II, Richard and John. But fittingly the two Norman castles that come nearest to the ideal of what such a castle should look like, and perhaps the two most complete survivals, are the two that guarded the contentious frontier between the Duchy of Normandy and the Kingdom of France: Gisors and Château Gaillard.

Gisors lies on the former eastern border, the river Epte, and even today the castle dominates the town that now sprawls over on to the 'French' bank of the little river. In 1097 William Rufus employed Robert of Bellême to throw up a steep conical motte and crown it with an eight-sided donjon. His brother, Henry I, added the impressive curtain wall with its twelve towers. Henry II added more stonework, but nevertheless Gisors and other parts of Normandy were often in French hands. Even under Richard the Lionheart, who retained most of it, Gisors fell into the grip of Philippe Auguste of France – which caused Richard to build that other great defensive bastion, Château Gaillard. The Epte was never a frontier between the Norman Vexin and the French Vexin in the modern sense. The Vexin was simply a piece of country over which both armies ranged, investing castles and being in turn invested in them.

My most recent visit to the keep found it under repair but there were guided tours to the rest, almost every hour on the hour, including the Prisoners' Tower with its evocative graffiti.

The car park and main entrance are in the Place de Blamont, but if you are on foot head for the T-junction in the town centre. An attractive alleyway facing the Rue de Paris leads to the old postern gate from which twisting stairs lead directly up into the castle. If you do not go on the official tour there is no charge for a quick wander round the delightful flower gardens in the bailey.

Of all the castles I have mentioned Château Gaillard at Les Andelys is the greatest; it is a Mont-St-Michel among castles. Routes south from Dieppe and Le Havre are quite likely to pass east of Rouen, near Les Andelys. It is worth building in a slight detour, and you can in any case cross the Seine here conveniently and for nothing. Strictly speaking it is an Angevin castle and not Norman at all, since it was built by Richard the Lionheart from scratch between 1196 and 1198. But many of its features are Norman, and its siege and capture by Philippe Auguste six years later effectively rounds off for a while the English involvement in Normandy that began in 1066.

Set on a high chalk spur overlooking a north-eastern loop of the Seine, it was intended by Richard, lately back from the Third Crusade and his long imprisonment in Durnstein, as a forward base from which he could recapture Gisors and those parts of the Norman Vexin lost to the French by his brother John. It was built not in one year, as many sources suggest, but within three, which is still fast in an age when a castle took on average eight to ten. No expense was spared: Richard lavished £10,000 on it, £3,000 more than he spent on all his other castles in England. It was part of an elaborate system of defences involving a palisade across the Seine to check French penetration downstream to Rouen and a bridge across from the south bank via a fortified mid-river island to a new, walled settlement at Petit Andely.

For the best first view today, this is the place to aim for, along the northern bank of the Seine to the more attractive of the two Andelys. Cars and castles quite often do not mix well, and I left my vehicle in the Place St-Sauveur and walked past the cemetery up the clearly signposted Rue Richard-Coeur-de-Lion, although there is a one-way system for the less energetic which involves a long drive through Grand Andely with all its rather faceless factories. You take the Rue Louis Pasteur up the hill, then turn right into the Allée du Roi de Rome which drops steeply down to the often crowded car park.

There are, however, two advantages in the approach by car: fine views over Les Andelys and the Seine, and the fact that you can better appreciate the problems of Philippe Auguste's besieging army in 1203–4.

Château Gaillard is sited on a spur with steep slopes on three sides that Richard made even steeper. The fourth side he defended by cutting through the spur to create a giant saddle. With this south-eastern approach regarded as the only possible line of attack the castle was then built by armies of ditchers, diggers, levellers, barrowmen, hodmen, carpenters, fence-makers, mortar-mixers, water-carriers, smiths, miners, quarriers, masons both rough and free, lime-burners, porters and the like. The castle had four components: first the outer ward, which was a separate, triangular redoubt or *châtelet*; then, across a moat and linked by a permanent, Z-shaped bridge, was the massively walled middle ward; within this lay an inner ward protected by another moat and a long, oval *chemise* wall; and within that was the final stronghold, the keep. This is the order in which besiegers would have to penetrate them, and also the ascending order of their importance.

In 1203 Château Gaillard lay in the August sun like a stone dreadnought. Richard had died of a gangrenous arrow wound in 1199. John, after half-hearted efforts to defend it, had returned to England, leaving Roger de Lacy as castellan with three hundred men and about a thousand refugees. Philippe Auguste, having neutralized the Seine defences and taken Petit Andely, set his sappers and miners to work on a piece of curtain wall between two of the five towers of the outer ward – presumably where you can see gaps today, to the right or left of the foremost tower. In the manner still practised by Fred Dibnah, Britain's most celebrated demolisher of old mill chimneys, they picked away at the foot of the wall, shoring up the roof with wooden props as they dug, then stuffed the hole with combustibles, fired them and watched the wall crash down.

Siege warfare is also a waiting game. How much food did Roger de Lacy have? For his men, about a year's supply; but not for the refugees from Petit Andely. As winter began to pinch he shoved them out of the gate – old men, women and children. But Philippe Auguste, hoping that they would quickly eat out the English stocks, refused to receive them. Neither side gave way, and so through the bitter February weeks they lay in no

The castle gate at Caen

View of Château Gaillard across the Seine (Selina Head)

man's land, the wretched jetsam of war, living in holes in the ground, eating rats, birds and then each other. Rained on by missiles from either side, they were soon too far gone to be of further use in this desperate game, so Philippe Auguste relented.

Then his men had problems with the middle ward, and tried in vain to scale the chalk walls of the moat by sticking daggers in as foot- and handholds. But an observant scout noticed the outflow of a garderobe built in the thickness of the curtain wall. Some brave spirits squirmed up this unspeakable passage and found themselves in the crypt of a chapel. Sadly the walls here have fallen away, so the feat can only be imagined. Once inside they found an unbarred window in the chapel and hauled up several of their fellows. John had added this chapel in 1202, so he was in a sense responsible for the fall of the fortress his brother had believed impregnable. Roger de Lacy tried smoking the French out, but they made a great noise to suggest they were a large force and in the confusion the English panicked and fled into the inner ward. The invaders sallied out of the chapel, let down the drawbridge and the middle ward was theirs.

The curved *chemise* wall now faced them, made up of gently curving buttresses like a vast jelly mould. Persistence, ingenuity and luck now combined to favour the French. Richard had left an arch of rock as a bridge over the moat and sappers hid under it and began to undermine the *chemise*. The English counter-mined while the French brought up a siege engine called Ca-bulus which hurled rocks at the wall above. In time cracks appeared and a breach was made. This point can be clearly seen on the north-eastern side.

At this juncture Roger and his knights might have been ex-pected to take to the keep, a formidable tower overlooking the Seine, circular on the outer side, but with a right-angled beak projecting into the inner ward. It was a grim place – no well, no garderobe, no fireplace – designed for a last despairing stand. Stone arches circled the top from behind which defenders could drop hot oil, water and other missiles to ricochet from the angled base into the faces of any attackers. These are the earliest examples of machicolation, but they were never used. Roger's men had had enough. They fled through a postern and were soon rounded up. Château Gaillard fell to the French and the rest of Normandy soon followed.

5 D-Day Normandy

Eastern Manche, Calvados and the Battle Areas

On 6 June 1944 an invading force of 156,000 Allied troops landed in Normandy and began the Liberation of western Europe from the Germans. Forty years on, about a million and a half visitors a year come to those areas – the department of Calvados and most of Manche – fought over so bitterly in the ensuing two months. Three-quarters of them are French, but that still leaves several hundred thousand from other countries. Few of them, of whatever nation, are oblivious of the events of those months or unaware of the effect the war had on the towns, villages, beaches and fields that they now peacefully visit. On the other hand, not all those who are drawn into the main battle areas are particularly interested in World War II. There is much else to attract them, some of which has been described in Chapter 4; more details will be found in this chapter, which is not exclusively about battlefields and war museums.

However, a great many people from Britain, especially those who fought here and those related to them, do find themselves exploring the D-Day beaches or the hinterland to the south. They can get there most conveniently by car, and generally from Cherbourg, Caen or Le Havre. I have found it easiest to arrive in Cherbourg, slip down the Cotentin and then turn the corner at Carentan and head eastwards to Bayeux and Caen before swinging south again.

Beginning, then, at Cherbourg, follow signs to the Fort du Roule with its fine views over town and harbour. The area round the fort was the only part of Cherbourg to be severely damaged during four years of aerial bombing and the ground onslaught by

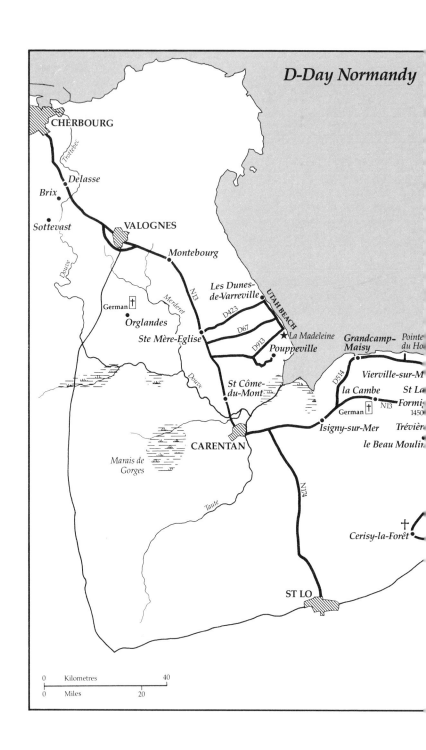

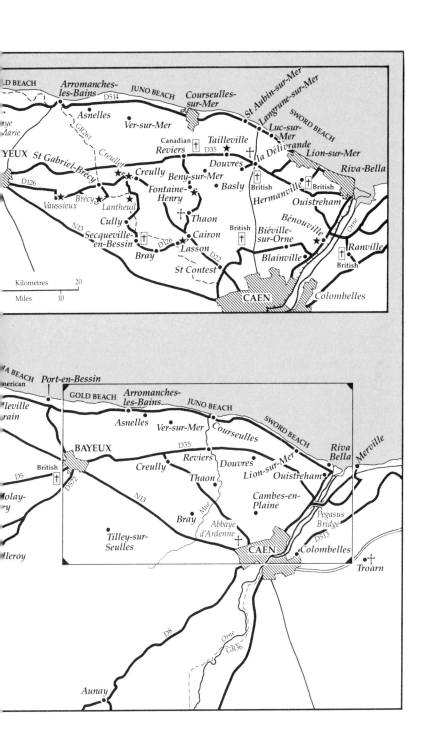

General J. Lawton Collins's three American divisions on 24 and
25 June. Cherbourg was important to the Allies. The first aim of
the American landing at Utah Beach was to secure it, for it was
understood that the Mulberry harbour, brought over the Channel
and erected in the sea off Arromanches, would not be able to
sustain the needs of the Allies as the invasion progressed. On
26 June General von Schlieben surrendered Cherbourg. Despite
German attempts to sabotage it the harbour was in use by the
Allies as early as 16 July and by November it was the umbilical
cord of the forces in Europe. The Pipe-Line Under The Ocean
(PLUTO) from the Isle of Wight to Cherbourg was begun soon
after the town's fall and oil was flowing through it by early
August. All this and more is documented in the War and Liberation Museum at the Fort du Roule, open during normal hours
except Tuesdays in winter.

Chapter 3 has suggested a wide range of interesting, more
leisurely routes from Cherbourg and down the Cotentin. You
may, nevertheless, simply take the N13, a dual carriageway for
much of its length. Leave the Fort du Roule on your left and
climb out of the town. In about 4 kms at a bend in the road
there is a fine view to the left over the Trottebec, which one is
tempted to take as an absolute equivalent of 'Troutbeck' and
was certainly named by the Vikings. After by-passing the village
of Delasse Scots motorists should turn right at the top of the hill
for a brief pilgrimage to the hamlet of Brix. Not only does it offer
a pretty view over a feeder stream of the Douve that you have
just crossed, but the castle ruins here are the original home of
the Bruce family who went on to provide kings of Scotland.
Robert de Brix (or Bruis) came over with the Conqueror, was
granted lands in Yorkshire and died about 1094. From here to
Valognes via Sottevast is not very far.

The town was General von Schlieben's headquarters in 1944
and was three-quarters destroyed between 6 and 10 June. Some
pleasant grey stone houses of the eighteenth-century *petite
bourgeoisie* survived, for example the Hôtel Beaumont with its
fine façade, which is open in the high season, afternoons only.
This town, ironically called the Versailles of Normandy because
of the social pretensions of its townsfolk, was once the Roman
station of Alauna, which surely gives us not only the name
Valognes but its suburb of Alleaume, to the north of the N13,
where there are Roman ruins. If you have inspected these you

deserve a visit to the Cider Museum in the Logis de Grand Quartier, open from mid-June to the end of September.

A very Roman road carries you on south-east to Montebourg and after slight deviation continues, equally Roman, to Ste-Mère-Eglise. During the night of 5 and 6 June Ste-Mère-Eglise became the first French town to be liberated. The D-Day landings were to be made in the Baie de la Seine between Montebourg and Cabourg. There were to be five separate bridgeheads: the Americans landing at Utah and Omaha beaches in the west, with the British and Canadians further east on Gold, Juno and Sword. The five divisions coming ashore on the morning of 6 June were to be helped to get a secure foothold and protected from German counter-attacks on their flanks by the landing of airborne divisions at each end – two American in the west, one British in the east – just a few hours before the main forces arrived on the beaches. So it was that twelve thousand paratroopers of the 82nd and 101st US Airborne Divisions parachuted into the southern Cotentin on the morning of 6 June.

The previous night, during the preliminary aerial attacks designed to make the Germans jittery, an incendiary bomb had set a house on fire in Ste-Mère-Eglise. Mayor Renaud roused several villagers who, under armed German guard, formed a chain of buckets from the pump by the church. They worked away, unaware that they were to be the first beneficiaries of a mammoth liberation force, at that very moment on its way by plane and ship. It is not difficult to imagine their astonishment and joy when they looked up and saw, caught in the light of the burning house, the first wave of parachutes ghosting down like giant snowflakes – two of them sadly landing in the burning house itself.

Later on, something almost as unfortunate happened to a paratrooper called John Steele. His parachute caught on the steeple of Ste-Mère-Eglise church and he hung there for two hours simulating death, until cut down by the Germans and made prisoner. This moment was immortalized in the film *The Longest Day*, when a mock church spire was built on the sports field outside the town. There is now a Hôtel John Steele as well as a Place du 6 Juin.

The church, if only for this extraordinary circumstance, is worth a visit. Two stained glass windows commemorate the airborne landings. The village pump is still there and opposite is the Musée des Troupes Aéroportées, an astonishing place shaped like a parachute and opened in 1964. It is looked after by an American war veteran, Philippe Jutras, who came here via Utah Beach and has written two books on this aspect of the war. It is open during normal hours. Next door is a second museum, housing a Douglas C47 aeroplane.

On 1 August, with the Battle of Normandy already won, General Leclerc's force of Free French, the 2e Division Blindée (Armoured Division) landed here and continued their progress 'from Chad to the Rhine'. In 1946 De Gaulle ordered pink marker stones to be put up every kilometre to trace out this *Voie de la Liberté 1944*. They show the flame of freedom rising from the sea and have the usual road number (now often out of date) and distances on the flanks. The one in Ste-Mère-Eglise is marked K 0 – kilometres 0. Behind it is a black marble memorial to the twenty-two local people who died in the fight for their town.

Utah Beach is 9 kms to the east through Turqueville and Audouville-la-Hubert. This is where the American 4th Division came in by sea, grey-gilled and shaken after far too long in their floating sardine tins. It is all well signposted and as you drive there along the D329, D913, D67 or D423 you will appreciate the problem the Americans faced. At the top of the beach is a long line of dunes. Behind that the fields are low and can easily be flooded. Across them, at right-angles to the beach, run the causeway roads, one of which you are perhaps on. The Germans did flood this and other low-lying areas in the southern Cotentin, and the 101st Airborne Division ('The Screaming Eagles') was dropped here specifically to secure these causeway roads so that the incoming 4th Division would have some way of getting off the beach and up to Ste-Mère-Eglise.

All sorts of things went wrong, yet not fatally. Some landing craft got into difficulties and tides carried them too far south. The oldest officer in the invading force, fifty-seven-year-old Brigadier-General Theodore Roosevelt Jnr, landing on the wrong beach, found it less heavily mined and defended by blockhouses than the right one. Sensibly, he settled for it and charged up and down swishing his walking stick and urging his men on into the dunes as wave after wave of landing craft came in.

The airborne landings of the 82nd ('The All-American') and 101st, too, had gone awry. They had come in over the west

One of the marker stones showing the flame of freedom rising from the sea (Sally-Anne Greville-Heygate)

coast of the Cotentin at Les Pieux. Cloud had confused the navigators and anti-aircraft fire knocked them off course. Instead of dropping in concentration they were spread over 30 kms. Many, sadly, fell into flooded fields and, heavily weighed down with kit, drowned under their parachutes. Yet this very chaos confused the Germans, and American units did manage to co-alesce and establish themselves on the Carentan–Cherbourg road.

At Utah Beach (La Madeleine) the Musée du Débarquement with films, exhibits and a diorama has been established in the former German blockhouse W5. It is open in summer during normal hours and is a very evocative museum, a place of reflection for ex-soldiers and their families. There are plenty of other memorials round about and another *Voie de la Liberté* marker stone, this time K 00.

You should then drive up the D421 to Les Dunes-de-Varreville where there is a monument to General Leclerc, bunkers, blockhouses and ruined bits of the Atlantic Wall with which Rommel tried to encircle the whole north French coast. All the insane, expensive and ultimately useless apparatus of Fortress Europe can be well understood here.

Then proceed inland, like the 4th Division, to Ste-Mère-Eglise again, via St-Martin-de-Varreville, where many Germans retreating from the beaches were caught and killed by paratroopers of the 3rd Battalion of the 101st. The toll on the Germans was very heavy and due east, about 8 kms from Ste-Mère-Eglise, in the vast, stone-walled cemetery at Orglandes, lie 10,152 German dead.

If you carry on down the N13 from Ste-Mère-Eglise via St-Côme-de-Mont you will see at some distance, in this flattest of terrains, the fine surviving tower and spire of Carentan church. This important point at which the Douve, Taute and other streams join and are bridged is a rich centre for dairy farming. It was a key point, too, for the Americans to secure, and fell on D-Day+6. Here the troops from Utah Beach joined with those from Omaha.

You may have to head south at this stage. If so, you should take the N174 to St-Lô. This unfortunate place earned the title in 1944 of the most devastated of all towns: it was a German Corps HQ and occupied a dominant position. The town is named after its founder, a sixth-century bishop of Coutances, and its old ramparts overlook the Vire. It had to be taken before the Americans could move on to liberate Avranches and Brittany. After a terrible eight-day siege they entered the almost totally demolished town on 19 July. The hero of the hour was Major Thomas D. Howie, killed in the final assault and carried by his men into the ruins of the church of Ste-Croix – he had wished to be the first soldier into St-Lô. Eight thousand of his comrades died here. The town is now, of course, entirely new, and as at Caen, you can see the ramparts more easily as a result. Howie has a square named after him and there is a Franco-American Memorial Hospital with an interesting mosaic by Fernand Léger.

From Carentan, most visitors will cross the Vire, still on the N13, and enter Calvados at Isigny-sur-Mer, which is the butter capital of the province. Like Carentan, it is a small port, reminiscent of some of those near the Wash, in Fen country. The main interest in the area ahead is, once again, the invasion beaches. From Grandcamp-Maisy to Port-en-Bessin stretches Omaha Beach – 'Bloody Omaha' as it became known. There were just 210 American casualties on Utah Beach on D-Day itself; at Omaha there were 3,880. It was the costliest D-Day battle, and very nearly lost. The other half of the 1st American Army, made up of the 29th and 1st Divisions, landed on Omaha and three factors contributed to their setback: the assault was not so intelligently planned as elsewhere, luck ran against them, and the Germans had geographical advantages on their side and very well defended positions.

After Isigny turn off left from the N13 up the D514, which will be your road for most of the way along the rest of the D-Day beaches. Grandcamp-les-Bains, or Grandcamp-Maisy, is a small fishing harbour and seaside resort. Shortly after it, turn left along the Chemin des Rangers for the Pointe du Hoc. This is a high, sheer-sided limestone bluff with fine views over the Vire estuary and the bay. The scene of one of the most desperate conflicts of the invasion, it remains a sealed off corner of the Normandy battlefield and still, despite the softening effects of erosion, evidently scarred by war. The Germans were believed to have fortified it with concrete bunkers containing several 155- and 88-mm guns which, if left in working order, could have wrought havoc on the invaders on Utah Beach, only 17 kms away, and Omaha. Intelligence was vague as the French Resistance could not gain access to this highly secret strong-

point. At all events, the position had been strafed from the air
for two months and in June two battalions of Rangers, the
American Special Forces, were tasked to neutralize the guns.
Equipped with extensible ladders and rocket-propelled grappling irons, they set off in their landing craft in the pre-dawn of
6 June. But the sea was strong and the tides contrary: they lost
three landing craft, arrived late and in the wrong place.
Lieutenant-Colonel James E. Rudder got 225 of his men ashore
to a hot reception, but the supporting fire from the battleship
Texas had so churned up the shore that he could not get his
ladders to the cliff, and seawater had made the ropes so heavy
that the rockets could not propel the grappling hooks to the top
of it. His men contrived somehow to struggle up while the Germans rolled grenades or suspended shells on time-fuses over
the edge. The televized re-enactment of this on the fortieth anniversary of D-Day showed young US Rangers clambering up
the western side of the cliff (the side Rudder should have
attacked if they had landed in the right place) against a thin fire
of blanks. The reality was very different.

They got to the top to enter a pockmarked, lunar landscape,
choking with gas and already smashed into ruin. And to their
amazement there were no guns there. The Germans had secretly
withdrawn them during the previous two months of bombing.
The Rangers' difficulties were now compounded, for they were
bombed and fired on by their own side. Strong German
counter-attacks began and went on for two days and nights, by
which time only ninety of the 225 were left. Today an obelisk
on top of a reconstructed blockhouse commemorates those
Rangers who died.

From the Pointe eastwards to Vierville runs the Sentier du
Littoral, and an excellent way of seeing Omaha Beach is simply
to walk down this well marked route – the whole path, from
Grandcamp-Maisy to Colleville-sur-Mer, is 15 kms long. Alternatively you may drive back to the D514 and follow it to
Vierville-sur-Mer. Here you will find the first of many monuments – to the American National Guard. The D517 should then
be followed to Les Moulins.

All along this coast, from 0630 on 6 June, the assault troops
struggled for a toehold. Most of them had been in landing craft
for too long. The seas were rough and there was much calling
for 'bags, brown, vomit'. Some men and tanks were launched

into the water too early and had to swim or sink. If they reached the beach they encountered a murderous enfilading fire from German bunkers and pillboxes, none of which the offshore battleship *Nevada* had much damaged. Twenty-seven out of twenty-nine amphibious tanks sank, so the Poor Bloody Infantry had to make a frontal assault without armoured support. Furthermore, the Americans had eschewed all the gadgetry that the British had developed for clearing the beaches of mines and other obstacles. Some men sheltered behind these obstacles, while others lay in the sea with only their heads protruding. When the successive waves of troops arrived they found the first wave still pinned on the beach. Men and equipment began to pile up. It was a grim moment. The German commander radioed to his HQ that the invasion tide had been stemmed. General Omar Bradley prepared orders to evacuate, though mercifully he did not give them. It was a near-run thing.

Destroyers came in within a kilometre of the shore to give support. The American 1st Division ('The Big Red One'), many of them veterans of Sicily and Salerno, rallied and pushed through the sea wall to attack Colleville. The 29th reached Vierville and St-Laurent. By nightfall they had a precarious bridgehead 9 kms long and – 3 kms deep, but the losses were awful – 3,880 men, over fifty tanks and much else besides.

The Vierville museum, Exposition Omaha 6 Juin, tells the full story graphically and is open during normal hours in summer. At Les Moulins there is, among others, a Monument du Débarquement and a memorial on the site of the first, temporary, American burial ground. Turn up to St-Laurent and on to Colleville. Here is the imposing and beautifully maintained American Military Cemetery in which lie nearly 9,400 dead. There is an orientation table here and a belvedere overlooking the sea and the 1st Division and the 5th Engineer Special Brigade have their own monuments nearby.

Seven kilometres along the D514 brings you to Port-en-Bessin, where the American Omaha Beach ended and the British Gold began. However if your interest in World War II is not so strong you might prefer to go from Isigny to Bayeux by the N13, making an occasional foray into the D-Day battlefield area. Or if you came by the coast road you could return by this more direct *route nationale*. This road should have been secured by the Allies on the evening of D-Day but it took a day or two longer. Shortly after leaving Isigny you come to another German cemetery at La Cambe. Here lie 21,160 soldiers of the Wehrmacht, including 296 in the conical ossuary surmounted by a heavy stone cross overshadowing two figures. Not all are German, for many units in France were made up of Russians, Ukrainians, Caucasians, Balts and others.

After 8 kms you will arrive in Formigny and find a monument out of keeping with all the others in this area. It was put up in 1903 to commemorate a battle fought here in 1450. England had held Normandy since 1418 but since the death of Henry V in 1422 France had been nibbling her way slowly back until by 1450 England retained only the Caen–Bayeux area and the Cotentin. An anxious Parliament sent an army of rather less than three thousand men under Sir Thomas Kyriell, who had fought at Agincourt thirty-five years before. He secured Valognes and went on towards Bayeux, but the French stood in his way at Formigny. On 15 April the English were vanquished. Before Sir John Fastolf could raise another army the French took Caen, Bayeux and Falaise and drove the English into the Cotentin, where only Cherbourg was left.

A fierce siege began. Cannon and bombard threw shot into the town and the fire was returned. Enguerrand de Monstrelet gives a lively picture of this fifteenth-century assault on Cherbourg:

There were even bombards situated on the seashore between high and low tide which were loaded with boulders; although they were under water when the tide was in, they were covered with greased skins so that the sea did no harm to their powder and as soon as the tide went out the cannoneers removed the coverings and continued firing into the town, to the great astonishment of the English, who had never seen anything like it.

This French ingenuity had its parallels in 1944, but this time it is not clear which side was the more inventive – the Germans or the British. The Germans had driven pointed wooden stakes into the beach at low water. Mines and other explosive charges were often fixed to them – 2,500 were collected up afterwards on Gold Beach alone. Bits of old railway line, concrete tetrahedrons and giant caltrops made of steel girders and known as 'Czech hedgehogs' were sown in parallel rows along the beaches from Antwerp to Cherbourg so as to tear out the

134

bottoms of incoming landing craft. The Atlantic Wall ran along the head of the beaches and behind the wall wooden piles were driven into open fields to impede gliders. To counter these devices the British landing craft arrived just two hours after low tide when much of the beach furniture was still exposed; the other hazards were dealt with using various contraptions such as Churchill tanks with flame-throwers, others with chain flails on revolving drums to clear a path through the minefields, and special ditch-crossing apparatus.

And so the British were back in Normandy for the first time since 1450 – this time only temporarily, and as the allies of the French. As you come into Formigny from the west you will find the chapel of St-Louis, built in 1486 as a gesture of thanksgiving by the Comte de Clermont, and the later monument by the N13. Just south of Formigny is the pleasant town of Trévières with its fine twelfth-century belfry; Le Beau Moulin and other small châteaux and manor houses are situated in the countryside around. At Surrain, a further 3 kms down the N13 to Bayeux, is the privately owned Musée de la Libération de la Normandie with vehicles, uniforms, arms and equipment. It is open during normal hours and has souvenirs for sale.

And so you come to Bayeux, which must detain any visitor for two or three hours and could well do so for two or three days. It is pre-eminently notable for the Tapestry and the cathedral for which it was designed, both described in Chapter 4 (see p. 114).

Your ticket to the Tapestry will admit you equally to the Baron Gérard Museum on the north side of the cathedral in the Place des Tribunaux. Rouen and Bayeux porcelain, locally made lace and Italian primitives are its speciality.

As you wander about old Bayeux you will see several elegant *Hôtels* or town houses of the nobility: the tourist office is situated in a fourteenth-century house *à pans de bois* in the Rue des Cuisiniers; there are four similar buildings in the parallel Rue Franche and seven or eight other notable examples – Bayeux was fortunate in being evacuated by General Kraiss and liberated undamaged on 7 June. South-west of the cathedral, on the ring road first built by the Allies to facilitate troop movements round the city, are grouped the British Military Cemetery, biggest of all with 4,655 burials, and, opposite, the memorial to the 1,837 men who have no known grave. Close by is the futuristic-looking and very well laid out Memorial Museum of the Battle of Normandy, opened in 1981. Vehicles, uniforms, weapons and documents are on display and there is a film, diorama and bookstall. It complements Arromanches, Ste-Mère-Eglise and Bénouville, which concentrate on the seaborne and airborne landings.

Bayeux keeps alive the crafts of embroidery and lacemaking, paramount in the nineteenth century. Schools teach these skills and mount exhibitions. In the Place aux Pommes are the Centre Normand de la Dentelle aux Fuseaux (Norman Bobbin Lacemaking Centre), which exhibits and sells work during normal opening times, and the next door Norman Craft Centre, which keeps much the same hours. The Atelier de l'Horloge covers embroidery and weaving as well as lacemaking and is at No. 2 Rue de la Poissonerie.

The four roads leading south off the ring road all offer interesting excursions which can be made from Bayeux in half a day each. Take the D5 to Le Molay-Littry, 14 kms away, for an interesting contrast after the intricacies of lacemaking and the bombardments of World War II. Here is the Musée de la Mine, where the visitor can sample some French industrial history. An eighteenth-century Marquis de Balleroy was a forgemaster but found local wood too expensive. He exploited the discovery at Littry in 1741 of a vein of coal, and in the nineteenth century up to six hundred men were at work in thirty shafts here. The Museum (open from April to the end of September during normal hours, except Wednesday, less often in winter) has a 1790 fire engine and assorted items of coal-mining equipment. In another building is a 1:10 model made in 1893 of a Picardy coalmine. Finally you can walk along a mine gallery.

About 8 kms further south-west is the eleventh-century abbey church of Cerisy-la-Forêt (see p. 105) which offers an evening *son et lumière*. Completing the triangle, 8 kms to the west, and more accessible directly from Bayeux down the D572 and D73, is the gem of the collection, the Château de Balleroy. It is worth bending your route quite a long way to see it and its associated Balloon Museum. The twenty-eight-year-old François Mansart spent ten years building the château, 1626–36, and the harmonious and mutually enhancing proportions of its elements testify to his infinite care. The village of Balleroy and the château were designed together, so the wide main street leads up to the big house, through formal gardens – arabesques and scrolls of trim box with gravel between, flanked by handsome annexes. The drive then crosses a dry moat and rises to a *cour d'honneur.* Two pavilions stand guard on either side, and finally there is the château itself in pinkish schist and white stone. It has a central *corps de logis* crowned with a simple lantern, and two wings. The interior is sheer magnificence: panelling, painted ceilings, an immense library, portraits – notably Pierre Mignard's Louis XIII. Built for Jean de Choisy, it stayed in the female line of the family and its *seigneurs* from 1704 to 1789 were marquises. The Balleroy family held it until 1970 when it was acquired by the Forbes Investors Advisory Institute Inc.

Malcolm Forbes founded the Balloon Museum in one of the annexes in 1975. The whole history of ballooning is here, from the Montgolfier brothers to today's long-distance high-flyers, with several exhibits. Every year for two days in June there is an international gathering of balloons and balloonists in the park. The museum and château are closed on Wednesdays, otherwise open in summer during normal hours except for those two days in June. Eat at the Hôtel des Biards in the village.

The department of Calvados has designated eleven *promenades* and signposted them. They vary in length from 20 to 40 kms and follow some of the quieter lanes of Normandy. They could be walked or driven or, perhaps best of all, cycled. Leaflets on all eleven are available from tourist offices. The three places just described – Le Molay-Littry, Cerisy-la-Forêt and Balleroy – make up the Route de la Forêt des Biards. West of Bayeux the Route des Trois Rivières reaches Trévières. The Route des Moulins circles round Creully and Thaon, east of Bayeux. Further south, the Route des Genêts meanders around south of Aunay-sur-Odon. So the countryside of the *bocage Normand* offers as much gentle, rural interest to today's walker or cyclist as it represented frustration and danger to the Allied tank commanders in June and July 1944.

The British and Canadian landing beaches lie to the north of Bayeux and Caen. An interesting tour along the coast road covers Gold, Juno and Sword – it is the D514 once more, all the way to Cabourg. Port-en-Bessin, the start of Gold, is the archetypal French fishing port, where two basins penetrate deep inland up the valley of the Dromme and everything revolves round the arrival and departure of trawlers. From time to time the French have tried to build it up as a port (Vauban gave it a fort in 1694), but its great day came in June 1944 when it was the petrol and oil terminal for the Allies before PLUTO came on stream. Since then the fishing industry has prospered so much that in 1972 the inner basin was enlarged and new auction sheds built. The harbour is protected by two stone jetties which curve out into the sea and are occupied at most hours by serious-looking, flat-capped sea anglers who look as if they are waiting for Edward Ardizzone to come along and sketch them. It is a charming town and would make a good base for the touring motorist; Bayeux is very near.

The monument on an arm of the outer harbour is dedicated to those who died in the landings there. Below Vauban's fort is a German bunker, built with the slave labour of the Todt organization. Here, inland of Port-en-Bessin, the important link-up was made between the British 50th Northumbrian Division on Gold and the US 1st Division on Omaha. HMS *Emerald* bombarded the town; then 47 Commando, Royal Marines, captured it on D-Day+1.

Five kilometres east is Longues-sur-Mer, and if you happen to be there on a Thursday afternoon you can visit the twelfth-century Abbaye de Ste-Marie. Otherwise you can turn north up the D104 to Le Chaos, a tumble of rocks where the cliff has fallen into the sea. There is a fine surviving battery here, whose four 155-mm guns were silenced by naval bombardment from HMS *Ajax* and the French cruiser *Georges Leygues* and taken on D-Day+1 by 47 Commando on their way to Port-en-Bessin.

They had come earlier from Arromanches, which is the next and perhaps most important place on this part of the invasion coast. Arromanches-les-Bains had, as its name implies, a modest reputation as a watering place when World War II began. Along the way it had had its moments of fame: in 1588 the Spanish galleon *San Salvador* was wrecked on a reef nearby, which thereafter bore the name Plâteau du Calvados. The name, in this corrupted form, was gradually attached to the whole region and, at the Revolution, the department – and indeed the excellent form of apple brandy produced within it. Arromanches was fortified with cannon by Vauban during the Seven Years' War in the mid-eighteenth century, but its essentially sleepy, sedate character was not shattered until Rommel's Atlantic Wall came after 1940, and it was selected as the site of one of the two Mulberry harbours that were to sustain the Allied landings. These events transformed the town: for a while afterwards it was known as Arromanches-Port Winston and adopted a new coat of arms, with the British lion, the American eagle and the star of liberty breaking the chains of occupation.

The Allies knew after the Dieppe raid of 1942 that they would not easily be able to capture a working French port, and so developed the audacious plan of bringing their own with them. The presence of the Plâteau du Calvados and the deep-water Fosse d'Espagne (Spanish grave) inshore of it pointed to Arromanches as a good site for the harbour, protected from Atlantic weather as it was by the Cotentin peninsula. It was not protection enough for Mulberry A (American), built off Omaha Beach, for a particularly bad storm shattered it on 19 June. But Mulberry B (British) survived, operated for eight months instead of the expected three, and a good bit of it is there still, albeit dispersed.

The Exposition Permanente du Débarquement in Arromanches is one of the finest museums of its kind anywhere. While other museums, such as the American one at Utah Beach, are homely, personal places for sombre reflection, the one at Arromanches astonishes by its attention to technical detail. It contains brilliant working models of the harbour and the landing beaches as well as a diorama of the disembarkation and a Royal Navy film. The harbour consisted of an outer ring of breakwaters made out of 146 concrete caissons together with sixty old merchant ships intentionally scuttled. The caissons were dragged across the Channel at 4 mph and set in place in the ten days between 7 and 17 June. Inside the miniature Cherbourg thus created were a number of floating steel pontoons, held in place on the sea bed and rising and falling with the tides. At these pierheads merchant ships discharged a million men, half a million vehicles and half a million tons of supplies, which were driven ashore along four floating pontoon bridges – in all 16 kms long. Port Winston exceeded all expectations, and the museum does so still for its many visitors. It is open every day during normal hours, but it is crowded and so it is best to go early in the morning or after lunch.

You can walk along this famous beach on the GR261 from

Port-en-Bessin to Caen, but at Arromanches the path turns inland through the sprinkling of châteaux east of Bayeux. Normandy battle sites are equally thick on the ground there, so you might arrange a circular tour to cover this interior zone as well as the coast. But to take the coast route first, proceed along the D514 towards Courseulles-sur-Mer. After Arromanches and Asnelles you come to Ver-sur-Mer, with its interesting four-storeyed eleventh-century church tower. The 50th Northumbrian Division came up the sand dunes west of here at 0725 on D-Day. It was for capturing thirty prisoners and silencing two German pillboxes and an anti-tank gun near Mont Fleury that CSM Stan Hollis of the Green Howards won the only VC awarded for action on D-Day.

In due course great men landed on the coast a little further east – at Graye, Winston Churchill on 12 June and King George VI on 16 June; at Courseulles, General de Gaulle on 14 June, to inaugurate the first provisional government of the Fourth Republic. A monument in the Place 6 Juin marks this occasion. Courseulles is a drying harbour, poor in bad weather, but it is popular among yachtsmen nevertheless – perhaps because it is a great centre for oysters. In 1944 it was a vital port before Arromanches really got going, and to protect it twelve old ships were sunk to make a miniature Mulberry – or Gooseberry – harbour.

The coast eastwards – the Côte de Nacre – or Pearl Coast – becomes increasingly built up with small, family seaside resorts, and Gold Beach has now given way to Juno, where the Canadian Division landed. Bernières-sur-Mer, which has a 67-m-high clock tower, was liberated by the French Canadians – a strange reversal of the Norman achievements of Samuel Champlain in 1608. This division did best of all in terms of distance gained on D-Day – by nightfall they were only 5 kms short of Caen. It was on Bernières beach, one and a half kilometres to the sea at low tide, that a pillbox with a persistent German sniper in it was silenced by a sapper bulldozer driving up behind and shovelling sand over it. At St-Aubin-sur-Mer, famed for its shrimps and crabs available on a catch-them-yourself basis on the plateau of drying rocks which lines this whole coast, are a number of monuments to French Canadian units. Locals in 1944 are said to have been astonished at the diligence with which the British army had taught its soldiers such excellent French!

You will then run immediately into Langrune-sur-Mer, whose etymology is of some interest: the Vikings, seeing an abundance of seaweed on the rocks, called it Land-groen, or Greenland. Langrune was well fortified and bitterly defended by the Germans and the monument you will pass is to 48 Commando, Royal Marines, who took two days to capture it. This is the western end of the last beach – Sword, a British responsibility. Luc-sur-Mer, Le Petit Enfer (not the most helpful name for the local *office de tourisme*), and Lion-sur-Mer now run into one another practically indistinguishably. On 6 and 7 June they were taken, with difficulty, by 48, 46 and 41 Commandos. Luc has a safe, sandy beach which makes it popular for children, and for rheumaticky adults it offers sea-water relief in Normandy's premier thalassotherapy centre. Styled the *'Capitale du Vareck'* – kelp capital – from the invigorating airs that are supposed to blow in over the seaweed, it has a casino and in its municipal park the skeleton of a whale beached here in 1885. Lion-sur-Mer has a sixteenth-century château (not open) with one of Philip II's cannon, perhaps recovered from the ill-fated *San Salvador*, and an interesting church with an eleventh-century tower.

At La Brèche d'Hermanville there is a memorial bearing the names of the old ships sunk to make a protective Gooseberry harbour for Sword Beach – like the French battleship *Le Courbet*, filled with concrete, whose remains you may be able to see at low tide. The D60A leads inland to the Hermanville cemetery with its 1,005 dead, mainly Lancastrians. Colleville-Montgomery-Plage comes next and, 2 kms inland, Colleville-Montgomery, both of which after the war added the very Norman name of the Commander-in-Chief of the 21st Army Group in his honour (see p. 50). The D514 here is called Rue Amiral Wietzel (captain of *Le Courbet*) and it leads to two memorials, one to Commandant Kieffer and the Free French element in 4 Commando, which drove the Germans out of the casino at Ouistreham-Riva-Bella.

Ouistreham is an ancient settlement at the mouth of the Orne, given the name 'West Ham' by the Saxons who first established themselves there. In the estuary William the Conqueror marshalled some of his fleet for the invasion of England and, in seeming retaliation, the English landed here many times in the following centuries on their way to attack Caen. So when Lord Lovat and 4 Commando followed the Free French in and swung round to Ouistreham it was a kind of reprise. Ouistreham and its seaside adjunct Riva-Bella, where the sea recedes over $1\frac{1}{2}$ kms at low tide, were too well fortified to be attacked frontally and so preserve their pre-war, slightly tatty, shanty-town look. But there are now new developments and sports facilities, and for yachtsmen it offers the only really reliable deep-water port between Cherbourg and Le Havre and accommodation in a marina for six hundred boats. Vessels may proceed to Caen 16 kms down the canal at a set time each day, when bridges will be opened, but at other times only in the company of a merchant ship. From 1986 Ouistreham will be the terminal point of a new Brittany Ferries service from Portsmouth. The Musée du Débarquement on the beach, near the casino and the tourist information office, opens daily during normal hours from June to mid-September, otherwise weekends only. The twelfth-century church of St-Samson is much restored, but has an unusual west front with three tiers of blind arcades.

If you are returning to Bayeux you should take the D35 and the D12 which run parallel to the coast road and 3–8 kms south of it. Alternatively you may choose to come out from Bayeux by this inland route and return by the coast. Leave Ouistreham by the D35A for Colleville-Montgomery (Colleville is a common Norman placename and leads to confusion: Colleville-sur-Mer is the site of the great American cemetery just inland of Omaha Beach, and there is another Colleville in the Valmont valley, east of Fécamp). As you move west down the D35 you will see the tall spires of the Basilica of Our Lady of La Délivrande, a notable Catholic shrine with a black madonna. Great pilgrimages take place on the feast days of the Virgin Mary. South of the village on the D7 is a mixed cemetery – 1,123 graves of British, Canadians, Australians, Belgians, Poles and Germans, and south-west, on the way to Basly, are the impressive ruins of the blockhouses of the German radar station at Douvres, an important objective, but one found too difficult to overcome until D-Day + 11. If you continue west along the D35 through Tailleville, where the Germans had a telephone exchange in the local château, you will come, just short of Reviers, to the Canadian cemetery at Bény-sur-Mer. Despite the name it is well inland, but high enough to offer good views over Juno Beach. Over two thousand Canadians lie here.

Between it and Bayeux, and not much disturbed by the shock of war, is a small nest of châteaux, abbeys and churches that are worth a pilgrimage in their own right. They can be seen, most of them, by making a U-shaped detour off the main east–west axis. Turn down the D170 and follow the valley of the Mue to Fontaine-Henry, the star of them all and arguably the best Renaissance architecture in Normandy. It was built in the late fifteenth and early sixteenth centuries on the site of a medieval fortress, and its lofty, steeply pitched slate roofs have become its trademark: their pitch is deeper than the actual stonework supporting them. While the Harcourts owned it, it was known as Fontaine-Harcourt. Later owners chose to recall its medieval originator, Henri de Tilly. Inside are paintings by many well-known French masters, a fine entrance hall and spiral staircase. The present owner, the Comtesse de Oilliamson, descended from one Williamson, a Scot in the service of Louis XI, opens the château at complicated times, essentially afternoons, except Tuesdays and Fridays. If it is closed or the cost seems high or time is short, just enjoy the sublime exterior, for some people find the interior disappointing.

Only 1 km to the south is the disused, twelfth-century church at Thaon, remote and beautiful in its setting. Dwindle down through Cairon, and just beyond, at Lasson, is another Renaissance château, thought to be by Hector Sohier, the architect of the church of St-Pierre at Caen. Thread west through Bray, past the (mainly) British cemetery with its 117 dead, to Secqueville-en-Bessin. Here you will find a fine Romanesque church and tower with a thirteenth-century spire, typical of many in the Caen region. A bit of judicious map-reading will bring you, heading north for 5 kms, to the decorous seventeenth-century Château de Lantheuil. Home of the Marquis de Naurois-Turgot, whose ancestor was the great financier Turgot, it operates guided tours in the afternoon, except Tuesday and Friday. Continue to Creully, where today's *mairie* is in fact an attractive château, once a feudal fortress given by Henry I to his bastard son, Robert of Kent, later the property of the Colbert family. Creully is open mornings and afternoons, but has rather longer hours in winter, oddly enough.

Very close by, somewhat confusingly, is Creullet, in the grounds of whose seventeenth-century château General Montgomery parked his caravan and set up his Tactical HQ. He found one deficiency, and sent an embarrassed aide-de-camp to borrow a chamber-pot from the *châtelaine*. In the middle of June he entertained Churchill, Smuts and King George VI there.

Take the D35 out of Creully, heading west to St-Gabriel-Brécy with its interesting ruins of an eleventh-century priory, a dependant house of the Benedictine monastery at Fécamp. Now a horticultural training centre, the former rectory, prior's house and choir – all of thirteenth- to fifteenth-century date – can be visited during normal opening hours except at weekends. Just 1 km south at Brécy the novelist Jacques de Lacretelle lives in a seventeenth-century château possibly built by François Mansart while engaged on the larger work at Balleroy (see p.136) and also remarkable for its ornate gardens, its wrought ironwork and its fine chimneypieces. It is open in the afternoons, except Wednesdays, and standing smack next to it is a fine little thirteenth-century church. Three kilometres west, still heading for Bayeux, is Vaussieux, which is a monument to the eighteenth-century Franco-American *entente*. In 1778 the Maréchal de Broglie borrowed it and the Comte de Rochambeau and forty thousand French soldiers exercised there to deceive the British, who had to tie down military and naval forces just in case France invaded. It cannot be visited.

A further 6 kms brings you back to Bayeux. I know of few other areas of France so thickly endowed with architectural treasures, secular and spiritual. The Loire valley is rich, but its riches are spread. Here, within a triangle of which the N13 between Bayeux and Caen is the base, I have referred to sixteen. An interesting walking holiday could be planned, in which you might take about a week wandering from Ouistreham or Lion-sur-Mer to Bayeux by way of all these places.

At Ouistreham my route across the D-Day landing beaches stopped just short of an area on the far eastern flank which saw some of the most stirring events of all. This chapter began with the American airborne landings on the western flank. Similar landings were made by the British 6th Airborne Division with the similar purpose of protecting the left flank of the main infantry beachhead, and additionally of securing intact the vital Bénouville bridges over the canal from Caen to the sea and the river Orne. The former, now renamed Pegasus Bridge, was taken in the middle of the night of 5–6 June, and the first house in

France to be liberated, the Café Gondrée, which stands close by the bridge, welcomed glider-borne British paratroopers at about twenty minutes past midnight.

A visit to the Pegasus Bridge is certain to be rewarding for enthusiasts or those with personal memories. You can still see much that is redolent of this brilliant action. Esplanade Major John Howard commemorates the commander of the force of six gliders who landed at 0016 in a field by the canal. Information boards in the field show just how accurately they were piloted in the darkness. Happily, during the fortieth anniversary celebrations in 1984 Mme Gondrée was still running the famous café, though she died shortly afterwards. The café became a medical centre on 6 June and is now virtually an Airborne Forces shrine. The canal bridge taken by Lieutenant Brotheridge and men of the Oxfordshire and Buckinghamshire Light Infantry is the original one, and the dent in the counterweight housing caused by a German bomb, fortunately dud, can still be seen. The German anti-tank gun in the pit opposite the Café Gondrée is the one that some of Howard's men used to dislodge German snipers from a nearby water-tower. Monuments abound, but most important of them is the Pegasus Bridge Museum opened in 1974 in what was the Gondrées' garden by General Sir Richard Gale, who commanded the 6th Airborne Division. There are models of the area, several personally donated exhibits and a guidebook written by Sir Huw Weldon, who came in with the 6th. It is open from April to the end of October during normal hours.

Equally evocative is the village of Ranville, just across the Pegasus and river Orne bridges. Two thousand men of 5 Parachute Brigade dropped into the fields around here in the small hours of 6 June. Ranville, secured by the 13th (Lancashire) Parachute Battalion at 0230, was the first village to be liberated, and Major-General Gale established his Command Post there. It is now the site of the Airborne cemetery, housing 2,563 dead. The now ruined tower of the church was used by spotters to bring down naval gunfire from HMS *Belfast* on to German positions in Colombelles to the south; the Germans replied by raking the tower with 88 mm artillery fire. A list of the units involved and a useful map can be found near the entrance to the cemetery. A good base here would be the Auberge Les Platanes on the Route d'Hérouvillette, which is highly recommended.

The Merville Battery is another site worth looking at. Follow the D514 towards Cabourg and turn off in Merville-Franceville on a road marked *'Batteries'*. Here was a well-defended position believed to contain four 150-mm guns, each in its casemate of 2-metre-thick concrete and facing down the line of Sword Beach. As the guns on the Pointe du Hoc threatened the American landings on Omaha Beach, so would these be disastrous to the British 3rd Division. In an elaborate plan the 9th Parachute Battalion were to neutralize the guns before the landings. Things went badly. A heavy preliminary pasting by Lancaster bombers was mostly off-target and left the batteries undamaged. With their planes deflected by wind and German anti-aircraft fire, and mistaking the Dives for the Orne, many of the 735 officers and men who jumped with Lieutenant-Colonel Otway fell off-course, some as far as 45 kms away. Gliders carrying other men and vital equipment never got there. Otway only mustered 150 men but nevertheless pressed home the attack. He took the batteries in thirty minutes but with the loss of half his depleted force. Just as the Americans found no guns on the Pointe du Hoc, Otway found no 150-mm guns but only much less far-ranging 75s, and had to abandon the position after taking it. There is a museum in one of the casemates, opened in 1982 by General Sir Nigel Poett, who had commanded the 5th Parachute Brigade. It is open from June to August, except on Tuesdays, during normal hours.

An alternative route to Merville, the inland D223, passes through Bréville. This had been an original objective of the 6th Airborne Division, but Rommel had personally noticed that its position on a ridge of higher ground overlooking Ranville and the Orne made it of great importance, and for many days the Germans held on to it. On D-Day+6 General Gale sent two battalions of the Parachute and the Devonshire Regiments to take Bréville, with Sherman tank support from 13th/18th Hussars. The British artillery fire fell short and killed many officers and men forming up in a wood near Amfréville. The survivors and some tanks pressed on to take the village, where the church was burning and there were scenes of terrible carnage. Ironically, having secured the central crossroads and church, the remaining troops were for a second time pulverized by a barrage of fire from their own artillery. But the Germans did not counter-attack and at a cost of about 180 lives Bréville was held. Most of the dead are in the Ranville cemetery, but two graves can be found in the shadow of the rebuilt village church

Actions like this took place in numberless trim villages in the broken, wooded country around Caen. Montgomery's plan, however, was that if the Anglo-Canadian advance was checked before the city fell it would attract German reserves from other parts of France and enable the Americans to break out in the west. This is what happened. The Warwickshire Regiment, for example, was checked at Blainville, just south of Pegasus Bridge on the D515, and Caen did not fall until after terrible attrition (Operation Goodwood) ending on 19 July.

It has been rebuilt with considerable care and skill, and there is still much to see in and around this charming city, whose main Norman architectural treasures survived and have been described on pages 111–114. Supposedly the Roman Cadamus or Cadomus, the city is now essentially a mixture of Norman and mid twentieth century. The Abbaye aux Hommes is at its western side, the Abbaye aux Dames to the east, built respectively by Wiliam the Conqueror and his Queen Mathilda. They must have made a strange couple – she just four feet two inches, he tall for his time at five feet nine (we know this from his thighbone) – but they loved Caen and endowed it in rich expiation of their supposedly wrongful marriage with the two abbeys, churches and hospitals; and William built a castle, too, whose successor lies on rising ground between two abbeys.

After exploring Caen's Norman treasures, return to Place St-Sauveur where there are good eighteenth-century houses, then thread through past much attractive half-timbering to the Rue St-Pierre, Caen's main shopping street. Heading north-east, you will come to the church of St-Sauveur, sometimes called Notre-Dame-de-Froide-Rue and a mixture of Gothic and Renaissance. A couple more sixteenth-century houses *à pans de bois*, Nos 52 and 54, survived 1944. When you see the church of St-Pierre on the right you are at the centre of Caen. The church itself is imposing and still has very good fragments of Gothic and Flamboyant stone carving, but on 9 June 1944 a shell from HMS *Rodney* struck the spire and sent it cascading through the nave roof. What you see today is largely a painstaking reconstruction.

The tourist information centre opposite is housed in the beau-

147

tiful, but also carefully restored, Hôtel d'Escoville, built by Nicolas le Valois d'Escoville between 1533 and 1538. Look at the courtyard before you go. Then cross the Rue St-Pierre and pass through pleasant gardens to the castle's Town Gate. The medieval castle walls, since the war cleared of the clutter of intervening centuries, are a fine prospect and above them a row of the attractive flags of Normandy – two golden lions one above the other on a red field – often snap in the breeze.

The Normandy Museum is inside the castle in the former Governor's House beyond well-groomed flower beds to the west. It contains a good collection of artefacts illustrating Norman life, arts and crafts – the making of lace, butter, cheese and pottery – through the ages. Open at the same times (daily, except Tuesdays and holidays, during normal hours, though it shuts early in winter) is the modern Musée des Beaux-Arts. This is excellent for a rainy day and I noted a Perugino, a Roger van der Weyden, a Nicholas Poussin (a Norman) and two Veroneses. There are also the fine Mancel collection of Dutch seventeenth-century masters and some good Impressionists – Manet, Corot and the like. Outside, good views over the city can be enjoyed from the ramparts on the south side. Note especially the fifteenth-century half-timbered Maison des Quatrans in the Rue de Geôle, the church of St-Pierre and the Tour Guillaume. You should remember that there are often troupes of school-children being shepherded around and when I was last there the castle was shrill with teachers' cries: 'Laisse les cailloux, Nicole! Marche normalement, Philippe!'

To the north of the castle is the university, founded by Henry VI in 1432, now specializing in science. Its ultra-modern buildings accommodate fifteen thousand students. Close by, beyond the modern church of St-Julien, is the Jardin des Plantes, started in 1736. It holds a varied collection of flowers, succulents and grasses, and the tropical house supports the enormous South American lilies *Victoria cruziana*.

There are plenty of trees and flowers in Caen itself. The replanned Caen is spacious and the *prairie* is a wedge of greenery which penetrates to the city's heart. After all this you may want to relax. There is a square pedestrian area opposite the Town Gate of the castle where you may sit on the pavement outside La Taverne Flamande or the next door L'Etoile and watch *la jeunesse Caennaise* trying to astonish the bourgeois.

Memorial at the Croix de Médavy in the Fôret D'Ecouves
(Sally-Anne Greville-Heygate)

I have always intended to try the local dish – *tripes à la mode de Caen* – but never yet achieved it. It is often to be seen on menus hereabouts and indeed if you are in Caen during any of the three or four *foires* held each year you may see the solemn procession of the Brotherhood of the Golden Tripe Sellers in their red gowns and white bibs. You could eat at the Poële d'Or at 7 Rue Laplace, or La Pomme d'Api, 127 Rue Saint-Jean – both offer good food and good value.

Caen has a ring of varied sites on its northern edge which would make a good afternoon tour. Head for Bénouville on the banks of the Canal Maritime de Caen à la Mer. Built by Baron Cachin in the 1850s, this 16-km ship canal makes Caen France's twelfth port. Apart from the Pegasus Bridge and museum Bénouville has an eighteenth-century château; the chapel and the garden may be visited and you should ask to see the splendid *escalier d'honneur* – worthy of a royal palace, some say. Pass through Blainville and take the D141 to Biéville, which was reached on the afternoon of D-Day and held. A narrow country lane leads to Epron on the D7. French Radio organized a public collection to rebuild a Norman village after the war and Epron won the jackpot. At next-door Cambes-en-Plaine there is a small cemetery with 224 British dead in it, mainly Staffordshire men. Pass through St-Contest (which should surely have won the jackpot), cross the D22 and you will come to Ardenne. Here are the ruins of a Norman abbey (see p. 105) which played their part in the war. Oberführer Kurt Meyer, a commander in a Hitler Youth division, used one of the turrets as an observation post in an attempt to check the Canadian advance on 7 June, and shortly afterwards forty-five Canadian prisoners were summarily murdered by the 12th SS against the abbey walls.

South and east of Caen lie pleasant areas for *promenades*, by car, bicycle or on foot, which are just a little further out than this northern ring. Leaflets on these waymarked *promenades* are available in the Caen tourist office. La Route des Genêts begins 30 kms from Caen at Aunay-sur-Odon in the more wooded country on the fringe of the true *bocage*. The town, reached by the D8, was destroyed in three days and took three years to rebuild, the church even longer. The very attractive road heads to Champandré Valcongrain and Mont Pinçon, the high point of Calvados at 365 m, which the 43rd Division took so decisively on 6 August. The former priory of Le Plessis-Grimault can be visited on the way to Ondefontaine and back to Aunay.

Thury-Harcourt is about the same distance from Caen – for motorists down the D561, for keen walkers along the GR36. It is the northern gate to the pretty but curiously misnamed Suisse Normande. I suppose it is a bit like parts of the Swiss Jura, but that is as far as it goes. Thury-Harcourt was the site of the eighteenth-century Château d'Harcourt, property of the Ducs d'Harcourt and totally destroyed, with its art collection, by the retreating Germans. The d'Harcourt family now live at Champ-de-Bataille (see p. 56). The park and gardens at Thury-Harcourt have survived (not to be confused with the arboretum at Harcourt near Brionne in the valley of the Risle) and are a *monument historique* open in the afternoons on Sundays and holidays until the end of June, thereafter daily until 'the first frosts'.

The Route de la Suisse Normande proceeds from Thury-Harcourt south-west to the D298 and the sixteenth-century Château de Pontécoulant, which belongs to Calvados and has a museum of old furniture and a landscaped park. Château and museum are open at the usual hours, except on Tuesdays and in October. The road meanders east to Clécy-le-Vey through very attractive wooded, watered country, with high, rocky points like l'Eminence along the way. You can even do some rock-climbing at Clécy. This is the most 'Swiss' part of this rather ambitiously named region and has the trim, manicured look of the Jura. The sixteenth-century Manoir de Placy contains a Norman folk art museum and in the Parc des Loisirs there is a miniature railway museum. Return to Thury-Harcourt by the Route des Crêtes (D133).

From Switzerland to Holland: east of Caen is the region of the Route des Marais. The marshes in question are those on either side of the Dives which claimed the lives of so many hapless paratroopers in June 1944. The Germans had flooded the area purposely, but since the battle of Varaville in 1057 – where Duke William cut off the rearguard of King Henri I of France as they struggled across the Dives on their way to sack Caen – the marshes have been progressively drained of seawater and turned to pasture. From Varaville the D95 runs south under the autoroute to Troarn, where there are abbey ruins (see p. 105). Various

151

departmental roads swing anti-clockwise past the Château de Beauquemare to Putot-en-Auge and Grangues. This is all flat going – *La Petite Hollande*, they call it – and would make a good day's cycle ride.

Lastly, La Route du Cidre, which is tangential to the previous route and could start at Beuvron-en-Auge, a most attractive *village sauvegardé* due east of Caen and south of Dozulé. The route, like the others, has directional arrows, this time with the sign of an apple, and leads through orchards and past manor houses to Cambremer, Bonnebosq and Beaufour-Druval. This is the area which produces some of the province's finest cider. The apple trees you see everywhere in the Pays d'Auge descend from those probably brought in by the kings of Navarre in the fourteenth century. Today they exist in an astonishing number of varieties, and it is said that the smallest and least sweet apples make the best cider. Such varieties as Tranquil, Yarlington Mill and Fieldmouse Red are mixed and pressed for their juices, which then slowly ferment and mature into cider.

As in Britain, it comes in many forms – sparkling or still, sweet, medium or dry, high or low in alcohol content. Farm cider (*bon bère*) is still until poured from the bottle, and tastes like scrumpy. Bottled cider (*cidre bouché*) is corked like champagne, though it is less fizzy. You have a choice between *brut* (very dry), *demi-sec* (medium-dry), or *doux* (medium-sweet). It goes well with most Norman dishes, especially with sea-food and *crêpes*. Many discerning Frenchmen drink Norman cider in preference to wine. It is cheaper, and in any case goes well with the often apple-orientated cuisine. There is nothing wrong with the stuff you can buy in supermarkets, but Britons should remember that if they take it home it counts in their duty-free allowance as a bottle of wine.

In the Pays d'Auge the industry's equivalent of *appellation contrôlée* is bestowed annually by competition on certain local farms and is called *Cru de Cambremer*. Those farms that can be visited exhibit the green and white *Cru de Cambremer* sign, and here you can see the cellars and presses with their heavy wooden or granite mills. And the smell! A tank corps officer once said that his abiding memory of the Normandy campaign was the heavy bouquet of apples crushed by his vehicle's tracks as he ploughed through an orchard. They even had their tanks turned unwittingly into cider presses when apples fell and became jammed under the revolving turrets.

Dégustation of the product is, of course, possible, indeed positively encouraged. Each one is subtly different. 'As the cider varies from place to place,' the leaflet says, 'it is advisable to taste it each time.' Since there are getting on for twenty selected farms on the list I am not sure whether to recommend you even to take a bicycle.

6 Innermost Normandy

Southern Manche, Orne, Eure

Normandy as a whole is relatively neglected by the British. Most of us prefer to dash down to the Loire Valley, the Dordogne or the Midi – on the Sloane Rangers' map of the world France is blank, apart from Paris, until you get to the Dordogne ('Friends have a farmhouse'). But some parts of Normandy are more neglected than others. Deauville, Trouville, Honfleur, Caen, Bayeux and the D-Day beaches are popular, but southern Normandy normally catches motorists at full tilt, on the first or second day out of St-Malo, Cherbourg, Le Havre or Dieppe. This was certainly my experience of the area for twenty years – I perhaps paused in Flers on the way through, I may have camped in a wood near Carrouges, I sent a postcard home from Barenton. But I never stayed anywhere long, to get the feel of a place.

The interior of Normandy breaks broadly into two: to the west, south of the Cotentin, is the heart of the *bocage Normand*, a hilly region of small, hedged fields, high rainfall and consequently lush grass, contented cows and miry lanes. Further east are the plains and plateaux of Orne and Eure, the Perche Normand and the Pays d'Ouche, flat uplands with vast, unhedged fields of arable crops and pasture, dotted with orchards and woodland and intersected by the often steep valleys of northward-flowing rivers – the Orne, Dives, Touques, Charentonne, Risle, Iton and Eure. Lately I have found these two areas full of interest in their own right.

I went across this hinterland belt of country from west to east, from Avranches on the bay of Mont-St-Michel to the river Seine. As I left Avranches I was in Lower Normandy, although the land is on average higher than in Upper Normandy further to the east. Lower Normandy is geologically different from Upper. If you draw a curving line from Cherbourg to Alençon, everything to

154

The bocage Normand (Sally-Anne Greville-Heygate)

The Tour de Bonvouloir at Lessart

Inner Normandy

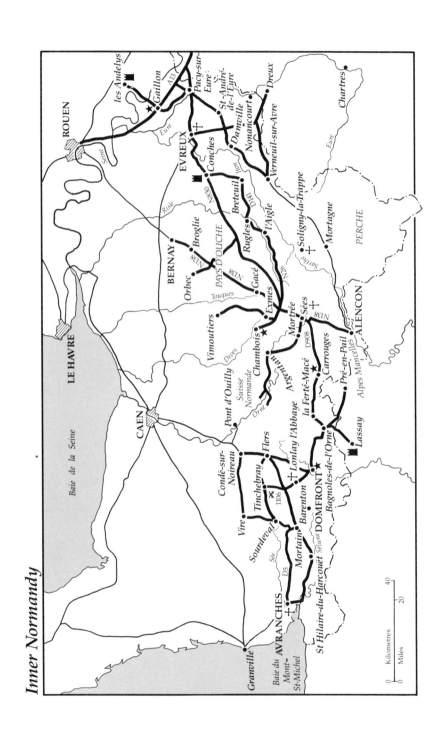

the left of it, including Brittany, is part of the so-called Armorican massif – shales and sandstone with great granite outcrops running in parallel east–west lines. Running out westwards between these ridges of granite are the four Ss – the Soulles and the Sienne, which find their way to the Channel near Coutances, and the Sée and the Sélune, which converge into the bay of Mont-St-Michel at Avranches.

The proximity of the granite ridges which hem in the Sélune has enabled it to be dammed, creating two attractive reservoirs which now fill the valley. If you take the D78 out of Ducey, five miles south-east of Avranches, you can weave back and forth across the Sélune three times and see it all before reaching St-Hilaire-du-Harcouët. It is a picturesque if meandering way of getting you on course for Mortain.

A more direct route to that deathly-sounding place is the D5, but this brings you into the town from above, and in a way that gives no sense of its unusual position. For Mortain, scene of savage fighting in World War II, is halfway up a hillside and straggles along a slope above the tumbling river Cance. There is something of the Derbyshire Dales about it, or the Devil's Bridge near Aberystwyth. The cascades below are a popular beauty spot.

There is a Place du Château so I presume there are signs of a castle there, though the Michelin green guide does not mention one. There must surely have been some fortification once, for William the Conqueror made his half-brother Robert Comte de Mortain, and its *comtes* were, with the Bellêmes of nearby Domfront, the traditional guardians of the marches of this part of southern Normandy from the depredations of the Angevins from Maine, which is only 13 kms to the south. What you *can* see, however, for two months in the summer, is the White Abbey crowning the ridge at the top of the town (see p.104) with its museum of Africana. Otherwise there is just the rather gloomy granite church of St-Evroult in the town centre, built in the thirteenth century.

When I last stopped in Mortain it was to do a bit of Christmas shopping, and this quiet little town had adopted the deplorable practice of relaying pop music through loudspeakers attached to every street lamp standard. This was happening in most of the small Norman towns I visited at that time. In Mortain two old men with several metres of bread under their arms and dead

Gauloises adhering to their lower lips stood looking baffled as Duran Duran blared out into the crisp morning air.

Drop away down the hill and an attractive road south-east skirts the Forêt de Mortain, passes Barenton and brings you to the foot of the sharp ridge occupied by the town of Domfront and its stern-looking castle ruins and ramparts. If Brionne in Orne had not got there first it might be twinned with Shaftesbury in Dorset, for its situation is almost identical. This is the town of the beastly Bellême family, who originated from the place of the same name in the Perche. They became Comtes d'Alençon, held Domfront and the bishoprics of Sées and Le Mans, and were powerful subjects of Duke William before the Conquest. Most of this complicatedly large clan were probably not much more foul than their fellows, but Robert of Bellême, born about 1052, the younger son of Roger de Montgomery, 1st Earl of Shrewsbury, seems to have become an exemplar of medieval villainy. Robert's 'contemporary reputation for sadism', one writer says, 'was extreme, even among the cruel Normans'. His life is a muddled catalogue of fealty and betrayal, of sieges and battles.

He was an outstanding military architect – the builder of Gisors – and horse-breeder, bringing Spanish horses to Wales and the famous Percheron breed (from the Perche) to England. But like Vlad the Impaler of Wallachia, immortalized as Count Dracula, he is remembered most as a byword for beastliness. After his wife had borne him a son, he locked her up in the Château de Bellême (luckily she managed to escape to Chartres). He personally gouged out the eyes of his own godson, whose father had displeased him. An irreligious man, he once starved three hundred prisoners to death during Lent. He had men and women impaled. He so maltreated his vassals that his enforced departure from his Welsh marcher estates around Bridgnorth occasioned widespread rejoicing, matched only by the gloom of his vassals near Domfront to whom he returned. When Henry I finally seized him and imprisoned him in 1112 any tears were probably ones of relief. He was incarcerated at Wareham and died an unrecorded death some time after 1130.

It would be sacrilege to climb up to Domfront before looking at the gem of a Romanesque church, Notre-Dame sur l'Eau, built at the time that Robert of Bellême was at the peak of his career, and still standing by the bridge over the Varenne. One hundred and fifty years ago road improvers lopped off most of its nave but what is left is quite delightful despite the constant traffic.

One's eye then travels up to the ridge and the remains of William of Bellême's very early eleventh-century donjon. To get there, climb the hill to the town centre. Press straight across into the old quarter (not old, sadly, but a slightly too twee and tidy post-war reconstruction). Pass under a bridge and then instinct will make you turn left – the only other option drops down off the crest northwards to Flers. The lofty, modern church of St-Julien appears on the left. The road turns right past the hôtel de ville and suddenly you will emerge by the public gardens which now surround the ruined donjon of the Bellêmes. The conviction that castles are generally built on the highest ground will guide you, as it did me, to this airy eminence with its views over the small fields and high hedges of Passais. Domfront's houses grow out of the living rock: it has the exposed, beleaguered look of a frontier town.

Tinchebray to the north is rebuilt and unremarkable, except as the site of a little-known battle between Henry I and the traitorous Robert of Bellême in 1106.

It lies now in the middle of the grandly titled Industrial Quadrilateral of the Central Bocage, bounded by Vire, Condé-sur-Noireau, Flers and Sourdeval. While the rest of the Normandy *bocage* has slowly depopulated, this area has grown astonishingly in the last fifty years: Flers has doubled in size, Vire trebled. Car parts, machinery, metalwork, textiles, asbestos for brake linings, clothing, biscuits and confectionery, as well as the expected milk, butter and cheeses, are produced. Tinchebray itself turns out metal goods and sweets – I recommend the excellent chocolates from the Chocolaterie de l'Abbaye, available in most *pâtisseries* in the province.

But this is only light industry and mostly concentrated in the small towns. The countryside is still the main resource and it is as attractive as anywhere else – do not anticipate anything like the road between Sheffield and Rotherham. This is the Bocage Virois and further north lies the Bocage du Cotentin, further east the Bocage Ornais. These *bocages* are slightly more open – still the small fields, high hedges and muddy lanes between, but not so corrugated, thicketed and close as the *bocage Normand* proper, or *bocage profond* as it is sometimes called, of the Mortain–

Domfront region, with its higher rainfall and more medieval, forested, rock-strewn aspect.

Agriculturally, the *bocage profond* is poor country, with quiet, isolated almost dead villages like Ger on the Mortain–Flers road, which I had to visit on account of its odd name. The authorities hope to arrest its depopulation by attracting more tourists to its existing, lesser-known treasures like nearby Lonlay l'Abbaye (see p.105), and by offering them various newer country pur- suits. To encourage all this the Normandy–Maine Regional Na- ture Park has been set up, which has its headquarters in the Château de Carrouges. A heavily wooded, T-shaped area be- tween Mortain and Sées, with a leg dropping down into Maine to include Sillé-le-Guillaume, it is at the moment still little more than a project.

It is an attractive 16-km walk down the GR22 from Domfront through the Forêt des Andaines to Bagnoles-de-l'Orne, one of the Regional Park's more interesting centres. Alternatively you can drive through the forest on the D908, Roman and spear- straight, turning off at L'Etoile, where nine equally straight roads or footpaths come together at the centre of the star. It is actually worth turning off more sharply on a *route forestière* to Lessart – near there is one of Normandy's oddest monuments and not to be missed by those with a taste for *curiosa*. The Tour de Bon- vouloir is almost all that is left of a fifteenth-century château built as a celebration by the then lord, who had for many years longed for heirs but was impotent. After taking a course of baths in the thermal springs at Bagnoles de l'Orne he sired ten children in as many years. As an expression of his joy he built an erect obser- vation tower some 25 m high, which rises alongside a small, thicker, conventionally rounded bastion. Euphemistically called a tower, beacon, even lighthouse in maps and guide books, it is in fact an impressive phallic symbol.

'*S'adresser au fermière,*' the notice said boldly, but surely un- grammatically. I did, and a cheery, rose-cheeked woman emerged carrying buckets of swill. There was a twinkle in her eye as she nodded towards the tower and said, '*On ne monte plus de l'haut.*' I could well see why. The tiles on the realistic pepper-pot roof had begun to drop off like autumn leaves. The whole attractive ensemble is free. There are farm buildings all round, the former bailey being now a muddy yard where cider can be supped on rustic benches in the summer. Behind a fine cylindrical *colombier* were several rows of cages containing vast rabbits. The breeding theme continues.

Bagnoles-de-l'Orne is a rural spa, supposedly the biggest in western France. But like all spa towns, and indeed the waters they dispense, it is an acquired taste. In summer I dare say it is quite lively, with droves of old ladies tottering into the *Etablisse-ment Thermale* for the cure, or moving decorously across the large lake in pedalos. In winter – but this is probably true of rural spas everywhere – it is dead, its streets empty, its hotels closed: like Wigan in Wakes Week. However I found a restaurant which would have earned my recommendation even had it not been the only one open. La Toque Blanche in the Place de la République gave us a good *terrine maison* and *filet de l'hareng*, followed by a seasonable turkey dish – *escalope de dinde*. The forests, amid which the spa town developed in the 1840s are still very evident. The river Vée runs into its lake in which are reflected stately nineteenth-century casinos and hotels. The sulphurous waters, to be both bathed in and drunk, are efficacious, so the town claims, in treating *affections veineuses*, obesity, phlebitis and a whole lot besides. It is a place worth considering as a point at which to pause for a day or two on the way south from the Channel ports.

Some interesting excursions can be made from Bagnoles. The Château de Couterne (only the exterior can be looked at), built in the 1540s and extended in the eighteenth century, lies 5 kms to the south. You can go via Pré-en-Pail to the Alpes Mancelles and the attractive upper valley of the Sarthe in Maine. Those who have time or patience for only one château should go to Carrouges, via La Ferté-Macé. Better than Couterne because it is open, Renaissance Carrouges dates from Henri IV's time; it is large, moated, atmospheric and finely furnished. If you happen to be heading south from Domfront or Bagnoles a pleasant place to pause would be the old town of Lassay, across the river Mayenne and thus strictly in Maine. There are two châteaux here. The first is a stark Renaissance ruin at Bois-Thibault with patched up walls of different periods and unglazed windows like empty eye sockets. In the town itself and overlooking a small tributary of the Mayenne is a formidable, multi-turreted fifteenth-century castle, a fairytale place of drawbridges, garderobes and machicolation. (Beware of some possible confusion here. This is Lassay, but there is also Lessay in Manche, with its abbey. Barenton and Barentin are both in Normandy, and while we have looked at Mortain, Mortagne lies ahead in the Perche Normand.)

Moving east towards Sées to the heart of the vast Forêt d'Ecouves you will come across another *étoile*, of seven straight roads this time, at the Carrefour de la Croix de Médavi. A Sherman tank of the 2nd Free French Armoured Division reminds visitors that we are still in the 1944 battle zone. The highest point in north-west France – 417 m – is not far from here.

Sées (which can also be spelt Séez) is a most attractive little city and worth an hour or two's stop. A declining town, really (it has been going down since the fourth century), it is the seat of one of the oldest of Normandy's six bishoprics with a fine thirteenth-century Gothic cathedral, and is thus, technically, a city.

The cathedral precincts offer everything to delight the eye – that harmonious blend of secular and ecclesiastical architecture so often found in France, yet so different on every occasion. At the top of the slope on which the cathedral stands is an elegant eighteenth-century hôtel de ville under which hides a sparsely stocked syndicat d'initiative office. Across the road lie shops and a hotel with some fine frontages. In the centre is a statue of the city's local worthy, Nicolas-Jacques Conté, engineer and chemist, born in the nearby hamlet of St-Cénéry and the inventor of the lead pencil. But looming over all this is the chief glory of Sées, that cathedral. Gallo-Roman Christians were the first to build here, and what we see is probably the fourth cathedral on the site. An early one was burnt down in 1048 by its own bishop, unable to dislodge a crowd of his enemies who had occupied and fortified it in his absence. The perpetrator of this dire remedy was Bishop Yves of – no prizes for guessing this – the Bellême family. The west end of the present structure looks a bit of a mess. This is because it began to sink in the sixteenth century and so two disproportionately massive buttresses were slapped up against it. But inside no adaptations have been made since the thirteenth century to mar the cold purity of the Gothic nave. The lines of its pillars rise clean and vertical to their gabled arches. The cathedral seems unusually empty, devoid almost of statuary, as if the iconoclasm of the Wars of Religion had never been reversed.

But there was one corner where I thought it had been. A young man in a mackintosh joined us in the south transept. He and a companion stood in front of an awful plastic-looking figure of Mary holding the infant Jesus. *'Voilà la Vierge,'* he said, and in reverential tones they began to cluck over its beauty. I mentally scorned them in my Protestant way. How could they, amid all that airy Gothic simplicity, home in on this vulgar object? Later I discovered in Michelin that it was the rare and beautiful fourteenth-century marble and gold Notre Dame de Sées....

All roads around the cathedral lead to fine church buildings now put to other use. Behind it is the eighteenth-century bishop's residence, today a school; there is a former abbey and a seminary. It is a place where you expect to see, not traffic, but crocodiles of choristers led by coifed nuns. I doubt that much ever happens in sleepy Sées.

The little city lies in what has been called Normandy's 'Fertile Crescent' – a swathe of land which swings in a boomerang shape from Alençon, up through Argentan and Falaise north to Caen, then along the coast to Honfleur.

Alençon is a large, prosperous town on the upper Sarthe and is always coloured in my mind, perhaps unfairly, by its dukes, who throughout history seem to have been a pretty feckless lot. Shakespeare may be partly to blame. He has one in the first part of *Henry VI* who spends a lot of time with other French notables bolstering up his courage by saying what a starved and pathetic bunch the English garrison at Orleans are, then charging madly at them and being soundly clobbered. Charles, Duc d'Alençon, 'contemptible.... ineffectual,' later fought for François I at Marignano and Pavia and fled the field on both occasions. An earlier Alençon had fallen at Crécy, Duc Jean at Agincourt. I should have thought it was a title to let lapse, but it kept being revived right up to Louis Philippe's time.

The castle of the former dukes, in the centre of the town, is a gloomy-looking place, and properly so, for the Germans did away with scores of French Resistance workers within its walls between 1940 and 1944, and it is still a prison. But there is more to Alençon than this.

Immediately to the north of the castle is Place Foch, a large, handsome square fringed by some good-looking buildings – the town hall, which houses an art gallery, and the Palais de Justice.

163

If you leave your car there it is an easy walk to the fine church of Notre-Dame, built in Flamboyant Gothic style in 1444. A lofty, three-sided porch, added in the early sixteenth century, rises from amid the half-timbered shop buildings that hem it in.

The lace museum is not far away, by the Pont Neuf which spans the Sarthe. Lace has been made in Alençon for over five hundred years but was given a boost in 1665 when Louis XIV's minister, Colbert, a Norman from Rouen, subsidized the craft in Alençon and Argentan. Intricate hand-made work is still produced but is, understandably, very expensive. The nimble fingers of Alençon girls are now more likely to be assembling kitchen mixers at the Moulinex factory, which employs over two thousand people.

The most famous *Alençonnaise* was undoubtedly Marie Françoise Thérèse Martin, who became Ste-Thérèse of Lisieux. She was born in 1873 in Rue St-Blaise and devotees can enter her former room from an adjoining chapel.

If you take the attractive D26 due north of Alençon you will recross the Forêt d'Ecouves and come again to the Carrefour de la Croix de Médavi, a watershed between the Biscay and Channel river systems. From here a green-line (scenic) road runs all the way north to Montmorrei, near Mortrée. This village is worth starring on any itinerary, for just north of the Sées–Argentan main road is the exquisite Château d'O, I must admit that it was its name that first drew me to it: it is thought to be German in origin, and a d'O is said to have fought in the Crusades.

The château rises sheer from the waters of a small lake. The natural moat is narrow enough on two sides for it to be spanned. The main entrance bridge brings the visitor to the oldest of the three wings, built about 1500, probably by Jean d'O, Charles VIII's Chamberlain, when he had recovered his lands from the English after the Hundred Year's War. This building represents an important transitional moment in domestic architecture, which is why the entrance wing is Gothic and defensible in plan, but Renaissance in actual construction, with large glazed windows and no element of fortification.

The buildings occupy three sides of a rectangle surrounding a courtyard which opens on to the lake. The south range was built in the sixteenth century when Charles d'O and his grandson François brought further fame to the family. François was Master of the Wardrobe to Henri III and Minister of Finances from 1578 to 1594. He was one of the wealthiest men in France during his life but died bankrupt in 1594, after which the property began its passage through many hands. The de Montagus added the final west wing in the eighteenth century, but almost all the castle lands were sold off in the nineteenth. After World War II it became a holiday home for sailors' children until bought in 1973 by Jacques de Lacretelle, whose son and daughter-in-law now run a summer school where young people study art, sculpture and music. The château is a favourite of French advertising agencies and is often seen on television.

Visitors to O should arrive in the late morning and first eat lunch at the excellent Ferme d'O restaurant, run by the château owners in a converted thirteenth-century barn in a nearby court-yard. Try the *poularde au cidre, sole Ferme d'O, filet de boeuf Monglas* or the *fricassée de caïon* – any day except Wednesdays.

Near neighbours are the Médavy-Grancey family, who occupy the attractive eighteenth-century Château de Médavy. Two vast towers with slated roofs mark the remains of an earlier fortified town. The family are chary of unannounced visitors and I got no further than an impressive wrought-iron gate with a frieze of spikes fashioned like antlers to deter intruders. The château does, in fact, open to the public between 14 July and the end of August.

Deviating up the Fertile Crescent a little further you pass the Château de Sassy, south of the main road and open in the high season. If you enjoy traffic jams and happen to be in the area on 25 July, or the Sunday after, head to the adjacent village of St-Christophe-le-Jajolet, because on that day, Christopher being the patron saint of travellers, the church will bless your car and all the others that have managed to fight their way there. It ought to be called St Christophe-le-Chevrolet.

After this you come to Argentan, a large town on the Paris–Granville railway line and the Alençon–Caen road. Part of the lower jaw of the pincer movement that trapped the German 7th Army in August 1944, it was devastated by the Americans and Free French. Two old churches survived the bombardment and there is a castle that was ruined already and is now a law court. It was here that four knights in 1170 heard Henry II complain of being 'mocked so shamefully by a certain low-born clerk' – a remark which led to their murder of Thomas à Becket at Canterbury. Argentan is one of the gateways to the region known rather flatteringly as the Suisse Normande. Take the D15 west-wards to Putanges-Pont-Ecrepin. Here the river Orne begins to cut its way into the landscape, creating some lofty rock cliffs with fine outlooks over wooded hillsides and the winding watercourse. Various *routes départementales* lead towards Pont d'Ouilly, past the odd-looking dam at Rabodanges. The climb to the Roche d'Oëtre and the walk to the Rouvrou meander are worth fifteen minutes each.

Return now to Sées and the axis of the west–east journey across Normandy's deep south. Leaving the prosperous Plaines de l'Orne, the lands of *grande culture*, you come towards the Pays d'Ouche, which is almost as prosperous.

North of Sées, on the N138 to Gacé, Bernay and Le Havre, you are in what – however prosperous – I am tempted to call bandit country. This was the road where, in January 1984, British lorries were hijacked and their cargoes of lamb and beef pillaged, given away or burned. Their drivers, ignored by watching gendarmes, were taken as hostages to Paris, where they were eventually freed. This modern Peasants' Revolt has been in progress for many years now and Brittany and Normandy have been two of the worst affected provinces. French farmers are not much different from farmers anywhere in western Europe, but they are the victims of an EEC system which has encouraged them to over-produce, and then supported their over-production with subsidies. This has so conditioned them that competition from other EEC members arouses anger. So while you admire the French countryside you might feel a little wary of those that work it. In Normandy and Brittany – where the farmers are the least efficient and thus most susceptible to the occasional chill wind from Brussels – you might well find the road blocked by demonstrating tractor drivers, smashed eggs, manure, burning tyres or rivers of intentionally spilled milk.

Driving east through Le Merlerault and down the valley of the Risle you will be clipping the top of the Perche Normand, where tall, black calvaries stand at road junctions and white water-towers dot the flat countryside like giant golf tees. This is horse-breeding country – the grass which grows on limestone is considered the best for building strong bones. Studs abound, like the famous one at Haras-du-Pin, north of Sées. The sturdy Percheron horse takes its name from the district and Mortagne and

Bellême, in hillier country to the south, are the centres of it. Everywhere there are neat, white-railed paddocks and sleek, well-groomed animals within.

You will have crossed through the Forêt de St-Evroult, the source of the river Charentonne, and the abbey town of St-Evroult-Notre-Dame-du-Bois (see page 105).

By-pass the steel mills of L'Aigle and you enter the department of Eure. The valley of the Risle is wooded for almost all its remaining course northwards. On the way to Evreux one can either cross the Forêt de Breteuil or the Forêt de Conches. The town of Conches, on the northern fringe of the Pays d'Ouche, offers more excitements than Breteuil.

Both the Gauls and Romans had settlements at Conches. A Norman motte and bailey castle was built in the 1030s on a spur round which the Rouloir meanders, and it was later a frontier fortress town in the Normandy–France border country. There is now a fine donjon in the town centre, all that is left of a once larger medieval castle with an *enceinte* of walls. The English and French occupied this alternately throughout the Hundred Years' War. The events of June and July 1356, are probably typical.

Henry, Duke of Lancaster, had landed at St Vaast-la-Hougue and with 2,500 men set off to relieve Pont-Audemer, then Breteuil, both being besieged by the French. His high-speed incursion, or *chevauchée*, was a resounding success. Averaging 35 kms per day for twenty-two days, they covered 531 kms in high summer, in the course of which Pont-Audemer and Breteuil were both secured. In between the two, Lancaster came to Conches. On 3 July, after riding 37 kms, he assaulted the walls, possibly using siege engines captured from the French at Pont-Audemer, got into the outer ward and burnt everything. For good measure they captured Verneuil, further south in the Pays d'Ouche, before turning for home. Challenged at L'Aigle by King John of France's army, ten times stronger, Lancaster cunningly carried out a silent night evacuation and escaped back to the Cotentin.

Michelin does not mention the surviving donjon, which I thought was interesting and maintained well. It is fun for the young at heart to climb about in. And for those with less martial tastes, Conches' main claim to fame is the stained glass in the nearby church of Ste-Foy, which is some of the finest of its kind. You could eat afterwards at La Toque Blanche in Place Carnot, or at Grand'Mare in the Avenue Croix de Fer.

A rather untidy road leads through thickening industrial clutter to the city of Evreux on the Iton. One of Normandy's smaller cities, it is not very well known to British visitors and somewhat by-passed (now, literally). It is *chef-lieu* of the department of Eure and has a fine cathedral, but alongside Caen, Bayeux and Rouen its fame is muted, its praises unsung.

The Gauls settled hereabouts and the name of their particular 'nation', the Eburovices, lingers in the names of Evreux itself and the nearby river, the Eure. It was Christianized in the fourth century, its first bishop being Taurinus, whose relics were once kept in a beautiful, still extant enamelled *chasse* in the former abbey church which bears his name. The first grant of 'Normandy' to the Viking leader, Hrôlfr, included the district around Evreux, but because of its proximity to the kingdom of France it lay in the firing line between English and French for four centuries. It has been burnt on at least six occasions, two of them during World War II. The destruction of 1944 at any rate enabled the city planners to reveal its surviving charms more pleasingly: the Iton with its willows and swans is now more photogenic; the Gallo-Roman ramparts have been opened up and now skirt an attractive riverside walk; the cathedral, a successful muddle of styles from the twelfth to the eighteenth centuries, and the adjoining fifteenth-century Bishop's Palace, are now much more visible. Since the 1950s it has doubled its population and attracted much high-tech industry – electronics, precision engineering, pharmaceuticals and car parts. Its nearness to Paris and its good communications account largely for its spectacular growth.

Evreux has good shops, as befits the centre of a region much more densely populated than those so far passed through on the route from Avranches. As I wove slowly through the traffic up the busy Rue Chartraine I saw a surrealistic group of four dead boars on the straw-covered pavement. Three were fixed so that they sat bolt upright, noses in the air, two with light bulbs in their snouts and one holding an umbrella. Bizarrely, three of them wore tutus, ribboned neck-scarves and tasselled party hats. I don't know what the message was, but Christmas was coming and perhaps a few Evreux tables were shortly to be groaning under the weight of roast *sanglier*. Although no wild boar

Wild boars on the pavement, part of a pre-Christmas display in Evreux (Sally-Anne Greville-Heygate)

The Château de Brécourt

has been killed in Britain since 1618, the hunt flourishes in France.

As you leave Evreux and drive across the flat fields of the Evrecin eastwards to Pacy-sur-Eure and the furthest confines of Normandy you will become aware of a final transformation in the landscape. Since leaving Avranches the tiny fields and high, wet ridges of the *bocage* have given way to the flat plateaux of Orne and Eure, with their vast fields hemmed in by big, gloomy clumps of forest, and the narrow, marshy river valleys between.

By the Autoroute de Normandie Pacy-sur-Eure is now an hour's drive from Paris, only a few minutes from the manufacturing centres of Mantes, Flins and Poissy. The country around, the valley of the Eure particularly, is pleasant, despite the higher density of population, the more evident infrastructure and the landscape pockmarked with gravel pits and quarries for the material to build it all. There always seems to be a motorway in sight, so beyond Evreux the dual carriageways, that all now lead to Paris, perceptibly converge. But there are still corners and triangles of deep rusticity between them, and the valley of the Eure, as those of the Iton and the Risle, are favourite sites for Parisians' second homes.

My only complaints about these fast highways are the sometimes poor directional signs, compared with those on the other classes of road, and the difficulties of turning off across the traffic into a minor road. Of course, it grew dark on my way to Pacy. And I might have known things would go wrong when I scanned the near side for signs directing me there and glimpsed one leading to the village of Miserey. Then with no apparent warning a single unlit sign pointed down an exit road. But I was already past. I plunged along into the teeth of an unbroken chain of oncoming yellow headlights, peering helplessly across the road as one after another unidentified village road led off.

I found Pacy-sur-Eure eventually. It is a small, lively town with touches of sophistication not so evident further west. Its interest for visitors is that it lies in the attractive Eure valley and would make a good centre for its exploration to north and south. The Eure is a considerable river which, like the Seine parallel to it, comes in from outside Normandy.

You are back in the land of châteaux and battle sites. You may think we have never left it, but the nearer the Seine the greater their concentration. South of Pacy the first is La Folletière – brick and sixteenth century. Further upstream lies Ivry-la-Bataille. On a hill to the west, where an obelisk now stands, in 1590 Henri IV defeated the army of the Catholic League led by the Duc de Mayenne. It is a busy valley and some old crafts persist: at La Couture-Boussey, the manufacture of oboes and other reed instruments, and at Ezy-sur-Eure, that of horn combs. Crossing the river at Ezy you are soon at Anet, whose château is one of the finest products of the French Renaissance. Begun in 1548 by Philibert de l'Orme, it was the home of Diane de Poitiers, mistress of Henri II. When the King died in 1559 and Queen Catherine de Médicis reasserted her authority and evicted Diane from the Château de Chenonceaux in the Loire valley, it was to Anet that she retired. Strictly it is across the Eure, and thus just outside Normandy, but not to be missed on that or any other account.

Return to the Norman bank and follow the Eure upstream past the hump-backed bridge to Saussay. Near Marcilly you will see the Château de Brazais and soon afterwards the ruins of the former Abbaye de Breuil-Benoit (see p. 105), which has connections with another abbey, La Grande Trappe, situated between L'Aigle and Mortagne.

I am always intrigued by a country's remote corners and its frontiers, and although it is difficult to get worked up about French departments the D143 here runs to the furthest southeast corner of Normandy before it crosses the Avre to enter the flat wheatlands of Eure-et-Loir. The Avre and the Eure, which join here, are Normandy's traditional border with France and were consequently well defended. Just before the frontier it was a little disappointing, therefore, to find 'Motel' marked boldly on the Michelin map. But I need not have worried; it is not a bungaloid box with cars parked all around, but the fine seventeenth-century Château de Motel. Sadly, it is not open to view.

A good circular route back to Pacy would be via Dreux, if you like, and Nonancourt. Or for a quieter route, omit Dreux and follow the line of the Avre westwards. Nonancourt has some castle remains dated from 1113 and a good church. If you have plenty of time, or are in any case heading west, do not miss the fine old town of Verneuil-sur-Avre. Another fortified frontier post, it has two richly furnished churches, interesting old houses and easily traceable ramparts. A good road back towards the Seine valley would be the D51 to Damville and St André, which gives its name to the surrounding *pays*.

Beyond Pacy I took the N181 to Vernon and turned off to the village of Douains. Here I began to feel that special tingle of expectation that travellers experience when they are shortly to arrive at a place of great comfort and luxury. The *ennui* of the journey is replaced by pleasurable anticipation.

Brittany Ferries have an excellent arrangement with the Relais et Châteaux group of hotels. They will ferry you to Caen, St-Malo or Roscoff and book you in for two, three or five nights at any permutation of eighteen châteaux or luxury hotels for a taste of gracious living and an evocative whiff of history. The hotels are all three- or four-star and most of them are dotted about the Breton coast and in the Loire valley. Three are in Normandy. The system does not operate in August, when French hotels tend to be full enough with French, and many of them close for varying lengths of time in the winter months.

I was to stay for a couple of nights at the seventeenth-century Château de Brécourt, just north of Douains. It is especially gratifying to locate something that has proved rather elusive, and so I was glad when the dark countryside ahead was suddenly glowing with light. No disfiguring signs in mock Gothic confirmed that we were there. They are not necessary. No *son* but plenty of *lumière*, hidden discreetly amid the topiary work, played on the warm, brown stone of an unmistakable Louis XIII château. Its buildings surround the main drive and the trim front lawns on three sides.

The large oak door opened into a warm stone-flagged hall. Everything has been most carefully modernized: the furnishings, pictures and tapestries are all in the style of the period, and the original hexagonal floor tiling, marble fireplaces and wooden shutters have survived. I kept expecting carriages to come clattering into the forecourt.

I suppose, out of season, my companion and I should not have been surprised to go into the restaurant for dinner and find it entirely empty except for an immaculately black-coated young maître d'. He showed us to our table and then with the measured care of a priest at the high altar moved to a sideboard and arranged various mysteries on its thick white napery. The log fire illuminated fine wall tapestries and a distant Vivaldi cassette played as he presented us with a plate of tiny savouries and two large menus.

We were in a substantial first-floor room, the width of the house, now warmly shuttered but looking out, by day, on to the entrance drive on one side and over extensive parkland on the other. Presently the maître d' returned carrying a tray with two silver domes which he placed on a small serving table. He put one before each of us. All fairly normal restaurant practice, you may say, but it was done with such studied elegance that it bears relating. He then stood between us, stretched out both arms with the steadiness of a Guards Staff-Sergeant and grasped the silver pommels of both lids. There was a pause-two-three and he raised them simultaneously with a certain flourish. I could tell before tasting it that the *sandre aux palourdes aux queues d'écrevisses* revealed in front of me would have been a culinary triumph if it had been dished up in a rusty mess tin, but my companion, who was staring mutely at her *escalope de truite de mer a l'étuvée d'endives*, agreed that the glorious theatricality had lifted it into altogether higher realms.

The correct selection of cutlery is not usually a problem but the maître d' had us beaten when he placed at our right hands a curiously flattened implement with a nick in its edge. There was nobody else from whom to take guidance, so, hoping it wasn't meant for some forthcoming delicacy, we slurped up the rich sauces with it.

We cleansed our palates with a *granité au citron vert* and then with the same elaborate ritual we were served *noisettes d'agneau aux zestes de pamplemousses confits* and *mignon de veau aux noix et aux amandes*. A memorable dinner, accompanied throughout by perfectly chilled Muscadet de Sèvre-et-Maine, was concluded with coffee and petits fours.

Two places close by may merit a short excursion: Cocherel and Bizy. Few today remember Aristide Briand, French statesman and apostle of peace in the 1920s. He lived in a succession of houses at Cocherel, just north of Brécourt, on the Eure, and died there in 1932; his burial place can be visited. Across the valley is the site of an obscure battle of the Hundred Years' War, between Bertrand du Guesclin and Captal de Buch, with troops from Navarre, England's ally. On the outskirts of Vernon is the Château

173

de Bizy, owned by the Duc d'Albuféra and fairly recently opened in summer to the public. Built in 1740, it was much modified in the nineteenth century, with a park largely designed by Louis-Philippe.

Go just a little further, either through Vernon or from Cocherel through Gaillon to Les Andelys, and you come to the end of this particular journey when you reach the Seine. Gaillon has a fine château, rebuilt by Cardinal Georges d'Amboise, one of Louis XII's ministers, in the very early sixteenth century. It is thought to be the first notable Renaissance work in Normandy. In June 1984 it was laced up in scaffolding, undergoing extensive restoration. Push on into one of the many tongues of land lapped about by the Seine to approach Tosny. From a high cliff just short of the village, there is a fine panorama of the Seine, often wreathed in mist, its stream divided by long, wooded islands.

Brittany

7 St-Malo and the Emerald Coast

The Pays du Rance, Dol and Dinan

The nine-hour cross-Channel ferry route from Portsmouth to St-Malo is the longest one from Britain to France. Yachtsmen usually allow two or three days and break their journeys at Cherbourg or in the Channel Islands. The day crossing by ferry is a pleasant one for unlike the shorter routes it offers something to look at. First the fateful Cap de la Hague lighthouse, seeming to stand in the sea off the Cotentin peninsula's north-west tip; then you see the nuclear power station complex at Beaumont-Hague on the hilltop. On the starboard side is the black-and-white striped Quenard light on Alderney's eastern end. In a vessel the size of Brittany Ferries' *Prince of Brittany* you will not be disturbed by the Alderney Race, and soon Sark's green table-top and jagged ends appear to starboard. After that, to port, the vast sweep of St-Ouen bay at Jersey's western end. Leaving behind La Corbière lighthouse at its southern tip it will still be a couple of hours before you are in St-Malo.

This is not surprisingly a much-visited place – holiday resort, favourite haunt of sailing enthusiasts, and a point of entry to Brittany and lower Normandy. It lies at the mouth of the Rance, originally confined to a rocky promontory on the eastern side and looking across to Dinard on the western. The old town, or Intramuros as it is called, is massively walled. Over a causeway are extensive industrial developments and a large commercial port.

Who was St-Malo, and what was his connection with this town whose church, a former cathedral, is dedicated to St-Vincent? The Breton church has always had a pleasant habit of making saints of whomsoever it wished without reference to

176

Rome. According to legend several of the priests and hermits who migrated from Wales, Ireland or Cornwall in the fifth and sixth centuries are said to have flown over or swum or paddled over on a stone or a lettuce leaf (a coracle?). In the post-Roman era Brittany was sprinkled with holy men – native-born, Welsh, Irish and Cornish – most of whom had been promoted by popular acclaim to be somebody's local saint. St-Malo came over from Wales in the sixth century and became Bishop of Aleth, the Gallo-Roman settlement that became St-Servan, now practically a suburb of St-Malo and just south of the port. For security the community later moved on to the rocky prominence on which the town of St-Malo grew up and was fortified.

A sense of independence developed and has been keenly felt by *Malouins* over the ages. They have a motto: *'Ni Français, ni Breton: Malouin suis!'* And once during the Wars of Religion, in 1590, they even managed briefly to set up a republic. Even today St-Malo flies its own flag, blue with a white cross, the top left-hand quarter red, with a large white dog.

They have good reason to be proud, for they have produced a fair stock of famous Frenchmen. On the walls overlooking the sea you will find the statue of Jacques Cartier, and in the church his tomb and stone to mark where he stood to receive his bishop's blessing before his first transatlantic expedition in 1534. He passed Newfoundland and its cod banks and in 1535 was the first to round the Gaspé peninsula and find the St Lawrence river and the site of present-day Quebec.

One man's freedom fighter is another man's terrorist. The French style St-Malo *'La Cité Corsaire'*; the English in time past called it a nest of pirates. Foremost of these was René Duguay-Trouin, whose statue also stands on the ramparts. It was to check the likes of him that Admiral Benbow led an attack on St-Malo in 1693. He launched a specially primed old frigate against the western wall, but it blew up 50 yards short and killed six English sailors. Other *Malouins* whom the British had cause to oppose were Mahé de la Bourdonnais, who took Madras in 1746 in that ding-dong battle between the British and the French on India's Coromandel coast, and Robert Surcouf, a successful privateer during the Napoleonic Wars.

In the eighteenth century one minor area of contention between Britain and France was the Falkland Islands. In 1982 we were reminded that the Spanish-speaking world knows these islands as Las Malvinas. 'Las Malvinas' is Spanish for 'Les Malouines' – the name given to the islands sighted in 1767 by sailors of Louis Antoine de Bougainville's fleet, to honour the girls of St-Malo that they had left behind them. A gallant gesture but perhaps a little hypocritical, for there was a convention, recognized in St-Malo even by the church, that once a corsair had cleared Cap Fréhel outward bound his marital obligations could sit fairly lightly upon him.

But the town has produced not only sailors and fighters. Lamennais, the philosopher, and François-René de Chateaubriand, the writer, who cast his own solitary, gloomy spell over the French literary scene, were born here, and it is worth the walk (at low tide only) to Chateaubriand's tomb on the offshore Ile de Grand Bé. He also has a better-known memorial in the form of steak Chateaubriand – a favourite dish of his, prepared by his own chef, Montmireil.

One thing must be made clear – the 'old' town of St-Malo is a painstaking and generally successful post-war reconstruction. In August 1944 the occupying Germans decided to hold out, and so for a fortnight the town was slowly devastated by Patton's artillery. The ramparts, some fourteenth-century, some seventeenth-century, and the castle of Duchess Anne largely survived this assault, but the houses and shops within did not. The postwar architect Arretche stuck to the original street plan, but cast the new town in a uniform, functional, modern mould, all in rich grey granite.

Newcomers should find an hour in which to walk round the walls. For several centuries the city walls were guarded at night by packs of mastiffs which roamed about outside, savaging potential intruders and curfew breakers until called off by trumpet in the morning. It is a bracing walk, full of interest, and the views are striking. Start at the entrance gate in Place Chateaubriand. Try to find time, too, for the museum in the castle, now also the town hall. It contains mementoes of the redoubtable Duchess Anne, last ruler of an independent Brittany, whom Charles VIII married in 1491 in order to attach the duchy to the kingdom of France, where it has remained. There are also many exhibits relating to St-Malo's seafaring heroes. In the castle tower nearest the sea, called Quic-en-Groigne, is a waxworks museum with effigies of all the notables of St-Malo, open at the usual hours every day from April to September. *'Qui qu' en groigne'*, said the authoritarian Duchess Anne, *'ainsi sera, car tel est mon plaisir'*, or, roughly, 'Whoever may complain, this is how it's going to be, for such is my wish.'

The maritime links are still evident: the port is always busy, there is a lively cod-fishing industry and in summer the capacious yacht basin with its nine hundred moorings is always thronged. It is admirably placed – just by the tourist office and only a cable's-length from the castle gate. Just inside, and to the left, is Rue Jacques Cartier, a street full of splendid, colourful seafood restaurants tucked under the ramparts themselves. These are packed with holidaymakers and ships' crews. The whole scene is animated, piratical almost. Squashed yachting caps, rumpled blazers and trousers recently liberated, mouldy and sea-salty, from their lockers, proclaim *les yachtmen anglais*. One of these restaurants, the Gargantua, is especially good and open out of season. Exotic fish can be ordered as well as reliable steaks. Try a local dish, *choufleur à la St-Malo*, which consists of potatoes and cauliflower, those solid Breton vegetables, covered in a rich mayonnaise and heaps of shrimps. The Muscadet de Sèvre-et-Maine will wash it all down delightfully.

Once clear of the swirling traffic on the Esplanade St-Vincent it is a pleasant summer's walk to the fine beaches in nearby Paramé, the plage de Rochebonne and the plage de Minihic. Beyond is the attractive holiday village of Rothéneuf, and further still the Pointe de Grouin.

Just inland of the coast road, the D201, lies the pleasant village of St-Coulomb. This village and St-Columb, near Newquay in Cornwall, are both named after St Columba, founder of the monastery at Iona, converter of Picts in northern Scotland and the Western Isles, and champion of Celtic Christianity. A cross on the beach nearby marks the point where some disciple of his (perhaps) landed in Brittany in the sixth century.

A less Christian figure who spent some time from 1911 onwards in St-Coulomb was the writer Colette. It was the setting for her novel *Le Blé en herbe*. She is still just remembered, but more for her capacity to shock – wearing trousers and smoking cigarettes in a ten-inch-long holder as she and her dazzling Parisian friends shopped in the village. Occasionally they may have taken the steam tram into Cancale.

This picturesque fishing port is the domain of the oyster. If you stand on the cliffs above Cancale you can see, at low tide, the rows of wooden stakes marking the oyster beds. All over the bay of Mont-St-Michel various types – *pieds de cheval, plates, creuses* – are cultivated in *parcs* to which the local fishermen chug out regularly in their flat *chalands*. The magic of the oyster has always escaped me but it is clearly the basis of a big business, and so when a parasite attacked the north Breton beds in the 1970s it was a great blow from which the industry is still recovering. A notable by-product of it all was Claude Debussy's orchestral work *La Mer*. In 1905, after lunching at Cancale – no doubt on oysters – he returned by boat through a storm to St-Enogat, where *La Mer* was born on an old harmonium in the local church.

If you leave St-Malo by the main road to Normandy you will miss out Cancale and reach the bay of Mont-St-Michel at St-Benoît-des-Ondes. Primitively painted signs outside roadside farms advertise *huitres, ail, chouxfleurs* and *carottes à sable*: wind-blown seawater carries over the levée and gives the carrots a salty tang. The grass that the sheep nibble makes possible, in the same way, *mouton pré-salé*.

It is always worth turning inland at Le Vivier and going east via Dol-de-Bretagne. This unusual little city originated in the mid-sixth century when St-Samson, one of Brittany's 'seven founding saints', came over from Cornwall. He set up a monastery, most likely on the site of today's cathedral, and became the first bishop of Dol.

The flat land to the north was then covered with forest, but in the eighth century the sea irrupted over it and washed right up to the walls of Dol. This left protruding from the waves 3 kms to the north the curious 65-m-high hummock known as Mont Dol. This sort of natural disaster had evidently happened before because the remains of many prehistoric animals have been disinterred there.

Dol was now somewhat cut off from St-Malo and became, rather oddly, both an archbishopric, seat of the Primate of Brittany, and a frontier city guarding the border with Normandy. Part of the border was the small but significant stream, the river Couësnon, which runs out into the Channel near Mont-St-Michel.

In 1064 Duke Conan of Brittany declared war on the Normans

Routes from St Malo

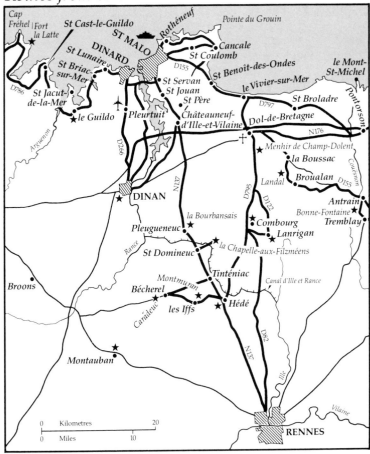

and Duke William responded by invading Brittany. It is because of this that Dol features prominently in the Bayeux Tapestry, according to which (and remember that it gives very much a Norman view) King Edward the Confessor had sent Duke Harold to Normandy in 1064, ostensibly to confirm an earlier arrangement whereby William was to be Edward's successor. Harold was in reality probably attempting to rescue his brother and nephew, currently held hostage by William. Harold's ship landed short of Normandy in Ponthieu and he was duly seized. William arranged his release, and Harold rode to Rouen full of gratitude.

181

His indebtedness was reinforced when William betrothed his daughter Aelfgifu to Harold.

So it was that when the Bretons rose and William marched, Duke Harold went along with him. The tapestry is at pains to show how Harold served William well and was properly rewarded by a grant of arms. The intention is to emphasize the enormity of his sacrilege and treachery when, after swearing over holy relics that William was indeed heir to the English throne, Harold had himself crowned king on the death of Edward in 1066.

The tapestry graphically shows the Norman force crossing the Couësnon, where men and horses fall into quicksands. A neat touch has Harold bravely dragging a Norman soldier by the wrist while carrying another one clear of the danger on piggy-back. Then they came to Dol, whose motte and bailey castle is clearly shown. This has been identified with Mont Dol, but as the hillock was now an island in the sea it seems more likely that the castle was in today's Dol on some piece of rising ground. The motte is crowned by a wooden keep reached from the bailey by a long shallow ladder up which the Norman cavalry seem to be charging. Duke Conan eventually finds the fight too hot and escapes from the keep by sliding down a rope, which the embroidress, for clarity's sake, depicts, in splendid defiance of gravity, hanging at an angle.

The Bretons must later have strengthened their border at Dol, because when William came again in 1075 the defenders held out there. Henry II took it in 1164 and John destroyed the Romanesque cathedral in 1203. The present Norman-Gothic edifice replaced it later that century, at the same time as the work of draining the marshes and driving back the sea was initiated. The main street, later called Grande-Rue-des-Stuarts in honour of the exiled James II, was filling up with the houses of prosperous medieval merchants, some of which survive. All this makes Dol worth not only a few hours of your time, but consideration as a possible base from which to radiate to St-Malo, Dinan, Mont-St-Michel and Fougères.

The road out to the Couësnon and the dull Normandy border town of Pontorson on the other side is unremarkable, as is the northern route via St-Broladre and the drained marshlands or polders, as the French have correctly termed them. It is all very

Fougères, the castle (Victoria Southwell)

The medieval castle at Fort La Latte (Victoria Southwell)

flat. An express route bypassing Pontorson and Dol now links Avranches and Dinan. Pontorson should certainly be avoided in the high season: it is clogged with cars and caravans.

A more interesting route from St-Malo and Dol runs inland to Fougères. On the way to Antrain there are the ruins of a fifteenth-century castle at Landal and a pretty hill-top chapel at Broualan. Leave Antrain by a *voie ordinaire* to the sixteenth-century fortified manor of Bonne-Fontaine at the confluence of the Couësnon and the Loisance. The Romanesque church at Tremblay is a rare sight in Brittany. Then St-Brice-en-Coglès with *two* castles, and Fougères, whose massive *château-fort* is the historic gateway to Brittany from Maine and out-tops them all.

I was first attracted to Fougères by a postage stamp – one of a series showing historic buildings, cathedrals, abbeys, châteaux and the like that have maintained excellent artistic standards since World War II. It showed the walls of the fine castle reconstructed in 1173 by Raoul II after the original had been slighted by Henry II in 1166. Although it occupies a textbook position in an acute meander of the river Nançon, now partially dried out, and although it was formidably fortified with its thirteen towers, it nevertheless fell at least six times to besiegers. The upper town which overlooks the castle was itself defended by ramparts and it is from these, in the Place aux Arbres, that there is the best view of the castle. Fougères' other main architectural feature is the Flamboyant church of St-Sulpice.

Victor Hugo and Balzac both used Fougères as the setting for historical novels: the research for *Quatre-Vingt-Treize* and *Les Chouans* was done there, and both books deal with the anti-Revolutionary rising in La Vendée which sputtered on for ten years after 1793. The revolt of the Chouans – so called because they used the hoot of a screech-owl (*chat-huant*) as a secret call, was begun by a native of Fougères, the Marquis de la Rouërie. There is a Musée des Chouans near St-Etienne-les-Coglès on the D155 to Dol.

Fougères is nowadays France's greatest shoe-producing centre, turning out 4 million pairs of women's shoes per year. The town museum features shoes from 1600 to 1930, with examples from other countries.

If you want to drive southwards from St-Malo to Rennes, the provincial capital, the prettiest route is by Dol and Combourg.

Just outside Dol pause to look at the massive Menhir de Champ-Dolent, a 9-metre-high shaft of stone (nearly twice that size if you count the portion under the ground). Menhirs are standing stones several thousand years old, associated with the people who preceded the Gauls. The stones have a symbolic, probably religious, significance. (See p. 270 for more about these extraordinary structures.)

The grim *château-fort* at Combourg is open in the afternoon from 1 March to 30 November, daily except Tuesdays, and merits a visit. Begun in the eleventh century, it was the home briefly of two of Brittany's most famous sons: its greatest warlord, Bertrand du Guesclin, in the early fourteenth century, and Chateaubriand in the 1770s. The writer's room has been turned into a small museum. Purists who want an unsullied view of the castle should contrive to approach Combourg from Lanrigan (which has its own) to the east; they will see its machicolations and 'witch's hat' turrets nestling in a bed of trees from across the lake.

From Combourg a good road runs to Rennes via Hédé with its ruined castle, or you can amble down the valley of the Ille and the Canal d'Ille et Rance to Rennes where it joins the Vilaine. From these rivers derives the otherwise unclear name of the department – Ille et Vilaine. Hédé is on the fastest route from St-Malo to Rennes, the D137 – still marked N137 in places. If you leave St-Malo by this road and feel like a break half-way, look for the Château de la Bourbansais, just off the road to the north of the village of Pleugueneuc. It is a sixteenth- and eighteenth-century château and one of the most harmonious of Brittany's larger houses. It now has a little zoo in the park, open at the normal hours. There are guided tours of part of the château on summer afternoons.

Just a little further on there is a pleasant picnic place on the banks of the Canal d'Ille et Rance at St-Domineuc, where a road left leads to the Château de la Chapelle-aux-Filzméens. Tinténiac, next, once belonged to the Coligny family and has some attractive old houses. Just west of it is a piece of wooded country dotted with châteaux, churches and menhirs and rich in interest. 8 kms down the D20 is Bécherel, old, walled and designated a *Petite Cité de caractère*. On its outskirts is the seventeenth-century Château de Caradeuc, which can be visited. The drive is flanked by pyramidal topiary work and leads to a fine front court, but the chief charm of the château is the glorious park in which it is set. It is worth returning to the D137 via Les Iffs, which has an interesting church and the Château de Montmuran nearby. The château was begun in the eleventh century and still has two twelfth-century towers, one with an original oven. The medieval parts are open to the public but the seventeenth-and eighteenth-century bits are still habited.

For those heading out of St-Malo two significant routes remain, of most interest to the westbound traveller. The first goes up the valley of the Rance to Dinan, either direct or by Dinard; the second to Dinard and the so-called Emerald Coast and points west. I used to have some trouble distinguishing between these two similar-sounding names, and there is a Dinant in the Belgian Ardennes to complicate matters. Dinard is a relatively recent growth, by the sea at the mouth of the Rance. Dinan is ancient, walled and 19 kms up-river.

If you are in a hurry head straight for Dinan. It would be a pity to leave St-Malo, though, without having a look at St-Servan, just south of the ferry terminal. On the headland, very close to where the boats of Brittany Ferries nose in and out, is the site of the old city of Aleth, precursor of St-Malo. Leave your car in the Place St-Pierre by the ruins of the early cathedral and walk up to the Fort de la Cité, built during the Seven Years' War but much strengthened by the Germans in the 1940s. On another small headland nearby is the Tour Solidor. It is a tall, fourteenth-century donjon, in effect three towers joined together, built to keep watch over the Rance and now a museum (the Musée International du Long Cour Cap Hornier, which mystified me for a moment – it features sailing ships that used the Cape Horn route).

The new direct route south, the D137, then takes you through St-Jouan and round Châteauneuf to Dinan, with good views over an arm of the Rance between St-Père and St-Suliac. Deviations can give a better view of moored sailing craft from La Passagère, Mont Garrot and Port St-Jean. The Rance itself is quite a small river, but for centuries the tide has surged in and out to create a deep and indented valley. As early as the twelfth century retaining walls were built which were just submerged by the enormous tides, but on the ebb enabled escaping sea to drive watermills. The same principle is applied today by the vast

186

hydro-electric power station, the first of its kind and highly experimental, which since 1966 has spanned the Rance just south of St-Servan. And it goes one better, for it harnesses the rising tide as well as the falling. A lock admits shipping at high water and is bridged by the D168, which today runs across the top of the barrage.

A few years ago I took the attractive route to Dinan over the dam – there is parking on the west bank for those of a mechanical turn of mind who want to visit the installations and boggle at the annual kilowattage produced – and down the D114 to La Richardais and the D12. The route south from the barrage, whether by the D12 or the faster D266 offers the least imposing entrance to Dinan: it is better to come up-river by boat or, taking the east bank route, pause at Lanvallay. This way the full majesty of the ramparts and the castle is revealed.

Dinan is a striking place and full of history. Its large motte and bailey castle features in the Bayeux Tapestry. Breton foot-soldiers are shown defending the wooden ladder, but some Normans run up the motte and set fire to the wooden walls of the keep. Duke Conan, who had escaped from Dol, leans over the palisade and surrenders Dinan by handing out the keys of the castle on the end of his lance to be picked up on the tip of a waiting Norman lance.

Walking across the Place du Champ-Clos, a large open space within the old walls covered now with parked cars, I recalled the ancient associations of what was once, as its name indicates, an enclosed field in which tournaments were held. It had been the scene of deeds of medieval pageantry and chivalry so perfectly archetypal that they might almost have been the work of a Victorian novelist or a Hollywood scriptwriter.

In 1364 the Breton hero, Bertrand du Guesclin, and his brother Olivier were defending Dinan against a superior force of English led by Henry, Duke of Lancaster. Bertrand made a forty-day truce, at the end of which the town would surrender if it had not been relieved in the meantime. Olivier then went out of the town unarmed, but was nevertheless taken prisoner by an English knight, Sir Thomas of Canterbury, who extracted a ransom of a thousand florins. Enraged at this, Bertrand challenged the knight to fight him in the lists (*champ-clos*). Henry of Lancaster watched Sir Thomas lose, return the thousand florins and surrender his arms to du Guesclin, and then banished him from the English army. Watching the triumph of the courageous but physically ill-favoured Breton was Tiphaine Raguenel, a Dinan girl as beautiful as her name, and scholarly too; she later married him.

After such a dénouement you will not need to be told that Bertrand du Guesclin's heart is buried in the church of St-Sauveur. But there the romantic tale ends, because after his death in the Auvergne in 1380 the rest of his body, though embalmed at Le Puy, decomposed so badly in the July heat that bits of it had to be buried at three different places on the way back to Dinan.

It must have been the devil of a place to besiege. The English tried at least three times, in 1342, 1357 and 1364, and failed (though they did get in to burn the place in 1344). Its walls are on cliffs looming over the Rance on all sides except the north and west. The beautiful oval donjon of Duchess Anne – now a historical museum – is set in them. The *vieille ville* is a delightful place to stroll around. The English, since they ceased to invest it, have loved it and there was a flourishing English colony there, like the one at Avranches, in the 1830s. They are described, somewhat disparagingly, by Thomas Adolphus Trollope, Anthony's brother, in his *A Summer in Brittany*, published in 1840, the first good English book on the province and one which had a marked effect on our awareness of Brittany. They had their own church and clergyman, and the Jardin Anglais still offers the best vantage point over the Rance and the imposing viaduct which carries in the road from the east.

After lunching, perhaps on *poulet grillé à la diable* at the Hôtel de la Poste in the Place du Guesclin (the Hôtel Marguerite in the same square also does a memorable galantine of salmon), you could walk it off a bit by doing a tour of the ramparts which, as at St-Malo, should take about an hour. The more energetic could walk through the *vieille ville*, down the picturesque Rue du Jerzual, out of a town gate and down the steep Rue du Petit Port, lined with exquisite half-timbered and jettied houses, to the Gothic bridge (a faithful post-war copy) over the Rance. The old port itself is tiny and charming and has several waterside restaurants. The catch is, of course, that unless you are taking the boat back to St-Malo you have to toil back up again.

*   *   *

188

Apart from Dinan, the other obvious destination if you drive westwards across the Rance barrage is nearby Dinard. Not quite Torquay, not quite Frinton, but with much of both, Dinard has a trim, respectable air about it. Never more than just a residential and holiday town, it was founded by an American called Coppinger in the 1850s and patronized by waves of rich expatriates. It reached its apogee just before and after World War I. Its very street names give the clue: Boulevard Albert-1er, Avenue Edouard-VII, Rue G. Clemenceau, Avenue George-V, Boulevard Président-Wilson. There was once a British consul and there still is an English church and library. All this, of course, has attraction for those who want a quieter holiday. No vehicles are allowed to sully parts of the road along its sea frontage. It does not feature in the brochures of package tour operators. But its charms are not merely faded ones – witness its modern casino and its heated, seawater, Olympic-size swimming pool. It is also a place that you can visit easily if you happen to be in the Channel Islands. Aurigny Airways operate a service from Jersey to Dinard's airport, 5 kms to the south at Pleurtuit.

Dinard is the gateway to the western part of the Emerald Coast, which stretches almost to St-Brieuc. If you leave your car in St-Malo you can get over by ferry and see some of the prettier villages along the coast. St-Enogat is the first, in effect a suburb of Dinard with an attractive beach. St-Lunaire, St-Briac-sur-Mer and Lancieux come next, all rocky beaches with mussel beds, then St-Jacut-de-la-Mer on its narrow headland, Le Guildo with its medieval castle, and St-Cast. Edward Mace, travel editor of the *Observer*, wrote in 1978 that this his favourite stretch of coast was between Dinard and St-Brieuc: 'Nowhere on reasonably accessible earth touches these few miles for a perfect family holiday,' he sums up.

Those who tire of the beach can drive from St-Cast down to the mouth of the Arguenon, cross over and look down river for the remains of the Château de Gilles de Bretagne at Le Guildo among the trees, and reflect in this martlet-haunted ruin on the machinations of the Hundred Years' War. Gilles de Bretagne was the youngest brother of the powerful Duke François de Bretagne, and the castle of Le Guildo came to him on his marriage to Françoise de Dinan in 1444. Brittany was still independent, but while Duke François currently favoured the French Gilles was an ardent anglophile. A letter he wrote to Henry VI of England promising continued support was intercepted and deemed treasonable, and Duke François' fury was only exacerbated when Henry VI offered Gilles the dukedom of Richmond in Yorkshire. Duke François enlisted the support of a French force of four hundred, and seized Gilles at Le Guildo as he was playing tennis with his English friends. The castle was sacked and Gilles imprisoned in it. But this was not enough for Arthur de Montauban, a powerful courtier in Duke François' train, who coveted Gilles' young wife. When Henry VI, in a misguided attempt to rescue his unfortunate supporter, took Fougères he only strengthened the alliance between France and Brittany. Fougères was soon retaken and Gilles moved inland to the dungeon of the castle of Le Hardouinais. After failing to poison him several times, Montauban's hirelings pressed Gilles to death under a mattress in 1450. The ivy of centuries has recently been pulled off and the castle restored by voluntary student labour.

Fort La Latte, beyond the rock-fringed Baie de la Frenaye, is another medieval castle with additions by Vauban and in far better repair than Le Guildo. It is dramatically situated just off the mainland, and access is only by drawbridge. Equally imposing, but completely undeveloped by man, is the bleak promontory of Cap Fréhel, one of the finest of many savage and exposed headlands in Brittany. Here you will find circling, wind-tossed gulls and the constant pounding of the waves and, if the weather is kind, unsurpassed views.

Further west, the Emerald Coast gets even better for beaches – Sables-d'Or-Les-Pins, Erquy-Plages (the names tell it all) and Pléneuf-Val-André. These are all quiet places, popular with the French during the school holidays, and ideal for children. Le Val-André also has ancient Breton history close at hand. Inland at Pléneuf there are mounds and standing stones, and Dahouët is on a creek used as a harbour by the Vikings. If you dine at Chez Gisèle at the right hour you can watch the tide go out spectacularly and dump all the pleasure craft on the mud. During the summer the double-moated Château de Bienassis can be visited, a seventeenth-century castle now embellished by a peaceful formal garden.

Like Erquy-Plages, Le Val-André faces west and benefits from the Gulf Stream. The local syndicat d'initiative claims an astonishingly low average monthly rainfall: 44 mm as compared to

The Emerald Coast, north of Sables-d'Or (Victoria Southwell)

94 mm in Biarritz, 61 mm on the Mediterranean coast and 56 mm in Algiers. Certainly there are sub-tropical gardens with flourishing palm trees, mimosa, figs, camellias and cacti. Three beautiful sandy beaches are protected by two rocky headlands. When the incoming afternoon tide covers the fine scorched sands the temperature of the sea can rise to 25°C. The town itself, from the Promenade to the Rue Amiral Charner with their interlocking lattice of short streets, has grown up precisely because the beaches are so excellent. It is the epitome of this delightful coast. There is everything the most *sportif* might want, sailing and riding schools, a centrally placed campsite, a casino and eleven tennis courts on any one of which I half expected to see Jacques Tati's Monsieur Hulot astonishing opponents with his unorthodox service. A bird sanctuary on the islet of Le Verdelet can be reached at low tide, but hurry back when the hooter warns that the tide is rushing in.

All these are outdoor pursuits, but on my last visit to the resort I had to take refuge from a day of steady rain in the Grand Hotel du Val-André, where we were elegantly served with oysters, a delicious *lotte* (a kind of eel, caught in the estuary of the Rance) and a huge crab. It struck me as well above its present two-star rating.

8 Upper Brittany

Rennes and the Eastern Argoat

The interior of Upper Brittany is within easy reach of St-Malo. It is wooded, but less so than the higher, wetter land of Lower Brittany to the west. The only large area of forest in the east is the Forêt de Paimpont. It is gentle, low-lying, well-watered country, and the single large city of Rennes dominates the region.

All roads and railways lead to that city, the undisputed capital of the province since the department of Loire-Atlantique and Nantes were hived off. Before the Romans came the Redones built Condate, their capital, at the confluence of the minor rivers Ille and Vilaine. Condate therefore grew up on a natural crossroads – the meeting of the route over the Armorican peninsula between Channel and Atlantic with the main route from the peninsula to the heart of Gaul. Eight Roman roads converged at Condate; now there are eleven main roads. As it is almost impossible to avoid Rennes a good ring road has been built, but the city itself is well worth investigating.

To my mind, ancient and modern combine happily. Driving in from the west you pass stylish new high-rise flats, then a belt of higgledy-piggledy medieval Breton, and arrive finally in the rather severe classical eighteenth century of the centre. This reversal of the normal order is explained by a disastrous fire in 1720 which over the Christmas period destroyed almost a thousand old timber houses. Patches of old Rennes can be found in the narrow lanes round the cathedral and one surviving city gate, the Porte Mordelaise; these ancient buildings are surrounded mainly by post-war replacements. Much of the centre has been pedestrianized. Civic pride takes the form of smartly kept public areas and brightly coloured flowerbeds, and as befits a university city, there are plenty of good bookshops. Although Rennes has long been the capital of Brittany it has also been a frontier city, close to France and French-speaking, and it does not seem to me to be characteristically Breton. The numerous churches are all rather ordinary, and the cathedral of St-Pierre, with its Renaissance façade, masks a gloomy, early nineteenth-century interior remarkable only for the tomb of St-Amand and a fine fifteenth-century retable in a chapel near the south transept.

The most impressive building in Rennes is the Palais de Justice, which was the work of Salomon de Brosse between 1618 and 1655 and escaped the fire. It occupies the northern side of a gently sloping square from which its noble and austere frontage may be appreciated. Now the law courts, it once housed the Breton *parlement*, and in the 1680s Mme de Sévigné used to drive in from the Château des Rochers to watch the proceedings from a special loggia for distinguished visitors. Adjoining the Place du Palais is the Place du Mairie and here, facing each other are the theatre and town hall, the latter completed in 1743. Under its central tower is a large, empty niche with a chequered history. First it contained a statue of Louis XV, which was destroyed in the Revolution. Then in 1911 a symbolic sculpture showing Brittany bending the knee in subjection to France was placed there. In 1932, the quatercentenary of the union of Brittany with France, Breton nationalists blew this one up.

Other noteworthy buildings include a splendidly ornate Préfecture, an Art Deco swimming pool and two good museums south of the Vilaine (since 1720 embanked and partly underground). There are two universities – Rennes and Upper Brittany – each covering its own fields of study and catering for over twenty thousand students. A few years ago I talked to an eminent Professor of Celtic Languages there when I was researching a BBC programme. He was a great champion of the Breton cause, and yet a sane and moderating influence in a movement which has always had an extensive lunatic fringe. He offered a balanced view of Breton nationalism, while remaining sceptical of the motives of Paris and central government.

In truth much has been done for Brittany and Rennes in the economic, political and cultural fields in the last quarter of a century. Once Rennes was just a military base and an intellectual centre with a penchant for legal studies (St-Yves, a Breton and the patron saint of lawyers, worked at Rennes in the thirteenth century). Even at the time of World War II it was an antiquated

Routes from Rennes

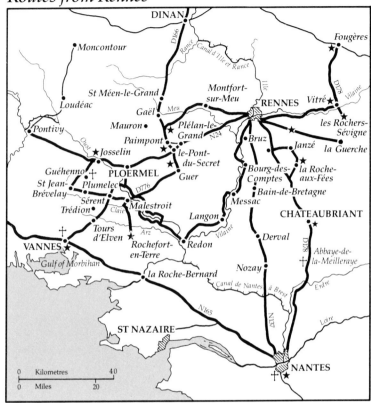

backwater with dusty, old-fashioned shops and inhabitants reluctant to venture east of Rennes on to 'foreign' soil. Now it is
a thrusting metropolis of a quarter of a million people, a considerable industrial centre – the big Citroën plant employs eight
thousand – and the heart of a prosperous agricultural and
market-gardening area. International airlines use the airport and
the A81 autoroute links the *Rennais* effortlessly with Paris.

When Napoléon scrapped the old provinces of the *Ancien
Régime* and instituted the ninety-one *départements* (most of them
named innocuously after rivers) Rennes became simply *chef-*

lieu of Ille-et-Vilaine. But in 1972 the concept of Brittany was revived politically when Rennes became the capital of a region embracing four of the five Breton departments, which more or less equates geographically with the old duchy. The regional system does not imply autonomy, let alone independence, but it offers a small step in that direction.

Of the many men who have worked for a better deal for Brittany and Rennes, two should be mentioned. Charles de Gaulle, the old soldier, loved the Bretons for their ready sacrifices in two world wars and tried to reward them in various small ways. He moved the French army's officer training school from its war-damaged premises at St-Cyr near Paris to Coëtquidan in the wilds of Brittany. When pressure on private industry had little effect, he arranged for various state-controlled space establishments and nuclear power stations to be set up in Brittany. The slow Breton revival begins during de Gaulle's final period in power, the first years of the Fifth Republic from 1958 to 1969. The other man is Henri Fréville, *maire* of Rennes from 1953 to 1977. He brought in the Citroën plant in 1953, built imaginative housing estates with good amenities, expanded the universities (in one of which he had been history professor before 1953). His twenty-four-year paternalist governance of the city helped to produce its present air of good order and prosperity. Perhaps his statue will one day fill that niche in front of the hôtel de ville and if it does I hope it fares better than its predecessors.

Driving through the city one spring day I had a fleeting glimpse of a street sign – Rue de la Fée Viviane. This – street of the Fairy Vivien – was a hint that there is magic country west of Rennes. Take the N12 out of the city and then just short of the ring road the D125 to the small town of Montfort-sur-Meu, then Iffendic, St-Gonlay and St-Malon-sur-Mel – all villages with square church towers surmounted by attractive slate lanterns. St-Malon has a smart grey telephone booth actually in the churchyard, up against the church wall and next to a grave, giving the faint impression that here one might communicate with the dead.

In fact, from this point on things become a bit spooky. And properly so, for you are approaching the Forêt Domaniale de Paimpont (not to be confused with Paimpol on the north coast), the last vestige of the ancient woodland that once clothed all of Upper Brittany, and the site of the legendary Brocéliande, forest birthplace of Sir Lancelot and scene of many an Arthurian romance. Take the road to Concoret and Mauron and you will soon enter the misty confines of the forest. Still ponds, beloved today of anglers, feed the stripling Meu and Mel. Swinging round a corner past dead-looking, lichen-covered trees you will come face to face with a moated medieval ruin, the Château de Comper, reputedly the birthplace of the Fairy Vivien, better known to us as Morgan Le Fay. It is private, but can be visited. Behind Comper fairy palaces are said to lie below the surface of the attractive *étang* where Vivien brought the infant Lancelot – Lancelot of the Lake. Vivien was an enchantress with whom the wizard Merlin fell dotingly in love. He came to Brocéliande and it pleased her to trap him in a magic circle and imprison him under a great rock. Though he had powers by which he could have freed himself he was happy to remain in thrall for eternity.

The route south from St-Malo to the Forêt de Paimpont would bring you via Dinan down the D766 to the N12 at St-Jouan-de-l'Isle and on to St-Méen-le-Grand. In the pleasant open square at St-Méen lie the remains of the sixth-century Abbaye de St-Mewan, the saint to whom you should pray to cure madness and whose tomb is in the nearby church. He came from Wales with his godson, St Austol, and curiously there are two adjoining parishes in Cornwall – St Mewan and St Austell. Deep in the Forêt de Paimpont ahead is a further supposed cure for madness. The waters of the Fontaine de Barenton, sacred to the druids, are supposed to ease disorders of the mind, and so they founded an early mental hospital at a village close by, appropriately called Folle Pensée. Merlin was taking the waters when the Fairy Vivien, using some of his own magic, ensnared him.

The next town on the D766 is Gaël, where everything is geared to agriculture. The narrow streets between the old houses are occasionally blocked by old farmers who seem to have been poured into their 2CVs, and who undulate along incredibly slowly stopping every now and then to stick their arms out of a window flap to argue a point with a kerbside friend. The evocatively named town of Gaël is pleasantly dilapidated and finds no place in any guidebook, yet it presents one facet of the essence of France.

Over the level crossing and down the D773 and you are once more in the Forêt de Paimpont. At Paimpont itself there is a sudden, surprising lake and a large, impressive abbey which may be visited in July and August when pedalos (a rare discordant note) may be hired. But Paimpont is a one-street town and soon you are amid trees again. All deep forests exude atmosphere, but this one specially so. When Christ was taken down from the cross Joseph of Arimathea is said to have collected his blood in the vessel Jesus used for wine at the Last Supper (the calvaries at St-Thégonnec and Cléden-Poher show angels doing this for him). Joseph is said then to have brought the vessel – the Holy Grail – to Brittany and to have lost it somewhere in Brocéliande. I can believe it.

But legends abound. Just after Plélan-le-Grand the D773 crosses the river Aff at Le Pont du Secret. What secret? It was supposedly here that Arthur's Queen Guinevere revealed her love for Sir Lancelot.

After all that it was difficult for me to buckle down to the prosaic business of military manoeuvring. But St-Cyr-Coëtquidan, the French Sandhurst or West Point, is nearby and of interest to some. A museum illustrates the history of the French army over the last two or three centuries. St-Cyr is open to the public every day during working hours. There are two entrances: one in the village of Bellevue, a miniature Camberley which has sprung up outside the gates on the D773 between Plélan-le-Grand and Guer; and a more imposing one on the N24 to the north, between Plélan and Ploërmel – look for a left turn just after the village of Beignon and pass between white statues of Bayard and du Guesclin. Both entrances are guarded by National Service soldiers but do not be put off by this. From the north you cross undulating heathland until you surmount the final rise to see a landscape filled with modern buildings. Ahead is the fine Cour de Rivoli, used for ceremonial parades, with an equestrian statue and the headquarters block facing you. It would be unwise to drive on to this. The museum, which is free, flanks the right hand side of the Cour and you can park nearby.

It would be pleasant to stay in this area. I noticed the Relais de Brocéliande at Paimpont (you might expect a rash of Arthurian establishments – Restaurant de la Fée Viviane, Chez Merlin and the like, but fortunately there has not been one), but since you cannot eat there in the summer months try the Manoir du Tertre (well signposted) which has vast old beams and a Great Dane.

The N24 through the Camp de Coëtquidan leads to Ploërmel. Just before Campénéac turn right and follow the rolling D312 to the Château de Trécesson. This looming, moated pile, built of brown stone in the fifteenth century, is now a farm and not open to visitors. Unfortunately I have only ever seen Ploërmel in pouring rain. Jutting, slender-bodied gargoyles directed cascades of water from St-Armel's church roof into the car park – Ploërmel is 'Plou-Armel', the parish of Armel, who founded it in the sixth century. The church, with a clock placed asymmetrically on its tower, is worth a visit whatever the weather. There are some fine stained glass windows, including a good Tree of Jesse and St-Armel towing off a captured dragon with his stole – a familiar piece of Breton symbolism indicating the defeat of paganism by Christian missionaries. Tucked away though it is, Ploërmel was bombed in 1944 and so the glass is much restored. The tomb of Jean II and Jean III, Dukes of Brittany, can be seen to the left of the altar. To the right is that of Philippe de Montauban, Grand Chancellor of Brittany, and his wife Anne, who died in 1514 and 1516. Outside the north door is some carved wood panelling of the four apostles and some elaborate Flamboyant Gothic stone carving, including some nice touches of rustic irreverence – a sow playing Breton bagpipes, a cobbler sewing up his wife's mouth, and two piggy-back, naked figures tooting horns. The House of Marmosets, built in 1586, is close to the church and worth tracking down, and in the nearby Place d'Armes is the statue of Ploërmel's most famous son, Dr Guérin, who perfected a lint surgical dressing in the Franco-Prussian War.

But the town may well be remembered more for the Ploërmel charter of April 1977, for it was in a speech made here that Giscard d'Estaing gave his support to Breton cultural development. He may have aimed partly to fob off the nationalists and win some moderate votes but it has meant that the Breton language should now be taught in schools for up to three hours per week and can be offered as a subject in the *baccalauréat* exams. But according to Per Denez, the Professor of Celtic Languages at Rennes University, it is all still somewhat cosmetic as there are not enough teachers of Breton to provide the service. TV and radio programmes in Breton have, however, burgeoned since 1977: Radio Bretagne Ouest, or Breizh Izel, now broadcasts sixty hours a week.

It would be a pity to visit Ploërmel without also seeing the small town of Josselin, 12 kms down the N24 to the west. The castle here is perhaps the most important ancient building in Brittany.

On the way I once wanted to look at a monument marked on the maps as the Column, or Obelisk or the Thirty. It marks the site of one of those bloody, pointless encounters that characterize the Middle Ages: after Edward III's renewal of the Anglo-French struggle at Crécy in 1346 there were some years of stalemate. The English in Ploërmel and the French at Josselin decided to settle the issue by an organized combat, thirty knights from each side. They met in 1351 midway between the two towns and a series of duels took place with a pause for refreshments in the middle. After nine English had been hacked to death the rest capitulated to the French. Unfortunately the N24 has been improved here and the obelisk is now trapped between two carriageways. After bumping inconclusively down several muddy lanes I, like the English commander, decided to give up. The hamlet of La Pyramide is the place only determined medievalists should aim for.

I wanted to cross the Oust and approach Josselin by the D4 from Malestroit. From here, on a bend just south of the town, is the most impressive view of the castle. It is a fairytale assemblage of walls and turrets rising almost sheer from the river. The first castle was built here by a local *vicomte* in about 1000 and finished off by his son Josselin, who gave his name to it. Olivier de Clisson, who succeeded du Guesclin as Constable of France, took the castle in 1370 and strengthened it. Through his wife it passed to the Ducs de Rohan, who still own it and live there. They turned it from a medieval fortress into a seigneurial residence and, although the exterior walls overlooking the Oust remain severe, those facing the inner court have much more delicately embellished gable windows in Flamboyant Gothic style. Henri de Rohan, leader of the Huguenot armies, was worsted in 1629 and Richelieu destroyed five of the castle's nine towers, leaving it much as you see it today. Inside there are fine furnishings, tapestries, paintings and fireplaces and many tributes to Anne of Brittany whose monogram appears everywhere. It is deservedly popular and guided tours process through the rooms from Easter to mid-September. Exact opening times should be checked with the syndicat d'initiative. De Clisson and Marguerite de Rohan are interred in the mainly fifteenth-century basilica of Notre-Dame-du-Roncier, which is well worth a few moments.

At Josselin you are in the broad valley of the Oust, a considerable river by Breton standards, which runs north-west to south-east to join the Vilaine at Redon. For most of its length it is also the Canal de Nantes à Brest. This great waterway was planned by Napoléon to link the two seaports by a route secure from the attentions of the Royal Navy. Its bed was in places lined, so the story goes, with old menhirs, and the task was completed in 1842. Its central lynchpin was the town of Pontivy, where a cut from the Oust joined the Blavet. This was a quiet provincial centre notable for sailcloth-making, with a castle built in 1485 by Jean II de Rohan (also *châtelain* of Josselin). In the days of the first Emperor it became a thriving place again and was for a time renamed Napoléonville: a lattice-work of streets – Rue Friedland, Rue Marengo, Quai Niémen – was built in his honour.

South-west of Josselin, and not so far as Pontivy, are two other sites of interest. Along the N24 and down the D778 is the village of Guéhenno where, far from those parts of Finistère most associated with calvaries, is a fine example first built in 1550 and an ossuary guarded by two Roman soldiers. A little further south is the Moulin de Plumelec with a memorial to World War II SAS parachutists. These two places are near the large village of St-Jean-Brévelay, which should be of interest to Yorkshire folk as its name derives from St John of Beverley, an Archbishop of York who died in 721 and whose remains were conveyed here.

A little way down the Oust is a *trouvaille* that might easily be missed, the Château de Crévy, overlooking the river near La Chapelle-Caro. Once a powerful medieval fortress, it was rebuilt on the original plan in 1697. Today it conserves its classical appearance, with four stout towers at the corners of an irregular quadrilateral, one of them fourteenth century the other three nineteenth and all topped with pointed slate roofs. Over the last twenty years the Bouquet-Nadauds, the present tenants, have totally restored it and have recently opened a Musée de Costume. Mme Bouquet-Nadaud built up the collection during the time she was a dress designer for French cinema and television. About ninety original costumes, covering the period 1720 to 1970 are displayed on models in twelve beautifully furnished rooms. Opening times are complex and should be checked in Ploërmel or La Chapelle-Caro. Nearby is one of Brittany's finest dolmens (supposed ancient burial chambers) – up a *voie ordinaire* towards La Ville au Voyer you will find La Maison Trouée.

Crévy is only 9 kms from Malestroit, an attractive town and a possible centre from which to see these and other places of interest. The Oust spills over a weir here and rejoins the Brest to Nantes canal. The old heart of the town is full of character. The church of St-Gilles stands in a maze of narrow streets, most of them with timbered medieval houses whose storeys overhang perilously. Many have carved and painted figures, including a townsman in a nightshirt belabouring his wife with a stick, a donkey playing bagpipes and a pig spinning yarn. St-Gilles is an interesting church with two parallel naves, one dark and Romanesque, the other late sixteenth-century. There is some good glass and a carved wooden seventeenth-century pulpit which has no visible means of entry (it is in the thickness of the wall). Outside over the south door are curious symbolic representations of the four evangelists. One of these, a passing old man told me, casts a shadow on the church wall which resembles the head of Voltaire when the sun is three hours past its apogee.

Take the Rue des Ponts and cross the river by the upstream bridge parallel to the one carrying the main road. This leads to the Ile Notre-Dame, where the old lords of Malestroit had their castle and later there was an Augustinian convent. The arms of the Malestroit family, once one of the nine baronies of Brittany, are now the arms of the town. The road leads on to the east bank where you will find the ruins of La Madeleine where the Truce of Malestroit was signed in the chapel in 1343. This is one of the many supremely unmemorable moments in history, when Philip VI of France and the English Edward III signed a three-year truce. Philip promptly went to a tournament in Paris where he was decapitated: a turning point in history when nothing turned. In fact, the Hundred Years' War had another 110 years to run.

The town, which rather grandly calls itself a city, has other points of interest. Pleasure boats ply on the canal and there is a landing stage here. A useful Intermarché can be found on the way to the railway station. Malestroit also allegedly has the biggest output of Emmenthal cheese in Europe, which makes me wonder what the good Swiss burgers of that town are doing. The restaurant at the Hotel Croix d'Or won a personal star from

A medieval timbered house in Malestroit

us, but is on the main through road and could be fairly noisy. The D776 is one of the new *Itinéraires Bis* holiday routes marked with a green blazon, this one for motorists heading from Rennes to southern Brittany. The most interesting short excursion from Malestroit is to the rebuilt and ultra-modern Museum of the Breton Resistance at St-Marcel, just 3 kms to the west. It is a model of its kind. In the surrounding woods there is a German 88-millimetre anti-tank gun disguised inside a reconstructed 'old' Breton house, and outside the museum a replica of part of the Atlantic wall beach defences. Inside, a video screen tells the story of the resistance in French, English and German. You will see a 14-tonne German range-finder from Brest, a rebuild of an old street with shops, whence come taped sounds redolent of the war. At the end are mirrors so that visitors become a part of the scene. Old cinema newsreels can be watched, and you can sit in the simulated gun-turret of a bomber and try to identify the larger Breton towns from World War II air photographs. There is even a corner devoted to the Black Market. Before or after your visit to this impressive museum you should try the popular Relais du Maquis in St-Marcel, where I recommend the excellent *saumon grillé sauce champagne.*

Somewhat further west is the rather isolated Château de Trédion. There are about 150 châteaux in Brittany and architecturally Josselin, Kerjean and Suscinio earn the most stars. Trédion must come about the middle. It is 8 kms west of the N166 in bosky country, the haunt of jay and owl. A former hunting lodge of the younger sons of the Dukes of Brittany, it is now being developed as time-sharing flats and a château-club. There is an attractive camp-site by a lake.

Just south of Malestroit is the wholly unremarkable little town of Pleucadeuc – 'pluck-a-duck' with an Inspector Clouseau accent. It is the sort of small town that few visitors pass through and none stop at. Yet there is about it something typically Breton that makes it interesting. The church is severely functional, with nineteenth-century furnishings and glass, and it stands four-square in the centre of the town. All roads converge on it. No churchyard surrounds it. Tarmac laps every buttress and tractors park their trailers in the angle of transept and aisle. There are a few shops, a very modern post office and the usual seedy bars where old men take their morning infusion of wine and younger ones play noisy games on the hand football machines. Sticking out in the middle of the road and causing minor traffic confusion to the uninitiated are well and a war memorial. And that is about all.

Geographically you are now in an area called the Landes de Lanvaux, a feature which runs west to east across the whole department of Morbihan. It is a narrow band of granite, denuded and unprofitable until the 1860s, then parcelled up, sold and planted with trees. Now you see pleasant clumps of gorse, broom and pines, flanked by the Claie to the north and the Arz, full of trout and pike, to the south, both running eastwards to the Oust. To north and south are other *landes*, agreeably wooded, with fertile, well-watered valleys between.

Following the Oust downstream from Malestroit there is an aggregation of saintly little villages where anglers gather: St-Laurent, where you will find the Café-Restaurant des Pêcheurs; then the fishy-sounding St-Congard; St-Martin, where the smart-looking Hôtel du Guélin faces the bridge over the Oust; and then St Gravé with the eighteenth-century auberge, the Lion d'Or, opposite its church. If you are lunching at any of these places the fish dishes are obviously the ones to go for.

Near here you will probably feel the magnetic pull of Rochefort-en-Terre, once a sleepy village like many others hereabouts but on an imposing spur and with many granite seventeenth-century houses. An American painter, Alfred Klots, owner of the twelfth-century château, put it on the map in 1911 with a competition for *maisons fleuries* which soon became nationwide. Since 1967 Rochefort has been in a class of its own. Somewhat over-prettified now, it is much visited, as the large car park halfway up the hill will testify. But the church, Notre-Dame-de-la-Tronchaye, has Flamboyant Gothic windows from 1533 on its north side and much good carved wood in its cool interior. There is a *pardon* (*pardons* are great religious processions, an important part of Breton traditional life) on the Sunday after 15 August. Restaurants and *crêperies* abound: La Chouannière (high summer only), Les Grées, Le Lion d'Or, Le Pélican and Le Vieux Logis.

A castle that is well worth a visit lies just off the N166 beyond Elven, conveniently on the road from Malestroit to Vannes. Maps call it Les Tours d'Elven, but on the fast N166 look for a right turn to the Forteresse de Largoët. You then follow a straight but positively medieval track through a deep wood leading past the ticket office to the tallest donjon in France. It has six storeys, rises 44 m and was built in the fourteenth century. Try to make the effort to trudge the 175 steps to the top for a pretty view over the smaller tower nearby, converted into a hunting lodge, and the wooded *landes* beyond. The townsfolk of Elven take part in a ninety-minute *Son et Lumière*, called *Lancelot du Lac*, on six evenings in the summer.

It is only a little way down the N166 to Vannes which, though strictly a port with access to the sea via the Gulf of Morbihan, can conveniently be dealt with here because it might well be the end of your route from St-Malo and, like Morlaix, it looks more towards its hinterland than out to sea.

It is undeniably an attractive city, modern but with a medieval heart, and an important one which has, like Rennes and Nantes, been at various times a capital of Brittany. Perhaps the best-known of the old Celtic 'nations', the Veneti of whom Caesar wrote (see p. 274), lived around the Gulf of Morbihan. The Roman city was called Darioritum, but the Gallo-Romans reverted to the old tribal name and Vannes derives from Veneti. The local chiefs became counts and one of them, Nominoë, was made first Duke of Brittany by Charlemagne's son Louis in 826. Vannes became the first capital of an independent Brittany in the tenth century and one of the dukes briefly made it a kingdom.

Ironically Vannes was where the Duchy of Brittany both began and ended. Claude, the daughter and heiress of Duchess Anne, the last truly independent ruler of Brittany, married François d'Angoulême who became King François I of France in 1515. Their son, the Dauphin, stood to inherit both France and Brittany and in 1532, at Vannes, the eternal union of Kingdom and Duchy was promulgated. Interestingly, Wales, which in so many ways resembles Brittany, was merged with England by François I's contemporary, Henry VIII, just four years later in 1536.

Vannes is an easy place to look round. Lose your car somewhere on the western side of the main vertical axis, Rue Thiers. It is a short walk into the maze of medieval streets around the cathedral, most of which are now pedestrianized. From here, a D-shaped tour will take you outside the well-maintained ramparts and back through the old city to the cathedral. Pass either side of it and through the Prison Gate, turn right and head southwards through the fine ornamental gardens that flank the

The medieval streets of Vannes

Rue Alexandre le Pontois. You can re-enter the old city either by the Postern Gate or, after reaching the head of the re-animated port with all its yachts, by the St-Vincent Gate. Strike up past the Maison de Vannes with its two carved stone figures of 'Vannes and his wife' into the Rue des Halles.

Here, at No. 9, is an excellent restaurant, La Benjamine. From a superb lunch I recommend *bisque d'étrilles* (soup of baby crab) followed by *jambon braisé Bourguignonne*. My companions at the time spoke well of the *mousseline de colin à l'oseille* (pollock with sorrel) and we all had an excellent Brie topped off by rich and creamy *île flottante*. Afterwards two of us took a turn round the cathedral with its mix of styles and mementoes of St Vincent Ferrier, a charismatic Anglo-Spanish missionary who died in Vannes in 1419. We vied with each other in translating the French and Latin inscriptions and found our performances much sharpened after two large glasses of Armagnac. Opposite the cathedral's west end is a covered market and exhibition hall known as La Cohue – the hubbub. You should now be back more or less where you began.

It may be that you do not intend to visit Vannes, because it lies too far west. If your route from St-Malo south through Rennes takes you to La Baule, Nantes or into the centre of France, there are other parts of Upper Brittany through which you might pass.

It is always dangerous to describe a region as having no interest – if I did so for anywhere in Brittany I would subsequently learn that it had a not-to-be-missed crêperie or a church with a remarkable fifteenth-century retable. But I think it safe to say that the triangle of country south of Rennes has less to distinguish it than its neighbouring regions.

It would be pleasant to strike down the Vilaine valley aiming for Redon. The D77 out of Rennes leads to Bruz with its interesting church. To the west, across the Vilaine, is the attractively sited Château de Blossac. A little further on you cross the river at Pont-Réan, where a lane to the left leads down to the bankside at Le Boël. Bourg-des-Comptes and Pléchâtel are two villages further south where good views over the water can be enjoyed. The Vilaine is navigable here – indeed it is a part of the system of Breton waterways that enables yachts to pass from the Channel at St-Malo to the Bay of Biscay at Lorient, La Roche-Bernard or Nantes. Beyond Guipry and Messac an attractive west

bank road leads to Langon, where Brittany's oldest intact building stands. This is the chapel of Ste-Agathe which, Gallo-
Roman in origin, was a shrine of Venus Genitrix. A fresco of
Venus rising from the sea can be dimly made out. The building
was converted to use as a Christian chapel in the sixth century.

Twenty kilometres further west is Redon, a delightful old
town, well inland but once a busy port. Its name, even more
than that of Rennes, reminds us that the Redones were the
Celtic nation here. Its heyday must have been the eighteenth
century when sailing ships lined the quays and the warehouses
flanking them bustled with activity. The old abbey church of
St-Sauveur has an unusually rounded twelfth-century tower
over the crossing and a separate Gothic bell-tower cut off from
the rest by fire in 1782. Redon is an important junction for river
traffic: the Vilaine and the Nantes–Brest canal cross here. South-
bound vessels execute complicated right and left turns into a
basin before locking out into the Vilaine at a lower level.

The N137, due south from Rennes, is for those in a real hurry
to get to Nantes. The D163, south-south-east, is slightly more
interesting and passes by St-Armel, where a tomb supposedly
houses the saint who founded Ploërmel. At the delightfully
named Corps Nuds strike off left to Janzé and Le Theil. Two
kilometres north-west is one of Brittany's finest megalithic monuments, La Roche-aux-Fées. Forty-two boulders, some enormous, form a covered corridor 21 m long.

Châteaubriant is the southernmost of three fortress towns
guarding the marches of Brittany from French attack – Vitré and
Fougères are the other two. It has in effect two castles put together: the feudal donjon was built around 1040 by Brient
(hence Châteaubriant), while the Renaissance wings were put
up between 1532 and 1538 by Jean de Laval for his young
wife, Françoise de Foix. She became the mistress of François I,
and her intensely jealous husband confined her for the rest of
her short life in a room hung with black. A lovely Italianate
stairway today leads up to governmental and legal offices –
sous-préfecture, greffier and so on; but the donjon is boarded up
and a plantation of saplings sprouts inside it. The town manu-
factures ploughs and has over fifteen thousand inhabitants. An
oval frame of forest surrounds it at about 12 kms distance and
large ponds dapple the landscape, pewter amid the green.

Take the D178 southwards for 12 kms to La Meilleraye, where

there is a Trappist abbey with a twelfth-century church; only men may visit it. Press on and you will reach Nantes, former capital of Brittany, but detached in 1956 when Loire Atlantique (the former Loire inférieure) became part of the Pays de Loire region. Industrial but interesting and fair of face, France's sixth city, though often by-passed, is worthy of closer examination.

Its two oldest buildings still dominate: the ducal castle, where the famous edict, permitting protestantism, was signed in 1598, and the cathedral of SS Peter and Paul. Old Nantes was built at the confluence of the Erdre with the Loire and the castle overlooks a former branch of the Loire, now filled in. The present cathedral, begun in 1434, took many centuries to build and was badly burned in 1972. Do not be put off by the unprepossessing west front. Inside, its white pillars are loftier than many in France, its predominantly modern glass gives it a light, ethereal air and you may be lucky enough to have the accompaniment of its deep, melodious bells.

There are at least ten museums in Nantes, three of them in the ducal castle. Among them are a maritime museum, highlighting the city's important role in the development of France's colonies and its part in the slave trade, a magnificent fine arts museum in Rue Georges-Clemenceau and one devoted to Jules Verne, who was born in the city in 1828.

By contrast, a refreshing and unusual outing can be made by taking a river trip up the Erdre. From the centre of the city northwards the banks are lined with delightful châteaux and *gentil-hommières*. One of a fleet of half a dozen boats, some of them most futuristic in design, could take you, in accordance with the season and the time of day, simply sightseeing or for a luncheon or a candlelit dinner cruise up the Erdre to Sucé and the Lac de Mazerolles. Bookings can be made at the Bateaux de l'Erdre office on the Quai de Versailles.

From Rennes, finally, a still more easterly line would take you to La Guerche-de-Bretagne or Vitré. Châteaugiron, only 25 kms from Rennes, is on the D463 and has an imposing donjon on a motte. Guerche contains some old houses and a church with amusing misericords in the choir stalls. But better than both is Vitré, with its fine triangular *château-fort*. It is always important how you arrive in these places. I first came into Vitré from Guerche to the south along the D178 and parked in the railway station yard.

Where was the castle? Sadly it was almost the last thing I stumbled across and from its least imposing side. It is better by far to come in on the D178 running south from Fougères, or the D857 from Rennes. Here you will see the castle at its best, on the end of its spur looming over the tranquil Vilaine.

Vitré has a well-kept medieval heart. The fifteenth-century church of Notre-Dame is interesting inside and out. On the south wall is an exterior pulpit, quite a common feature in Breton churches; in the late sixteenth century public debates were held here in which the Catholic clergy would dispute with Protestant divines on a platform, now gone, in the house opposite. Admiral Coligny was the doyen of the Huguenots in the sixteenth century, and since his family owned Vitré it became a nest of Calvinism. After seeing the church you should walk round the outside angle of the surviving stretch of rampart and then return into the heart of the town through a postern. I confess a disappointment with the castle's interior. Most of it is given over to municipal offices, and the public is only admitted to the much-restored tower of St-Lawrence. This houses an interesting, well laid out museum on several floors, but just when I was expecting to escape from fire extinguishers, glazing, temperature control, polished wooden floors and high-tech lighting and find a few draughty, genuinely medieval battlements it all petered out in a room full of pinned-down beetles and bottled snakes.

The best restaurants are to be found in and around the charming Rue Beaudrairie. I eyed the menus at the Bistrot du Chat Noir and the Taverne de l'Ecu, and they looked good. Unfortunately I had to lunch early and hurriedly in what proved to be a not so cheap but nevertheless nasty place in the Place de la République. I disliked the unnecessary and somewhat catchpenny reminder – *Service à l'appréciation de la clientèle* – which appeared several times on menu and bill. What's wrong with *non compris*?

Just over 6 kms down the D88 is the fine Château des Rochers, styled on the newer maps Rochers-Sévigné. This was the home, from time to time between 1654 and 1690, of Mme de Sévigné. My driver and I were shown round the strangely impressive, free-standing, octagonal chapel built in 1671, and three or four rooms in the cold, north-facing part of the house that the present owner, the Comte de Ternay, presumably does not want to use. Here it was, the lady guide told us, that Mme de Sévigné wrote many of the thousand or more letters, most of them to her daughter, the Comtesse de Grignan, which give such a detailed picture of aristocratic life in the time of Louis XIV. But I could not help asking myself if she really immured herself in these chill quarters when the sun was beaming down on the other side of the house. The rooms on show were full of the great lady's possessions, and we were particularly taken by the porcelain *bourdaloue*, shaped like a gravy boat with a lid, which, like all ladies of the time, she is said to have used for her relief during mass. The extensive gardens were originally laid out by Le Nôtre, but were redesigned in English style in 1982.

Just a little way further down the D88 and over the autoroute is another equally fine-looking château at Argentré-du-Plessis – the home of Mlle du Plessis, Mme de Sévigné's great rival. After that the D88 runs straight and true out of Brittany into Maine.

9 Inland from Roscoff

St-Pol-de-Léon and Morlaix

Only once have I walked into France, and that was in April 1976, from the car-deck of a Brittany Ferries vessel at Roscoff. I stepped out of the rather angular, modernistic comforts of the *Penn Ar Bed* (no longer in their fleet) on to the open road between the cauliflower and artichoke fields of the old region of Léon, now the department of Finistère. A major difficulty in France is distance: what appears on the map to be an evening's hike is sometimes a great deal more over the ground. On this occasion I did not, get very far – quite simply my feet were not up to the mileage I expected of them – and I had to alter my plans accordingly.

It reminded of the time before, when as a raw, untravelled undergraduate in 1952 I decided to cycle across France to the Mediterranean. I arbitrarily divided the road between Paris and Provence into daily stages, borrowed a bicycle and set off. Paris, even then, was perilous for cyclists. I had to circle the Arc de Triomphe three times, my extended arm in constant danger of being winged by passing taxis, before I could regain the peri-meter and pedal off down the avenue I wanted. Next day, still rather to my surprise in the suburbs of Paris, I hit the *pavé*. The cobbles weakened the frame of my overloaded bicycle and my teeth felt as if they had become disloged. Many miles short of my target headache and fatigue brought me to a stop and I slept fitfully and half-frozen by the road. Soon after dawn I was again pedalling towards a pale rising sun, cold, unfed and miserable. At Fontainebleau I made a reappraisal. It was going to take me four times as long as I had allowed to reach the Mediterranean and, of course, there was the return. I caught a train and cut back to the fleshpots of the Rive Gauche.

In Brittany in 1976 I was on foot, I had three weeks, I had no

213

firm, predetermined objective, just a hope of getting into the Monts d'Arrée in the interior, so, as I slung my pack and marched off, it did not really matter what happened. The cross-channel port at Roscoff is on the eastern edge of the town and since I took the road south I missed it. But I saw it subsequently in 1978 and 1979 and it must be the obvious place to begin this chapter.

When I first heard the name Roscoff I was puzzled – what was such a Russian-sounding place doing in France? But I learned later that '-iff' and '-off' as prefix or suffix are common in Brittany (Plogoff, Baie du Stiff, Iffendic) and have nothing to do with the Romanoffs. The town was put on the international map by an ardent Breton, Alexis Gourvennec, who farms near Morlaix in the north of Finistère. In 1961 he formed a farmers' co-operative which planned, uniquely in the farming world, to set up its own shipping company – Brittany Ferries. This was in anticipation of Britain's entry to the EEC, when a more convenient gateway to southern England than St-Malo for the area's potatoes, onions, cauliflowers, artichokes, meat, fish and eggs would become viable.

West of St-Malo there was no good port unaffected by tides, so Gourvennec wrung 6 million francs from the French government to build the deep-water quay at Roscoff. In 1973, the year Britain joined the Common Market, the port was finished and the daily ferry services (up to three a day in summer) to and from Plymouth began. There is in addition a weekly service between Roscoff and Cork, which, whatever its economic value, is dear to Gourvennec and other Bretons who aspire to revive old links between the Celtic nations.

Long before the construction of Gourvennec's Port Bloscon Roscoff was a seaport, though a rather hazardous one. Since the English were the habitual enemy some of the best-known early arrivals were Scots. In 1548 it was, most historians say, the landfall of the five-year-old Mary, Queen of Scots, on her way to be betrothed to the four-year-old Dauphin who was to become François II in 1559. After an eighteen-day voyage from the Clyde, and terrible storms off Land's End which the admiral of the flotilla, the Sieur de Brèze, reported that she survived cheerfully, her ship threaded in through the rocks to Roscoff. The places where supposedly she landed, stayed the night and dedicated a chapel are still to be seen. Then in 1746 came the defeated Bonnie Prince Charlie. He had slipped away from the battlefield of Culloden and, disguised as Flora Macdonald's maid, escaped to the Hebrides. From there he sailed to Roscoff, in a corsair's ship hotly pursued by George II's navy.

The small harbour, which dries out at low water, is a circular haven at the end of a northwards-facing promontory, sheltered to an extent by the Ile de Batz (pronounced 'Bah!') 5 kms away across a deep-water but quite treacherous channel. Roscoff was always the haunt of corsairs, a sort of miniature St-Malo. Its low granite houses seem to turn a protective shoulder to the sea and look inwards to the small Place Lacaze-Duthiers where stands the imposing sixteenth-century church, Notre-Dame de Kroaz-Baz, and to the maze of narrow streets beyond.

The richness, not to say occasional quirkiness, of what French towns have to offer never ceases to astonish. Most of them claim something worth stopping to look at, while many have a bizarre variety of things. Roscoff is one of the latter. Where else could you find two early seventeenth-century ossuaries, an internationally famous marine biology centre and aquarium and the biggest fig tree in the world? This last is a dangerous claim – *The Guinness Book of Records* neither confirms nor denies it – but the tree, which still bears fruit regularly, was planted by Capuchin monks in a convent garden in the 1620s and its branches, propped up by concrete pillars now, cover an area of 600 sq.m. It is near Roscoff's small railway terminus. The ossuaries you will find in the churchyard. The aquarium, often open, and the marine biology centre, founded by a Sorbonne zoology professor named Henri Lacaze-Duthiers over a century ago, are, like the church, in the square which bears his name.

Some of the best hotels and restaurants are found in this square, which is actually a triangle and as tranquil as the long main street fronting the port is animated. One can lunch exceedingly well at the Ar Maner restaurant in Le Brittany hotel, a fine eighteenth-century granite house with big arches now fully glazed and overlooking the old harbour. From the hotel you can see the Ile de Batz, which lies grey and mysterious, filling the north-western horizon.

Port Kernoch on the Ile de Batz faces Roscoff across the confusingly rock-strewn channel. You can make the crossing every hour by *vedette* in about fifteen minutes and at any state of the tide, which can fall 10 m here. At both ends of the crossing are long, sloping ramps leading down past weed-strewn boulders into the deep water.

The Ile de Batz is easily walkable – about 3 × 2 kms – and has character but not much else. Port Kernoch looks thriving from a distance but on closer inspection has the slightly beleaguered air of many island villages. There are narrow, winding lanes – almost traffic-free – some grey houses, a post office, a few shops and *pensions* and a camp site. It would make a good holiday spot for people who do not mind being thrown on their own resources – it is the place to write that novel. Men and women work in the small, stone-walled fields which they nourish with local seaweed. Two buildings are worth visiting: the lighthouse can be climbed and gives a view which in clear weather is superb and at low tide appalling to the sailor – to the west the sea is dotted with enormous reefs and isolated stacks between which the current can sluice at up to 5 knots; the church contains relics of the region's most famous local saint, St-Paul-Aurelian or St-Pol, a monk from south Wales who migrated in 517 to Ushant and then to the Ile de Batz and to nearby St-Pol-de-Léon, which assumed his name. He was Bishop of Léon and afterwards spent thirty years in retirement on the Ile de Batz. I suppose there wasn't anywhere much else to go. He must have been a tough old cleric – he lived for 104 years which, if true, is not bad for the sixth century.

There is almost no way out of Roscoff except through St-Pol-de-Léon, 5 kms down the road. In 1976 I had trudged off the ferry and followed the main road, with everyone else belting past in their cars. Soon I left behind the trim, white-washed bungalows, almost certainly second homes – *le petit log-cabin dans l'ouest*, but often of stark, uncompromising, severely modern design. The countryside is a mosaic of tiny fields of artichokes and cauliflowers. It is densely populated and there are few woods. This is *la ceinture dorée* – the golden belt, where every available square foot pushes up its vegetable.

The large main square of St-Pol-de-Léon is dominated by the splendid rough granite former cathedral, where repose other bits of St-Paul-Aurelian. A little further off is the imposing spire of the chapel of Kreisker ('Christ's house' in Breton) which is just 34 feet shorter than Salisbury Cathedral, Britain's tallest.

Routes from Roscoff and Morlaix

This must be the cauliflower capital of France. Down by the station I dodged past great lorries and trailers stuffed with them. Gourvennec's co-operative, the Société d'Intérêt Collectif Agricole (SICA), was formed to stop Breton farmers being ripped off by middlemen, and it now runs an experimental farm, controls production, fixes prices and regulates sales. Tons of produce can be bought by Dutch auction in a vast covered hall just south of St-Pol either by telephone or at the touch of a button. The days of the onion sellers who used to embark with their bicycles and

217

sell their strings door-to-door in southern England are gone for ever.

I strode on towards Morlaix and came to Keriven, by the banks of the Penzé, a beautiful tidal river running up into the bay of Morlaix. The D58, a new road and a boon for motorists, carries the St-Pol–Morlaix traffic across it by a modern bridge. I toiled laboriously over and up to the village of Henvic, a sleepy place with a fine granite church and calvary, and a Chinese restaurant. Chinese and Vietnamese restaurants, reflecting France's colonial past, can be found all over the country, but not usually in such small rural villages. I continued via Taulé, where the purest Breton is said to be spoken, to Morlaix.

The charm of Morlaix lies not in any single building – it has only vestiges of a château and no abbey or cathedral – but in its arrangement on its site. The town lies where two rivers, the Jarlo and the Queffleuth, come together in a long, steep-sided valley spanned by an enormous two-tiered viaduct built in the 1860s to carry the Paris–Brest railway line. Further downstream there is now another viaduct, over which the main east–west road runs in a semi-circular by-pass north of the town.

Near the confluence of the rivers is a maze of narrow lanes one of which, with the same logic that the Pont Neuf is the oldest bridge in Paris, is called the Grande Rue. Looming over them are the projecting storeys of gabled sixteenth-century houses; one of them proudly claims: 'Queen Anne slept here' – Anne of Brittany, on a pilgrimage in 1505.

Morlaix is 14 kms from the open sea but has always been a port. Sadly it is now much decayed commercially and the principal visitors are yachts, a great many of them from England. To create space for a bus station the town authorities have bridged over the river, so that it disappears underground south of the rail viaduct and only comes to light in the large yacht basin. Ironically, part of the open space is called Place Cornic, after an eighteenth-century corsair, the town's most celebrated seafarer.

The peaceful summertime invasion of Morlaix by English yachtsmen has another pleasant irony. There were earlier English incursions, one of which gave the town its well-known motto, a clever play upon its own name: *'S'ils te mordent, mords-les!'* ('If they bite you, bite them back!') In 1522 a fleet of sixty English vessels landed a force which found the town unde-

The charming port of Morlaix, dominated by the Paris-Brest railway viaduct

fended and its leading citizens at some festivities in the interior. The English sacked the place and got very satisfactorily drunk in the wine cellars, whereupon the townspeople returned and wrought terrible vengeance. The town's coat of arms features the French leopard confronting the English lion.

All this soon changed: to avoid the high cost of state monopoly tobacco, processed in the town in the eighteenth century as it still is today, the local smugglers developed a profitable English connection, which led them into many a coastal skirmish with their own excisemen. And in the twentieth century Morlaix sports a genteel 'English Shop' which sells sheepskins, decorated mirrors, tea-cosies, cushions and shell ornaments. There are good markets at both ends of the scale: on the *voie express* bypassing the town are two hypermarkets, Rallye and La Boissière on the St-Brieuc side and the Euromarché at St-Martin-des-Champs on the Brest side. And down in the town there is an occasional open market in the tree-lined Place Cornic with a wide range of good quality stuff and rosy-cheeked old ladies in their Breton coifs. Morlaix has over a dozen hotels and a camp site and would be a very good place from which to make excursions into Léon. It is very handily reached, not only by yacht direct or by car from Roscoff (or, indeed, on foot), but through its very convenient airport at Ploujean. Brymon Airways run a daily service (except Saturdays) to and from Plymouth, via Brest. Brit Air, Brittany's own air line, has a weekday service between Morlaix and Gatwick.

Perhaps the most tranquil way to explore the bay of Morlaix area is by boat. Morlaix is like an upside-down Truro, at the head of navigation of quite a long river. Slipping down a verdant tree-fringed canal you pass the attractive village of Locquénolé with its small harbour, sailing club, old church and calvary. Opposite it is the tributary river Dourduff, which comes in at the little port of the same name, and sounds like a minor character from *Macbeth*. The bay then opens out and to the west, on a limb, is the most agreeable little resort of Carantec. If you sail in from the open sea you can pick up a mooring off the projecting headland of Pen-Lann, reach the shore by dinghy and shop in Carantec.

Just off Pen-Lann is a reminder of those dark days of Anglo-French warfare: the Château du Taureau. To avoid a repeat of the 1522 surprise attack on Morlaix the town built a robust-

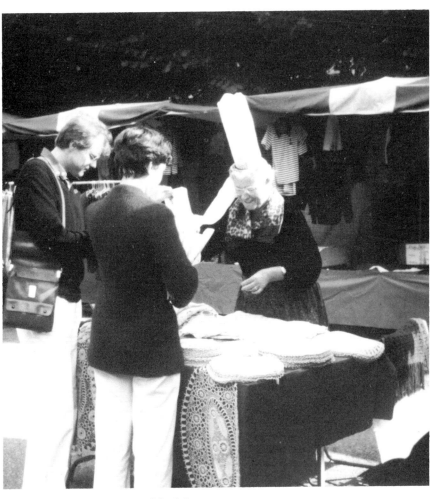

A Breton lace-seller at Morlaix

looking fortress on a rock in the approach roads. It rises clear out of the sea and the connection with a bull escapes me. In 1660 Louis XIV took it over as a state prison and it is now a sailing school – a fairly stern school, I would say, for whenever I have seen the little dinghies bobbing round it a stiffish wind has been blowing in.

Diametrically opposed to all this is a trip by car south of Morlaix, which would give all the flavour of the desolate but characterful Breton countryside. In just over 50 kms you could follow a three-sided route which would take you into the Monts d'Arrée. Head for the D9 south-east out of Morlaix to Plougonven (on Wednesdays and Saturdays a Cars de l'Argoat bus could take you out just after eleven and get you back after lunch). Plougonven follows the traditional Breton *enclos paroissial* (parish close) grouping of church, ossuary and calvary set around a cemetery, often reached through a triumphal arch. The intention was to link the spiritual world of the living with that of the dead, and in deeply religious Breton society there was intense rivalry between parishes to outdo each other in the magnificence of their *enclos paroissiaux*. Plougonven has an ossuary and an elaborate calvary raised in 1554.

Go on now to Lannéanou and turn right or take a different bus through Lannéanou to Carhaix – but that is dealt with in Chapter 10. The D111 is an attractive by-way and threads through the Monts d'Arrée to Le Relecq, with its ruins of a Cistercian abbey, music festival one Sunday every July and *pardon* in mid August. At the D785 head north to Pleyber-Christ, whose church has an interesting interior and forms part of an *enclos paroissial* with ossuary, and on back to Morlaix. After that you deserve a *crêpe* in one of the town's eight *crêperies*.

There are some noteworthy corners on the coast between Lannion bay and Morlaix bay, all within a leisurely day's run of Roscoff. If you take the Lannion road from Morlaix to Lanmeur, then turn off to Guimaëc, you will come to the attractive fishing port of Locquirec on the Corniche de l'Armorique, which has another fascinating church and nine sandy beaches around about, all differently orientated.

Nearer to Morlaix bay lie the pleasant villages of Plougasnou and St-Jean-du-Doigt. This area is best reached from Morlaix by the D76, which hugs the western bank of the river Morlaix to Dourduff, curls inland to Plouézoch, and then goes on north. Even those not particularly interested in history or archaeology should find it rewarding to make a detour on to a peninsula jutting out into Morlaix bay and look at the six-thousand-year-old tumulus of Barnenez. A superb piece of dry-stone walling in the form of a cairn, it has eleven funerary chambers of which two have been exposed. Their entrances all face the rising sun.

Further north everything is perfectly, typically Breton – rocks, views, pine trees, sandy beaches, granite churches. Out of the ordinary are the fish ponds at Primel and, for the faithful, a miracle-working relic at St-Jean-du-Doigt – no less, it is said, than a part of the index finger of John the Baptist, brought from St-Lô in the fifteenth century.

Of course, holiday-makers coming by ferry to Roscoff are not necessarily going to hover about in the immediate area of Morlaix. The Brittany Ferries route to Roscoff is also the ideal gateway to the south of Brittany and the west of France generally. From Morlaix famous holiday centres such as Quimper, Benodet and Concarneau can be reached by taking the D785 via Pleyben across the Monts d'Arrée. For the lower Loire and La Vendée you go to Morlaix again and take the D769 via Carhaix to Hennebont and points south. In that way important places such as Carnac, Auray and the Château de Josselin can all be reached, and time should be found for them. And crossing the neck of Brittany should not be regarded as a tedious, unavoidable slog because the interior, as Chapter 10 will show, has compensations of its own.

10 The Heart of Old Brittany

The Western Argoat and the Suisse Bretonne

There are at least four Brittanies. Upper Brittany, described in Chapter 8, is the eastern half, reasonably dry, closest to France and mainly French-speaking, and made up of the departments of Ille-et-Vilaine, Loire-Atlantique and half of Côtes-du-Nord. Lower Brittany, which is paradoxically higher above sea-level, is the western half, much wetter, where Breton is widely spoken; it embraces the departments of Finistère, most of Morbihan and the other half of Côtes-du-Nord. The Armor, the ancient name for the 'land of the sea', is the indented, island-strewn coastal fringe with its holiday resorts both fashionable and primitive, which is covered in Chapters 11 and 12. In between is the interior, the Argoat, the 'land of the woods' – dark, hilly and largely unvisited. The Argoat of Upper Brittany has already featured in Chapter 8, but the Western Argoat in Lower Brittany is a region which deserves to be explored more thoroughly, and it is easily reached from Roscoff.

I first came to this area some ten years ago. I was walking from Roscoff and arrived at Morlaix intending to cheat by taking the train south to Carhaix, which would run me swiftly into the Monts d'Arrée. After buying a ticket at the station I made for the platform, but the ticket collector stopped me. *'C'est un car,'* he said, and motioned towards a bus in the yard outside. Sure enough the railway line had long ago been ripped up. My map was clearly a decade or two out of date.

The windy little upland town of Carhaix-Plouguer is unremarkable but for La Tour d'Auvergne. I thought at first this was

Lower Brittany: The Argoat

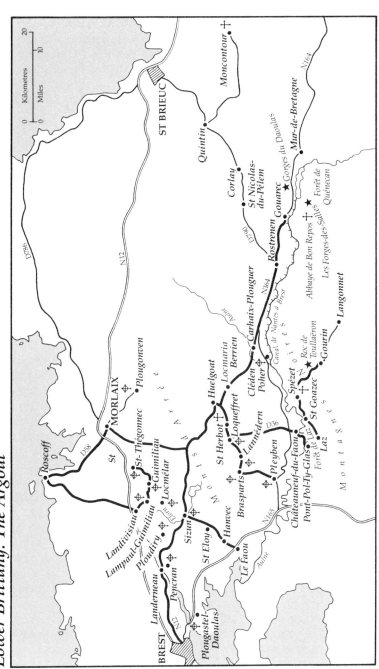

a wine, which is impossible for this part of Brittany. Nor is it a cheese or a bicycle race. La Tour d'Auvergne was an eighteenth-century soldier-scholar, and when I reached the spacious and rather desolate square I found his statue in solitary command.

His life was full of strange contradictions. Born Théophile-Malo Corret, he became a philologist and great enthusiast for the Breton tongue, but all his life he kept enlisting and re-enlisting in the French army. He had always wanted to be an officer and he contrived to show some connections with a noble family in order to gain preferment in the closed shop of the officer caste under the *ancien régime*. Yet, having established himself as La Tour d'Auvergne, he steadfastly refused promotion beyond junior rank. He soldiered for Louis XVI and then, with equal zeal, for the Revolution. He rarely saw active service, yet his loyalty, his eccentricity, his care for his men, his repeated returns to the field as a captain in his early fifties earned him the recognition of Napoléon, who honoured him as 'the First Grenadier of of France'. He was killed in battle at Oberhausen in Bavaria at the age of 57.

Carhaix where he had hoped to retire, began as the *chef-lieu* of the westernmost 'nation' of the Celts in Gaul, the Osisimi, and became known to the conquering Romans as Vorgium. My guess is that the name Carhaix derives, like Carfax in Oxford, from *quadrifurcus*, meaning a crossroads, for it was the centre of a network of Roman roads, the main ones possibly running from Rennes to Brest, and from Quimper to Lannion.

This happened again when Carhaix in the 1880s became the hub of a radiating system of narrow-gauge railway lines of which, with the general decline of the interior, only one arm – Carhaix to Guingamp – survives.

Next day I walked westwards to perhaps the best-known inland centre in Finistère. The small town of Huelgoat ('the high wood') may appear to receive fewer visitors than Carhaix but has more atmosphere. It lies on the edge of a lake, and the modest but ancient hills around it are clothed in thick pine forests in which streams tumble through agglomerations of vast, lichen-covered boulders and where the spirit of King Arthur lurks still.

More than any other people the medieval Bretons helped to propagate the notion of the Dark Ages as a time of high ideals

La Tour d'Auvergne at Carhaix (Victoria Southwell)

and chivalry, and Arthur as the exemplar of spiritual and military virtue. The Britons who crossed the Channel in the fifth and sixth centuries to colonize Armorica and become Bretons were his near-contemporaries. They brought with them their culture and their folk heroes. An Atlantic-facing stretch of the Armor they called Cornouaille after the Cornwall they had left, and Ile Tristan, off the coast, is a reminder of the great Cornish hero. The oral tradition of the Bretons regarded the Forêt de Paimpont, part of the once huge wooded region of Brocéliande, as the centre of Arthurian Brittany. Some members of the Arthurian canon – Lancelot, Galahad, Ector de Maris, Bors de Ganis – were pure Breton. Arthur's court is believed to have been established in Landerneau, near Brest, and he lies dead, they say, or perhaps just sleeping, on the Ile Daval, just off the north coast near Perros-Guirec.

Near the lake at Huelgoat are other places with Arthurian associations, though what he is said to have done there is nowhere made clear. I left the lake and followed the course of the little river Argent, whose name gives a clue to an important local activity of recent years: the smoke and clamour of leadmines were features of the area round Huelgoat up to World War I and silver was also found in some of these mines. The river plunges between huge granite monoliths into rock pools and nearby is the so-called Grotte d'Artus (Arthur's Cave), a natural formation of slab walls and capstones into which one can ascend. Crowning the summit of a hill is the Camp d'Artus, two concentric rings of Iron Age fortifications, of which the outer one is 3 kms in circumference. I was camping, and so I looked for a nest among the pine needles in which to bed down. It amused me to spend the night in the lee of an earthwork that might have been defended by some local Vercingetorix against the Romans. Demons are said to guard a treasure buried in the innermost ring, and their howlings can be heard down in Huelgoat. It does not do to push your luck, so I stayed outside.

On my next visit to Huelgoat I had a car and was recording material for a BBC programme. I left Brest rather late and headed for Sizun, 37 kms away, which looked like a handy stopping place. By the time we got there the dark interior was growing ever darker. The hotel seemed not to be open. Nobody was about. It began to drizzle. *'Une ville morte,'* said my companion. It is probably a pretty little place on a bright spring morning –

it has a very fine *enclos paroissial* with three triumphal arches and a church with an unusually colourful interior. But at night it was bleak, sinister even. So we pressed on into the mist-enshrouded Monts d'Arrée to Huelgoat.

It was after ten when I rolled into the long, rectangular Place Aristide Briand, which looked even more dead than Sizun. There were some hotels, but they all seemed closed. None of my cheery stories about the delightful dinner I had enjoyed on my earlier trip at the Restaurant du Lac (whose speciality is, predictably, fishy) seemed to mollify my BBC colleague, who was beginning to have presentiments that we might be forced to sleep in the car. There was just one bar open, where some young men were in noisy argument behind its steamed-up windows. We went in and conversation stopped – well, it probably would at some late-night caff in Bodmin if a French couple in a battered Alfa-Romeo had come stumbling in. The *patron* was too busy to be of much help. 'Have you tried the Hotel de la Bretagne next door?' he asked. We hadn't, so we did. The hotel was unlit but the door was wide open. There was a reception desk but no sign of the *direction*. I rang a bell twice. We peered into darkened rooms. I even went upstairs where there was a rack with a lot of keys hanging from nails. But we could raise nobody and so returned to the bar, which was quieter now.

The *patron* most obligingly began to telephone all the places he thought might take us in. No joy. We were getting desperate when another customer said he would guide us out to the house of Youenn Gwernig, a notable Breton poet, folk-singer and wood-carver whom we were expecting to interview for Radio 4 the following day. It was nearly midnight and this did not seem to be quite the way to conduct BBC business; however, we had little choice but to agree.

We drove out along dark lanes to the little village of Locmaria-Berrien and found his isolated farmhouse. Prolonged knocking eventually resulted in an upper window being thrown open. Bright light framed Mme Gwernig in hairnet and curlers. She was not pleased. Youenn was still out at a gig in St-Brieuc. After much reference to *le Bé-Bé-Cé*, whose audience we feared might be rather meagre in eastern Finistère, the latches were thrown back and the front door finally opened. We were given shakedowns in a cold spare room on the ground floor, where I slept like a Crusader with a Dalmatian crouched at my feet.

Next morning Youenn and I talked of the similarity of Brittany to Wales, where Youenn, his wife and daughters often went for their holidays. He recited some poems in Breton and English. And then, although it was the wrong end of the day for that sort of thing, Youenn fetched his guitar and he and his daughters sang a few plaintive Breton songs into the tape recorder.

For many people Locmaria-Berrien is only worth visiting for Mme Le Guillou's Auberge de la Truite, which is highly recommended for its Breton furnishings and its trout, lobster and quail dishes. The Gwernig family too are involved in the restaurant business – Youenn's wife, Suzig, runs a *crêperie* in Huelgoat. With its choice of twenty-one varieties Les Crêpes de Suzig provides a useful venue for lunch on this route.

I now took the D42 north-east which, if you can contrive it, is perhaps the best approach to Huelgoat. There are fine views as you bowl through the northern foothills of the Monts d'Arrée almost all the way to Plestin-les-Grèves and the shores of the baie de Lannion.

I was still searching for a glimpse of old Brittany, and north of Lannion I came to the manse of the Abbé Loeiz ar Floc'h, rector of Louannec, overlooking the rock-strewn bay near Perros-Guirec. I spent an agreeable afternoon discussing with him Breton history, Breton saints and Breton music. He has translated the Bible into Breton and is also a poet. He staunchly refuses to let his poems be translated into French. The Abbé Loeiz argued for yet another way of sub-dividing Brittany – not only Higher and Lower, and Armor and Argoat, but the north coast and the interior. He believes that the inhabitants of Léon and Trégor, the *Léonards* and *Trégorrois*, along the Channel coast are the direct descendants of those Cornish and Welsh who came over from Britain in the fifth and sixth centuries. It was their arrival that caused the region, previously called Armorica, to become known as Little Britain and later simply Brittany. The people of the interior he holds to be the descendants of the old Armoricans, and he told me that they still differ in temperament: the coastal 'migrants' are placid, while the older stock in the hinterland are more volatile. He illustrated this for us by singing the same Breton song in the way that people from the two regions might render it.

While I was there a fellow cleric, the Abbé du Bourg, said he would accompany me to the house of someone else whom I ought to see. At a farmhouse deep in the countryside around Plouaret, east of Morlaix, I met Anjela Duval, a celebrated Breton poetess and cult figure in her seventies, near a village which is, as she is herself, surprisingly French in name – Le Vieux Marché. Her tiny cottage was like a time capsule from an earlier age. It had no electricity. Chickens and dogs ran in and out on the earthen floor. Wooden chairs and benches polished smooth by decades of use surrounded an open wood fire, and along one wall of the dimly lit main room were the beautifully carved wooden panels and doors of a *lit clos*, the characteristic Breton bed, made up in a cupboard and, I should imagine, warm but claustrophobic. She recited poems in Breton for us (she has written over three hundred) and explained against a cacophony of barking dogs that she was one of those Breton souls living uncomfortably in a French skin.

Despite their often fiercely independent stance, the Bretons are not an unwelcoming people. They are particularly happy to see fellow Celts, and every few years enthusiasts from Kernow (Cornwall), Cymru (Wales), Alba (Gaelic Scotland), Mannin (the Isle of Man) and Eire gather together in Breizh or some other part of the Celtic fringe. But the welcome accorded to English and other holiday-makers is scarcely less warm.

Any look at Brittany's history would be incomplete without a visit to the foothills of the Monts d'Arrée, where the best examples of *enclos paroissiaux* (see p. 222) are to be found.

On the D14 leaving Huelgoat to the south-west I came across an interesting late fifteenth-century church at St-Herbot. A curious carved oak screen rings the choir and there are two stone tables nearby. Tufts of hair from the tails of cattle are laid on them the Friday before Trinity Sunday when the local *pardon* takes place. St-Herbot is the patron saint of horned beasts, and on that day all the draught oxen are given the day off. Further on, Loqueffret and Lannédern have small *enclos paroissiaux* and the curiously named Brasparts has a very good one of sixteenth-century date. Lovers of church architecture will certainly continue 11 kms south from Brasparts to Pleyben, whose *enclos* is one of the finest of all. There is a splendid Renaissance bell-tower, but perhaps the best thing here is the calvary, which in Brittany is not just a cross but an elaborate assemblage in stone (sometimes separate, sometimes part of the triumphal arch) of all the figures associated with the crucifixion, with a surrounding frieze illustrating many of the incidents in Christ's life. This one was reconstructed in 1743, and you can trace the events following the visitation of the Virgin Mary. The *pardon* here takes place on the first Sunday in August.

Coming from Roscoff you need not drive as far as Pleyben to see an *enclos paroissial* of the first order. Indeed, the best examples of this peculiarly Breton form of devotional art can be found quite near Morlaix and more or less due south of Roscoff. Take the road west out of St-Pol-de-Léon and then the D69 south to Landivisiau. Here in southern Léon, in the long valley of the Elorn, which runs fiord-like into the Rade de Brest, are the three finest – and signposts will guide you round the *Circuit des Trois Enclos*. Start at Landivisiau, which has an interestingly sculptured fifteenth-century well dedicated to its saint, Thivisiau. From here you can visit the three in logical order – Lampaul-Guimiliau, Guimiliau and St-Thégonnec – and be pointing back to Morlaix or Roscoff after two and a half or three hours.

At Lampaul-Guimiliau it is the church itself with its shorn-off spire (struck by lightning in 1809) which is most interesting. Scenes from the lives of St-Pol and St-Miliau, from both of whom the village gets its name, adorn the interior. Notice, too, the fine carved rood-beam. Outside stands also the usual ensemble of triumphal arch, ossuary and calvary.

Three kilometres away at Guimiliau it is the calvary which is supreme. Pillars X-shaped in plan support a platform with a surrounding frieze below it on which can be counted upwards of two hundred figures around the cross. They have weathered well since the 1580s when it was all built, and many are dressed in the style of the time. Christ is depicted at his birth, the most important moments of his life, his death and resurrection, together with apostles, holy women and Roman soldiers. But look also for the *Katel-Gollet*, a traditional Breton representation of Catherine the Damned and a cautionary tale in stern granite for all the young girls of Guimiliau. Catherine, a notorious strumpet, is shown being dragged naked to hell – the cavernous mouth of a beast from whence gloating demons emerge. Do not neglect the church itself with its extraordinary Renaissance south porch and, inside, a font surmounted by a carved oak baldaquin of consummate richness. The 1670s must have been prosperous times in Giumiliau, for that decade produced font, baldaquin, organ and pulpit.

As if to keep up with their neighbours at Guimiliau, the villagers of St-Thégonnec built an ossuary in the late 1670s which must have been the most glorious charnel-house in Christendom. Now it is a chapel. The calvary there is smaller but crowded with figures, including two angels collecting blood from Christ's wounds.

If you are not in this part of Léon, other characteristic *enclos* can be seen at Ploudiry, La Martyre, Pencran and Locmélar close by to the west, Pleyber-Christ and Plougonven south of Morlaix (see page 222), Commana in the foothills of the Monts d'Arrée, and Plougastel-Daoulas across the bay from Brest. Part of the calvary at Cléden-Poher, between Carhaix and Châteauneuf-du-Faou, shows more angels below the cross collecting Christ's blood in a vessel – presumably another representation of the Holy Grail, the quest for which, in Arthurian legend, took his knights to Brittany.

After Huelgoat we headed south to Châteauneuf-du-Faou, a neat town overlooking a loop in the Aulne, which from here on is also the Canal de Nantes à Brest. This stretch of the Aulne is Brittany's main salmon-fishing water, so it was no great surprise when running towards Quimper we came upon the Auberge du Saumon near the bridge at Pont-Pol-Ty-Glas – a name so Welsh that we might have been crossing the Teifi in Dyfed. It was easy to give in to the impulse to stop and lunch at the Auberge. Some meals are unforgettable, and the grilled salmon in Béarnaise sauce, washed down with a cool Muscadet, is one of them. Afterwards, we walked far down an attractive towpath, with the insects of midsummer humming among the tall riverside grasses, to a broad weir and an imposing lock.

This was nothing like the expected dark interior, even though the Montagnes Noires were not far distant. From Pont-Pol-Ty-Glas it is only five minutes' pleasant drive up to Laz and on into the Forêt de Laz. *Montagnes* is of course a misnomer; nothing in Brittany is over 400 metres high and the so-called black mountains only reach 326 metres at the Roc de Toullaëron – about a third of the height of the Black Mountains in Wales. Carrying on from St-Goazec to Spézet, the small chapel of Notre-Dame-du-Crann is worth visiting. It is usually a disincentive to have to 'address oneself to the guardian' and get a rusty old key to some ill-maintained relic, but this chapel is a gem hidden deep in the countryside. Built in 1532 it has magnificent stained glass windows and carved wooden shutters round the high altar.

From Spézet you can take the D17 across the Montagnes Noires, following the track up to the highest point if the weather promises a view, and then descend to Gourin. This is a typically Breton little town given over to slate-quarrying and mixed farming. Some might prefer to avoid Gourin on 1 May for the national championships of the *biniou* and the *bombarde*, the Breton pipes, take place then. On the last Sunday in September there is the *pardon* and a big procession of horses to the nearby chapel of St-Hervé. I had to record a *bombarde* for the BBC programme I was doing, and I found my subject without trouble some 10 kms from Gourin at Langonnet. The instrument was played by the owner of the local print shop and *quincaillerie* (that evocative word for an ironmonger's shop which sounds exactly like two buckets being clanged together). During the lunch break he most obligingly took up his *bombarde* and I dutifully recorded its strident, reedy tones.

Many attractive corners of the Argoat conceal holiday villages and the second homes of coast- or town-dwelling Bretons. In Lower Brittany the favourite site for these is the upper part of the Blavet valley around the Lac de Guerlédan. This is a really well-hidden part of the interior on the borders of Côtes-du-Nord and Morbihan. You could come upon it from Roscoff if you were heading south-east to Vannes, or from St-Malo if on the way to western Brittany: either way you would have to be careful not to miss it.

From Roscoff head for Carhaix, Rostrenen and Mur-de-Bretagne. From St-Malo head via St-Brieuc, Quintin and Corlay – where in the late 1970s I visited a factory still turning out wooden sabots. From the neat little town of Mur-de-Bretagne a 40 km tour encompasses the whole of the Lac de Guerlédan – in fact a man-made reservoir on the course of the Blavet. It is a picturesque circuit through hills covered in beech, oak, Norwegian pine, broom, gorse and heather, sloping down to the sinuous lake below. Near Mur there are vantage points over the barrage, below which is a power station. At the western end is the pretty village of Les Forges des Salles, once the centre of an

Little girl in Breton costume (Victoria Southwell)

Grotte d'Artus (Arthur's Cave) (Victoria Southwell)

iron-making industry. It is worth pausing to visit the ruined Château des Salles and the Abbaye de Bon Repos nearby. Gorges are plentiful. The whole region has a Tyrolean air and indeed is often called Suisse Bretonne. The Gorges de Daoulas are near the abbey and the Gorges du Poulancre near Mur, but the finest are the Gorges du Toul-Goulic 12 kms north of Rostrenen, where house-sized boulders tumble in mossy profusion. But the Argoat is the land of the woods and nothing better typifies it than the view from Keriven, looking over the lake to one of the biggest surviving swathes of woodland, the deep, dark Forêt de Quénécan.

Before leaving the hills of the Argoat in Lower Brittany I should say that the Monts d'Arrée (and indeed the Crozon peninsula and the Ushant archipelago) have since 1969 been designated the Parc Naturel Régional d'Armorique. This has helped to conserve wildlife, bridle paths and footpaths, and keep up traditional houses.

Between Sizun and Le Faou, on the D18, you will find Hanvec where there is a Maison d'Accueil and St-Eloy which has an Environment Centre. There is an ecomuseum at Commana and a crafts centre 7 kms north of Brasparts. There are restored mills at Kérouat, near Sizun, and a fine seventeenth-century farmhouse at St-Rivoal. Museums of the older sort display examples of Breton head-dress and costume, furniture, utensils and craftwork. You will find these at Dinan, Morlaix, Pont l'Abbé, and Quimper, and there is an especially good one at Rennes.

In wild country like this it is easy to fall prey to the seductive illusion that one is the first to undertake a particular walk, or sleep in a particular wood. When I went on foot from Roscoff to Carhaix I often had this self-indulgent fancy, but then I came across a delightful book called *Off Beaten Tracks in Brittany*, written in 1912 by Emil Davies. Emil and his friend Tom took off from their offices in the City on a ten-day walk from Brest to Dinan, on a course at right-angles to mine but covering some common ground. It is a book of a genre that no longer appears – slow-paced, amusing, discursive and trivial – very much a product of those leisured, sunlit Edwardian summers. It depicts a Brittany now largely gone, where regional costume is everywhere the rule and 'Parisian' fashions evoke comment, where in an area between Carhaix and Rostrenen no French at all was even understood, where only an occasional motor car rattled on to the scene in a cloud of dust, and where children stopped playing and villagers gaped at the sight of the two Englishmen with their knapsacks. Emil and Tom were both vegetarians and Fabians, and only rarely noted the churches they came across. They remarked on how 'priest-ridden' Brittany was, and preferred to inspect inns, cafés and pastry-shops. Huelgoat, which they describe as the Tunbridge Wells of Brittany, had three hotels, as it still has, and the same capacity to spring surprises – they were slung out of their hotel room when a more prestigious party arrived in a fly from the station. Breton women, shaped for the most part 'like water butts', seemed to run things entirely, but the two young men acknowledged the many kindnesses that were shown them and found everywhere 'a native grace that is charming'. Moncontour, south of St-Brieuc, was 'the most delightful town of all'. Its crumbled battlements still surround the spur which its château crowns and the sixteenth-century church of St Mathurin, still the scene of a Whitsuntide *pardon* of great magnificence, has fine Renaissance stained glass. The square, actually triangular, is a gem. Much that the book noted has disappeared, but some things remain: the lanes, even in summer, are fairly empty of traffic and the tranquil Brest–Nantes canal, lined with numberless plane trees, still curves silently through the countryside.

11 From Trégor
to Porzay

The North Brittany Coast

From St-Malo to St-Brieuc by the most direct route takes two hours in a car. Here the characteristically wild north Breton coast so popular among seaside holiday-makers and yachtsmen really begins, where Trégor humps its back up into the Channel. It is a region of deep fiords, remote and empty beaches, of stacks, reefs, shoals – dangerous waters but scenic – the Coast of Pink Granite.

St-Brieuc, an industrial and unlovely city, is the gateway to all this. My first experience of it was when I arrived one June evening, quite late and with no hotel booked. *Patron* after *patron* shook his head sadly and spread his hands in that wonderful Gallic gesture of resigned helplessness. In situations like this I always head for the station hotel. Often they are cheap, cheerful and have a room or two left. So it was this time. We found adequate lodging in the Hotel des Voyageurs. But it is not the kind of hotel that gets into the guide books. You have to go through the bar to reach the staircase and the *patron*'s wife unhooks a key for you and hands it over the counter as you stagger past with your suitcases.

St-Brieuc is the capital of Côtes-du-Nord, a very old city which now has an international airport and is an important station on the Paris–Brest main line. There is not much to detain the visitor. The cathedral, founded in the sixth century by St Brieuc, who came from west Wales via Cornwall (where there is a St Breock near Wadebridge), is fortress-like, dull and much restored. The Tertre Aubé offers a view over the estuary of the Gouët and the rather monotonous, treeless country beyond.

When leaving, you can stay on the N12, which carries you quickly past the old town centre and on to Guingamp and Morlaix, or turn up the coast road to Paimpol and Tréguier. The latter route, to start with, is featureless and rather boring. Some holiday-makers favour Binic and Etables, but St-Quay-Portrieux further on, whose name is curiously derived from the Welsh St Kea, offers more life. After Plouha, there is little of note before Paimpol, a resort of the old type, very redolent of Cornwall. It has a strong fishing tradition, though the cod has now yielded to the oyster. There are old, narrow streets and entertainment of the 'Any-more-for-the-*Skylark*?' variety. It would make a very good holiday centre as there are things to see around it. Two-kilometres out of town, at Beauport, are the ruins of a Premonstratensian abbey, begun in 1202. To the north, at the end of an attractive 6-km stretch of road, is the Pointe de l'Arcouest, looking out over a rocky archipelago whose chief component is the Ile de Bréhat. You can cross to the island from the point or from Paimpol. It much resembles the Ile de Batz or Ushant with its drystone walls, tiny villages of Port-Clos and Le Bourg, and important lighthouses. An intriguing tradition tells that it was a man from Bréhat, Coutanlen, living in Lisbon, who told Christopher Columbus of the existence of the New World eight years before his famous voyage to the Bahamas. It is just possible that fishermen using the Grand Banks had already seen Newfoundland. Bréhat, which is really two islands joined by a bridge, is only $3\frac{1}{2}$ kms long and $1\frac{1}{2}$ kms wide. It sensibly permits no cars. At weekends and on French holidays its narrow lanes are thronged with holidaymakers wandering among the mimosa-covered rocks, so it might be better to time a visit for a quieter weekday. Fig trees and palms grow in this astonishingly warm, rain-free oasis. Port-Clos must be one of the most beautiful natural harbours in north Brittany, and in the next bay to the east is the Plage du Guerzido, a fine bathing beach. Shops, syndicat d'initiative and post office are in Le Bourg. It is a yachtsman's paradise and vessels can find a deep-water anchorage in La Chambre, between Bréhat and the islet of Logodec off its south-eastern corner.

A yacht is almost as good as a car from which to see the Breton coast, and it would be possible to enjoy the advantages of both: anyone arriving by car ferry in St-Malo or Roscoff, with a sailing dinghy in tow, will find excellent places to combine an ordinary seaside holiday with some exciting sailing. West of St-Malo almost all the resorts mentioned in Chapter 6, and those west of St-Brieuc just described, have sailing clubs. The happy hunting ground for British boats, however, is just beyond Bréhat. Two parallel estuaries, the Trieux and the Jaudy, are a focus for craft coming in from the north-east. Lézardrieux is a lively yacht station 8–9 kms up the Trieux, and Tréguier the same distance up the Jaudy. Guernsey is only 70 kms away, but tides often make it a long crossing.

Once into it the passage to Lézardrieux is fascinating. The tide in or out can be strong but the course is well marked. It is perfectly manageable at night – in fact, where one outcrop of pink granite capped by trees can look much like any other, many yacht skippers prefer, if they can, to come in just before dawn, so good are the navigation lights. At high water robust stone bollards, with attractive names like LOSTMOR and PERDRIX, mark the channel. When the tide falls they are revealed as veritable towers of stone rising from rocks that pepper the mudflats everywhere. Woods and tiny fields come down to the river's edge and all is silent save for the lapping of water and the cries of seabirds. Following its sinuous course you suddenly see the Lézardrieux quay, its 200-berth marina and beyond a forest of granite beacons – LES CHAISES, BEC-AN-ARVOR, MIN KÉRAOUL – the suspension bridge carrying the road from Paimpol to Tréguier. One year we moored in the river, which gave the shopping party in the dinghy a demanding and often exciting row through the swirling current to the quay. Another time we motored under the bridge and dropped anchor where the Trieux begins to widen into a large inland lagoon. Unknown to us there was a superb restaurant, the Relais Brenner, just by the bridge. My shipmates and I rowed ashore to look for supper and in heavy rain climbed through undergrowth up to the road. As if by some miracle this widely recommended house, set in its beautiful flower garden, lay opposite, overlooking the river. We stumped in, dripping with water, and far from being politely told that all tables were booked, were served with great tact and adroitness as we sat in our muddy seaboots, steaming gently.

We then motored up-river a further 12 kms to Pontrieux. The peace and solitude were total. We rounded one bend to see at the head of the reach before us the magnificently sited Château de La Roche-Jagu. Built in the fifteenth century on a cliff top fringing the outside of a tight U-bend in the river, it looms over the wooded slopes of the valley. It can be visited in July, August and half of September – motorists should turn off the D787

Lézardrieux to Pontrieux road. Pontrieux is a pleasant, ordinary Breton town memorable to me for having a supermarket called God. After shopping there we dined, by way of contrast to the expensive delights of the Relais Brenner, at the Café de l'Abattoir by the quay.

For scenic beauty there is little to choose between the Trieux and the Jaudy. A similarly winding, wooded estuary leads 11 kms to its confluence with the Guindy, where Tréguier stands. Tréguier is more of a town than Lézardrieux. It was, in fact, once a cathedral city and the church of St-Tugdual should certainly be seen. Over the transepts and the crossing stand three towers of different styles and eras: the Tour d'Hastings to the north is Romanesque, but the one I always remember is the curiously perforated eighteenth-century spire over the south transept.

Like so many places in Brittany Tréguier, the *chef-lieu* of Trégor, was established in the sixth century, by St Tugdual or Tudwal, a Welsh prince's son. Three great names are associated with it: St Yves, buried at nearby Minihy; the Abbé Siéyès, a canon of the cathedral; and the nineteenth-century historian Ernest Renan, whose birthplace in a street of seventeenth-century houses below the cathedral is now a museum. They were all in their day churchmen, but controversial, innovative and avant-garde. Yves or Ivo Hélory de Ker-Martin (1253–1303) was patron saint of lawyers and protector of the poor. He is often depicted in churches standing between a rich man and a poor man, his hand raised deprecatingly to the rich man's proffered purse. On 19 May, his feast day, a procession leads from the town to the fifteenth-century church at Minihy. This is part of the *Pardon des Pauvres*, and the devout pass on their knees through a low archway under his tomb. Yves is still one of the most popular boys' names in Brittany. The Abbé, later Comte, Siéyès helped to draw up the Declaration of the Rights of Man in 1789. He was the most pro-Revolutionary French churchman, a pamphleteer, political leader, partner of Napoléon, and the man who had most hand in the division of France into *départements*. Ernest Renan began his career in the church, but in his subsequent work as an academic brought historical method to bear on the life of Jesus and the story of Israel and earned fierce criticism for his rational approach. When some townsfolk of Tréguier put up his statue in the Place du Martray, others, more conservative, erected a nearby calvary to atone for it.

On the north side of the church there are fine cloisters, and a hand-loom weaving workshop opposite Renan's house is worth a visit. There are drives from Tréguier to the northern headlands on either side of the Jaudy, with impressive views over the sea. Not far to the north-west is the *station balnéaire* and fishing centre of Port-Blanc.

Perros-Guirec is a smart, busy place with a port and yacht station on the south side of a headland and two fine beaches north of it. There are good walks along the coast by the *Sentier des Douaniers* past bizarrely eroded outcrops of roseate granite to next-door Ploumanac'h. Perros-Guirec is the only fully fledged seaside resort on the north-west Breton coast, with hotels in profusion, modernistic blocks of flats, restaurants, discothèques, snack bars and a casino. We dined at the Levant, a deservedly popular hotel-restaurant by the side of the port. You can equally get away to the wild and remote: each afternoon in summer a *vedette* leaves from the Plage de Trestraou for the Sept Iles, about 8 kms off the coast and inhabited only by lighthouse keepers, puffins, guillemots, cormorants, gannets and other seabirds (Ile de Bono is a bird sanctuary, but a landing can be made on the Ile aux Moines).

At Ploumanac'h the Corniche Bretonne begins – an attractive coast road through Trégastel-Plage to Trébeurden. Here you will find more secluded beaches and oddly shaped granite rocks. The French are very zoomorphic about stone formations – many a free-standing cave stalagmite is called *La Vierge* and hereabouts there are granite 'tortoises', a 'King Gradlon', a 'Death's Head' and 'Napoleon's Hat'. Amidst the natural rock shapes there are menhirs and dolmens too, and King Arthur is supposedly buried on the Ile Daval, France's Avalon. But to bring you back to reality visit the Space Telecommunications Centre at Pleumeur-Bodou, just inland, which offers a one-hour guided tour, mornings and afternoons except Tuesday.

Following the Corniche round you come to the old, characterful town of Lannion. It has a small airport (with twenty-minute Brit Air flights to Jersey on Wednesdays in August) and the nearest rail terminal to Perros-Guirec. But its charms relate more to the past. The twelfth-century Templar church of Brélévenez on the top of a hill has a holy water stoup on the left of the entrance that was once a receptacle for the corn tithe. There are several medieval and Renaissance houses in the narrow streets of the

Trégor to Porzay

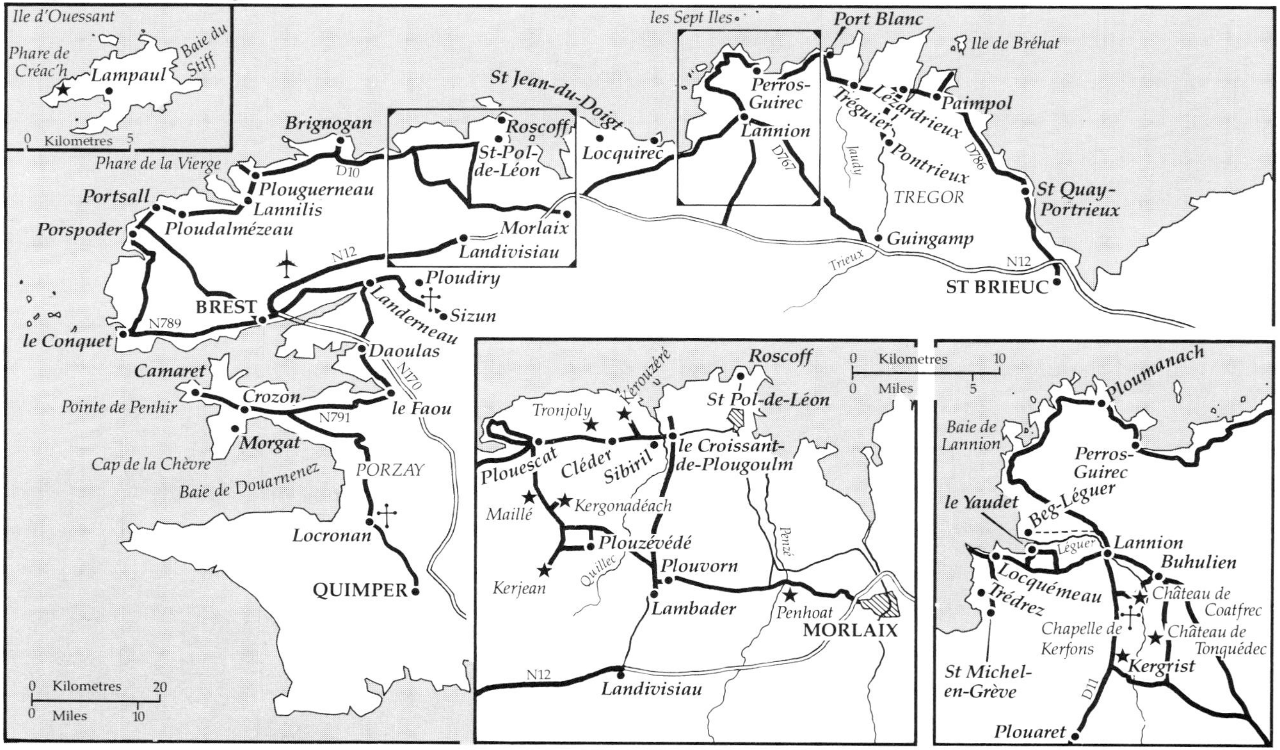

Ile d'Ouessant
Phare de Créac'h
Lampaul
Baie du Stiff
0 Kilometres 5
Brignogan
Phare de la Vierge
D10
Plouguerneau
Lannilis
Portsall
Ploudalmézeau
Porspoder
BREST
N789
le Conquet
N12
Roscoff
St-Pol-de-Léon
Morlaix
Landivisiau
Ploudiry
Sizun
Landerneau
Daoulas
N170
Camaret
Crozon
le Faou
Pointe de Penhir
N791
Morgat
Cap de la Chèvre
Baie de Douarnenez
PORZAY
Locronan
QUIMPER
0 Kilometres 20
0 Miles 10
St Jean-du-Doigt
Locquirec
les Sept Iles
Port Blanc
Ile de Bréhat
Perros-Guirec
Lannion
D767
Tréguier
Lézardrieux
Paimpol
Jaudy
Pontrieux
D786
TREGOR
St Quay-Portrieux
Guingamp
Trieux
N12
ST BRIEUC
Roscoff
0 Kilometres 10
0 Miles 5
Kérouzéré
St Pol-de-Léon
Tronjoly
Plouescat
Cléder
Sibiril
le Croissant-de-Plougoulm
Maillé
Kergonadéach
Plouzévédé
Quillec
Kerjean
Plouvorn
Penzé
Lambader
Penhoat
MORLAIX
N12
Landivisiau
Ploumanach
Baie de Lannion
Perros-Guirec
le Yaudet
Beg-Léguer
Léguer
Lannion
Buhulien
Locquémeau
Trédrez
Château de Coatfrec
Chapelle de Kerfons
Château de Tonquédec
Kergrist
St Michel-en-Grève
D11
Plouaret

town centre – such as the Rue Geoffroy-de-Pont-Blanc, commemorating a local hero mortally wounded defending the town against the English in 1346. Britons must have been as hated and feared as the Turks in these parts – at various times English troops occupied the Ile de Bréhat, and in 1591 Elizabeth I sent a small force to Paimpol to help Henri IV, still Protestant, against the Catholic League.

Perros-Guirec and Lannion are only 15 kms apart by the D788, but by sea the journey takes many hours.

It would make an ideal touring centre – in the Michelin Green Guide there is three times as much under *'Environs'* as there is under the town itself. For walkers it is an obvious base. The GR341 Sentier de Bretagne follows the Coast of Pink Granite from St-Brieuc and ends here, and there are numerous way-marked local routes up the wooded Léguer valley.

Several short walks radiate from Lannion. Follow the towpath along the north bank of the river and in 7 kms you will come to Beg-Léguer (*Beg* means point) where there is an excellent west-facing beach of fine sand, the Plage de Goalagorn, dominated by a lighthouse and two-star campsite. The companion route south of the river brings you after 2 kms to Loguivy-Lès-Lannion, which has an *enclos paroissial*. The statue of St-Ivy is the focal point of the *pardon* held on the first Sunday of May. The fine church has an external stairway to the bell-tower, while inside nativity scenes in carved wood show adoring shepherds in Breton dress blasting away on *binious*. Further along this road a headland, crowned by the village of Le Yaudet, projects into the Léguer estuary. This tiny place once had Roman walls and later sported a bishop, until destroyed in the ninth century. The chapel of Notre-Dame interested us, and we afterwards enjoyed an hour sitting in the sun quaffing *cidre bouché*. The hotel-restaurant Genêts d'Or is the place here.

A longer tour, in uncharacteristically gentle, wooded country, goes up the valley of the Léguer which breaks out into a sudden richness of châteaux and manor houses. A convenient circuit begins by taking the D767 as far as Buhulien. Turn off right and cross the Léguer to the castle of Coatfrec, a fifteenth-century ruin recently tidied up by enthusiasts. In the 1590s it was held by La Fontenelle, a local war-lord ostensibly supporting the Catholic League in their struggle against Henri IV. It was the banditry that appealed most to him, however, and after Henri's apostasy in 1593 La Fontenelle (see page 263) continued to terrorize most of Brittany, until he was caught, taken to Paris and broken on the wheel in 1602. Turn back to Buhulien and take the D31 south to Tonquédec. Here, off the D31B, by the Léguer, is one of Brittany's most evocative feudal ruins. Built in the thirteenth century, it was slighted on Richelieu's orders in 1622. Many towers and parapets survive and the donjon walls are 4 metres thick.

Kergrist, a castle in various styles begun in the fourteenth century, is only 4 kms away, off the D11. Visitors may only follow a marked route through the gardens. Two kms down the road to Plouaret is the motte of the very old castle at Runfrau; a chapel built in 1547 now crowns it. The name of Les Sept-Saints, a nearby hamlet nestling in the upper Léguer valley, has a strange origin. Legend has it that seven Christians buried alive in Ephesus in the fourth century were brought to life again on a dolmen here some centuries later. A pagan cult sprang up on the site which the Church, as was often the way, decided to take over. A curious chapel was built on top of the dolmen, and there is a crypt, and a nearby spring where water wells up in seven distinct places. By an odd coincidence, a seven-mouthed spring exists in Algeria at a place with a very similar name. On this slender ground, the *pardon* of Vieux-Marché (the nearest sizable village) on the fourth Sunday in July has since 1958 become an Islamic-Christian pilgrimage.

Plouaret, a little further on, is an important railway junction but a pleasant town. After seeing Anjela Duval at Traon an Dour (see page 231) I stayed at the Hôtel d'Arvon opposite the station and in my mind I still relish the *langoustine mayonnaise* and *steak grillé* offered in the modest restaurant there. Plouaret is on the fringes of the Argoat, but returning to Lannion on the D11 you will find near the Château de Tonquédec the enchanting fifteenth-century chapel of Kerfons. It contains an exquisitely carved rood-screen added in 1520. From here it is 7 kms back to Lannion, thus completing a circuit of about 40 kms.

A final sortie could be made westwards to Locquémeau, a small sardine port near the Pointe de Séhar, itself a fine place for a sea view. Trédrez to the south still takes pride in the fact that St-Yves was rector here in the 1280s; the church, of later date, is finely furnished. At the southernmost corner of the Baie de Lannion is

the village of St-Michel-en-Grève and a very attractive road, the
D786, runs along the beach, the Lieue de Grève, past green
valleys watered by trout streams. Here on these broad sands
King Arthur is thought to have battled with a dragon. They
fought inconclusively for a day, then Arthur enlisted the aid of
St Efflam in his seaside hermitage. A church and small settlement known as St Efflam exist today at the west end of the
beach. St Efflam prayed outside the dragon's cave, and next
morning the monster climbed to the top of a giant rock – the
Grand Rocher in the centre of the beach – and with much
rolling of the eyes and spewing of blood lumbered into the
sea and drowned. This corner of Brittany is heavily Arthurian: he
is believed to be buried on the Ile Daval, and his court at Carduel
is sited by etymologists at the Château de Kerduel just off the D21
north-west of Lannion. It is a grey stone house, very un-Arthurian,
and cannot be visited.

The D786 from the Lieue de Grève runs to Morlaix, and as it
leaves Côtes-du-Nord and enters Finistère it comes into areas
already looked at in Chapter 8. If therefore you cut straight
across to Morlaix and take the by-pass across the viaduct you
may be tempted to stop at the Euromarché at St-Martin-des-
Champs. This is the largest and best hypermarket in the region,
open from nine in the morning to ten at night. It has a large
restaurant and claims to be one of a new race of shops. Certainly
the range and choice are mind-boggling. You can ponder over
the respective merits of 40, 45 or 50 per cent fat content in the
Camemberts in the cheese section, and then after testing a few
boxes with a forefinger choose, as I do, the one with the most
appealing label. Most Camemberts are made in Calvados and
the best of all in the Pays d'Auge, but some are produced elsewhere, in neighbouring provinces: Brittany Camembert will most
likely come from Ille et Vilaine and might be called *Le Vieux
Druide*; the Maine variety may depict a rosy-cheeked old couple
– *Bons Mayennais*.
    Like most people, I suppose I spend most time by the drinks
shelves. There are amazingly cheap good wines and tempting
exotica – unheard of spirits and liqueurs in strangely shaped bot-
tles and flagons. The Morlaix Euromarché is always strong on
Muscadet, Brittany's only wine. Much of it is made at Le Pallet
in present-day Loire-Atlantique, historically part of Brittany.

Boxes of *galettes* and *crêpes* and delicate sweet biscuits such as *langues de chat* are favourite Breton products, too.

Make for the D19 to Plouvorn. Just as from Lannion there was an interesting circuit of the castles of Trégor – Coatfrec, Tonquédec, Kergrist – so from Morlaix a round tour can be made which covers many of the châteaux of Léon. There are many of them, but since few are open to the public the tour should not be an over-long one. An anti-clockwise progression will take you from Plouvorn to Kerouzéré, Tronjoly, Maillé, Kergournadeach and – leaving the best to the end – Kerjean.

On your way out of Morlaix you drop into the green valley of the Penzé; on your left stand ruins of the thirteenth-century castle of Penhoat. After 17 kms you will come to Plouvorn and see, rising from trees, the lofty bell-tower and steeple of the chapel of Lambader. Though much restored externally, inside there is a fine rood-loft dating from 1541. Head north here, up the D69, to the Croissant de Plougoulm; turn left and swoop down across the Quillec and up to Sibiril, from which any turning right leads to the castle at Kerouzéré (among the joys of Brittany are its rich, tongue-twisting placenames: these last five could not be more bizarre in their different ways). This fifteenth-century fortress is almost as difficult to get into now as when it was built – a formal letter has to be written a week in advance. This renders it available only to the determined medievalist, which is a pity, for it is a fine example of the military architecture of the day. It has everything – guardroom, tapestries, monumental chimneypieces, wall-walks above the machicolations, park, chapel and *colombier*.

A little further on is the picturesque lobster-fishing port of Moguériec, and if you follow the coast road round to Cléder you will pass the graceful Renaissance manor of Tronjoly (only the outside can be seen). It is best then to take the D10 to Plouescat, travelling through countryside thick with dolmens and menhirs. It is a pleasant town with a vast sixteenth-century market hall on oak pillars. If all this sounds deeply Breton, you should know about the Roxy – a multiple discothèque with two styles of music, three bars, four dance areas and fast food. If you feel like a swim take the D30 north to the Plages de Pors-Meur or Pors-Guen. If not, then the D30 runs south, too, to Maillé, an elegant sixteenth-century château whose exterior alone may be

admired. A short distance due east is the Château de Kergournadeach, which means, rather cumbersomely, 'the castle of the
man who did not run away', and is said to be the last fortified
château built in France – in 1630. It is now an imposing ruin.
And so to Kerjean, sometimes referred to as the 'Breton Versailles'. Drawbridge, moat, medieval walls and towers surround
a Renaissance *corps de logis* with two wings which house a
furniture museum. A finely decorated well adorns the *cour
d'honneur*. It is open during normal hours except on Tuesdays,
and during the summer there is *son et lumière* on Wednesdays
and Saturdays. On your way back to Morlaix, pause at Berven
to see the *enclos paroissial* and the church, which in 1573 was
a prototype of Renaissance work and much copied. From Berven
you can either return to Morlaix, driving east, or continue north
on the D30 towards Plouescat.

The D10 from Plouescat fringes the Grève de Goulven, which
might have been a good refuge for ships from westerly gales
were it not so rock-strewn and apt to dry out. This happens to
such an extent that the Baie de Kernic is a great centre for
sand-yachting. Brignogan-Plage lies on a headland and has
something of the rocky remoteness of Ploumanac'h or Roscoff;
the coast is just as tumbled with boulders but inland the country
is flatter and more featureless. Due west is the wild Léonard
coastland known as the Abers. These are three deep estuaries
running out into the Atlantic on Brittany's nose, L'Abervrac'h
(or Aberwrac'h), Aber-Benoit and Aber-Ildut (Aber, as in Welsh,
means mouth; Aberystwyth is the mouth of the river Ystwyth).
   Between Morlaix and the Abers there is really no safe anchorage for yachts, so the Abers are a favourite with British
skippers as an easily-found deep-water bolthole to lie up in
before moving round into the Bay of Biscay. They are easy to
home in on because La Vierge lighthouse, at 75 metres reputedly
the tallest stone tower in the world, throws out a light visible
for 52 kms. The lighthouse, on an islet at the mouth of
L'Abervrac'h, can be visited from Plouguerneau on the D71. The
roads that cross the Abers are pleasantly rural and earn the only
bit of green bordering that Michelin bestows on the whole region. A charming waterside park by L'Abervrac'h at Kerouartz,
near Lannilis, is open every day of the year. There is no big town
up these estuaries, just little, flat, windswept villages whose

names all seem to begin with 'Ker-' or 'Plou-' denoting a fortified farm or parish. This part of Finistère is undoubtedly desolate,
all grey houses and stunted trees and bleak seascapes, clearly
'the end of the earth' as its name indicates.

The D28 will carry you across the Abers to Ploudalmézeau;
another small, quiet town from where you take the D168 on to
Portsall. I was there in June 1978 when Portsall had recently hit
world headlines. The supertanker *Amoco Cadiz* had ploughed
on to the Roches de Portsall and spewed a quarter of a million
tons of crude into the sea. The oil had cast its filthy mantle over
fish, seabirds, rocks and beaches from Brest to St-Brieuc. The
Bretons had been justifiably enraged but their rage had been
expressed positively and cleaning-up operations had been con-
ducted with a furious energy. Four months afterwards the rocks
still had a black high-tide mark but the beaches were clear. I
could still smell oil on the wind, and out to sea, near the Corn
Carhai light, the rusting bows of the tanker protruded from the
waves, a visible reproach to the fishermen of Portsall.

Opposite Portsall's little harbour is Kersaint, with the
thirteenth-century ruins of the castle of Trémazan hard by; its
square keep is four storeys high. An attractive coast road leads
round to Argenton, another harbour which dries out, and Porspoder, high above the rocks, where in the sixth century St
Budoc is supposed to have floated in from Ireland on a stone.
It is here, as you look across the seething Chenal de la Helle to
distant Ushant, that the Channel is considered to merge with
the Atlantic. Aber-Ildut, exposed to westerly winds but a useful
deep anchorage, is the last of the Abers. On the way, north of
Brélès, are the massive menhir – 6 m high – at Kerouézel, Larret
with its pleasant church and old houses, and the Renaissance
Château de Kergroadès.

Brest has for a very long time been France's foremost naval base
and is one of the finest natural harbours in western Europe.
Entrance to the Rade de Brest is through Le Goulet, aptly named
and nearly 2 kms wide. Inside are 40 sq. miles of sheltered water
where, the 1909 Baedeker enthused, 'over four hundred men-
of-war can ride at anchor at one time'. There are fewer now, but
the French navy is still there in force, the mercantile marine is
equally evident, and yachtsmen find the Rade a pleasant cruising
ground. Six rivers flow into it, among them the Elorn, the Aulne,

the Daoulas and the Penfeld, at whose mouth Brest grew up. It is a prime site with low cliffs giving superb views across the Rade.

The castle, which survived World War II, stands where the Penfeld enters the Rade on the site of a Roman camp. Brest was a quiet fishing town until in 1631 Richelieu changed it for ever by designating it a dockyard and naval base; the Penfeld, in its gorge, offered good shelter from enemy attack or bad weather. Vauban redesigned the town and built defences. Colbert encouraged its commercial growth. In 1686 an embassy from Thailand made such an impact that the street from port to town centre was named Rue de Siam, and it still is. It grew in size and naval importance during the wars against the British in the eighteenth century, and great public works were made possible by chaingangs of convict labourers who lived in the *bagne*, or prison, built on the banks of the Penfeld in 1750. This vanished Brest comes to life in the excellent museum in the Tour Tanguy, built in the fifteenth century across the river from the castle by Tanguy de Chastel, the most important Breton of his day.

The nineteenth century saw the creation of many naval schools and a hospital, and in 1865 the arrival of the railway. After the fall of France in 1940 Brest became a prime target for Allied bombers, especially while the German battleships *Scharnhorst* and *Gneisenau* were sheltering there. Its destruction was completed during the six-week siege by the Americans and the tenacious German resistance of August–September 1944. Three-quarters of the buildings went up in smoke, so there is now virtually no 'Old Brest'. It now offers a rather soulless lattice-work of streets with white, flat-roofed concrete shops and offices, a new university and much industrialization, mainly in the electronics field. It is not therefore a place which draws many visitors for its own sake. The Cours Dajot is about the only pre-war street of any consequence to survive and still has fine views over the Rade. You can visit the castle, the municipal museum in the Rue Emile Zola and the Tour Tanguy, but the naval base is closed to non-French eyes and there really is not much else.

However there are places of interest in the vicinity, and as a lover of islands the one I would recommend first by way of contrast to modern Brest is the Ile d'Ouessant, generally anglicized as Ushant. This island, 19 kms from the French mainland, marks the southern entrance to the English Channel. It was often the first or last bit of land seen by windjammers on the Australia run; thirty thousand ships a year pass it these days and countless vessels have been wrecked on it. Some still are, despite its ample lighthouses, one of them the most powerful in the world. It is a by-word for remoteness, foul weather and danger, but what is it like?

A few years ago I went to find out. My companions and I sailed out of L'Abervrac'h, rounded the Roches de Portsall and headed south-west for the blob on the horizon which was Ushant – rising 65 m from the sea, 14 kms long, 7 wide and shaped rather like a turtle swimming up the Channel. It is surrounded by minor hazards but it is usually possible to land – if the wind is between north and east, head for the island's chief town and harbour, Lampaul, on the south-west side; if between south and west, make for the grimly named Baie du Stiff on the north-eastern side. A chain of islets and reefs, one – Molène – inhabited, links Ushant with the mainland. The sea, however, is always rather sinister here – in the Passage du Fromveur, south-east of Ushant, the tide races along at eight knots and even in calm conditions it seems to suck and bubble like boiling soup. It was comforting, though, to be able to see from the Passage no fewer than seven lighthouses at once.

We anchored in the Baie du Stiff, well clear of the areas used by the ferries from the mainland, and rowed ashore. It is only a 3-km walk, past the tiny airport, to Lampaul. The August afternoon was warm and tranquil, though I could imagine how in winter it might earn its Breton name – Enez Heussa, the Island of Terror – when fog descended and the six lighthouses on and around it set up their howling.

At Lampaul you can hire bicycles and push off a further $2\frac{1}{2}$ kms to the lighthouse at Créac'h – the world's most powerful, throwing out 500 million candelas and visible in good conditions well over 50 kms away. There has been a light there since 1638, but the present structure dates from 1939, is 50 metres high and can be visited. As we rested on our bicycles we looked down on an incredible chaos of rocks and the vast carcass of the *Olympic Bravery*, a 272,000-ton monster cast up on them, mercifully empty of oil, in 1976.

We pedalled back past the patchwork of potato fields, worked generally by the women while their men are away at sea. Tiny sheep crop the salty grass and produce delicious *mouton pré-salé*. In winter they roam free or shelter behind star-shaped dry-stone walls from whatever wind is blowing; in summer they are tethered. Since 1969 Ushant and its associated islets, which have a fascinating migratory birdlife, have formed part of the Parc Régional Naturel d'Armorique.

As we sailed off to Camaret we passed Les Pierres Vertes, where in 1886 the *Drummond Castle* foundered with the loss of four hundred lives. In Ushant we had seen more women in black than might have been expected to be widowed by natural causes, and it had been a sobering experience to count the number of *naufragés* in the graveyard in Lampaul. It is an evocative place and can be reached in three to four hours from Brest by a daily ferry (except Tuesdays out of season) which calls at Le Conquet and Ile Molène. Apart from anything else, this trip would be a good way of seeing the Goulet de Brest, the Pointe de St-Mathieu and Le Conquet.

Le Conquet is a small fishing port on a drying inlet at the western end of the mainland, the nearest port to Ushant. Eight old houses, left after the town was sacked by the English in 1558, are still there. The Plage des Blancs Sablons lies north of the Kermorvan peninsula with its lighthouse, and to the south on the headland is the Pointe de St-Mathieu light and a ruined Benedictine abbey. Breton sailors are thought to have recovered the head of St Matthew in Ethiopia and brought it here. Two other curiosities can be seen in the area: 4 kms east of Plouarzel, at Kerloas, is the biggest menhir in the department, all 13 m of it; and within handy distance of Brest, just off the D105, south of Guilers, is the ruined castle of Kéroual, the birthplace of Louise de Kéroualle, one of Charles II's mistresses, who later became Duchess of Portsmouth. Known as 'the baby-faced Breton', it was hoped that she would influence Charles to adopt a pro-French policy, but although she bore him a son, the Duke of Richmond, her influence was negligible. She was heartily disliked by the other courtiers, who had a hard time with her Breton name and knew her generally as 'Madame Carwell'.

There is much of interest on the eastern side of Brest, too. The D712, via Guipavas, south of Brest's airport, leads to Landerneau on the Elorn. North of the town, near the *voie-express* at

Pardon at the Chapelle de
la Fontaine Blanche
(Victoria Southwell)

*A typical French cheese
counter*

St-Eloy, is a sixteenth-century chapel dedicated to this patron saint of horses. On 24 June each year an equestrian *pardon* is held here. On the north bank of the Elorn, at La Forest-Landerneau, are the rather scruffy ruins of a castle thought to be the Château de Joyeuse-Garde, where Sir Lancelot lived. It seems a more likely site than Bamburgh or Alnwick, where Sir Thomas Malory placed it. Landerneau itself has a beautiful bridge, fine old houses and the church of St-Thomas-de-Cantorbéry – Thomas à Becket. It is a quiet place. When the French refer to something of very little importance, they have a saying, 'That'll cause a stir in Landerneau' (*Il y aura du bruit dans Landerneau*). It makes a very good jumping-off point for the *enclos paroissiaux*: Pencran is very near, as are La Martyre, Ploudiry and Sizun. Dirinon, just off the D770 to the south, is a place of pilgrimage for the Welsh; here is the sixteenth-century tomb of St Nonna, who was the mother of St David and fled here, Bretons say, in the sixth century.

Another route out of Brest would be across the Elorn by the Albert Louppe bridge, a two-tiered viaduct built in the late 1920s. It brings you to Plougastel-Daoulas, with its fine calvary of 1602–4 in thanksgiving for deliverance from plague. There is a fine *pardon* near here every 15 August. It takes place a little way south-east of the town at the Chapelle de la Fontaine Blanche. A cloth screen is slung up between two trees in the churchyard and priests officiate behind a portable altar. The congregation, about one third oldish ladies in black with tall coifs and tassels blowing in the breeze, sit on benches all around. A pleasant three-and-a-half-hour tour can be made by car in the Plougastel peninsula. This is deepest Brittany, with narrow, hedged lanes winding from hamlet to hamlet between strawberry fields. At the ends of the lanes beautiful vistas can often be enjoyed over the Rade de Brest. The pace of life is slow, and traditional costumes may still be glimpsed. Tourists are few, and those who visit the peninsula should do so sensitively and discreetly.

The Brest–Quimper *voie-express* by-passes Daoulas, Hôpital-Camfrout and Le Faou (pronounced 'Fou'), all interesting small towns on the innermost estuaries of the Rade de Brest. Daoulas has an abbey with fine twelfth-century cloisters, a rare bit of Romanesque in Finistère. It is open every day from 0900 to 1900.

Calvary at Plougastel-Daoulas (Victoria Southwell)

From Hôpital-Camfrout any of the roads leading west on to the peninsulas in the Rade de Brest will reveal rarely disturbed corners of Breton life. Le Faou, with its slate-hung houses, occupies a very attractive position at the head of its estuary. You can of course turn the perspectives inside out and explore these inlets by water in your own yacht or sailing dinghy. The Elorn can be penetrated as far as Landerneau and all the three small towns just mentioned can be reached by boat, though this whole area does dry out at low tide. At Le Faou the D791 turns westwards and climbs very prettily along the Corniche de Térénez. Its course is interrupted by the mouth of the second great river to empty into the Rade de Brest, the Aulne, which executes a sharp S-bend round the town of Landévennec. The Aulne is navigable by small craft for 70 kms, as far as Carhaix, and the first few of them offer delightful anchorages among bits of the French navy in mothballs. Around here a handsome suspension bridge, the Pont de Térénez, carries the D791 over on to the Crozon peninsula. Pause at Trégarvan to see an unusual museum, a preserved rural school.

The lower part of the Rade de Brest is closed by the Crozon peninsula. This much ramified headland separates the Brest roadstead from the Bay of Douarnenez to the south. Or to look at it even more distantly, if the whole of Brittany is like the head of a roaring animal, the Crozon peninsula is the tongue flickering in its open jaws.

There are really only two places to stay in the peninsula – Camaret and Morgat. Both are delightful and with yacht or car there is little to choose between them. You need your own transport as bus services are scanty, but excellent short walks can be made from either centre. Both are ideal places for yachts on passage, Morgat perhaps offering better facilities. Camaret is at the far western extremity, but is nearer to Britain by sea, and there are direct ferry services from Brest. It is an old prawn fishing port, while Morgat went in for sardines.

Take a drive round the Roscanvel peninsula to the north, which is the Rade de Brest's natural breakwater, and you will come to the Pointe des Espagnols, so called because a Spanish force dug in there in 1593–4 and Queen Elizabeth sent troops to help Marshal d'Aumont and the Huguenots drive them off. It was here that the explorer of the North-West Passage, Martin Frobisher, was fatally wounded in November 1594. A century later and the English were back again, this time joined by the Dutch in an assault on Brest. Their preliminary attack on Camaret was a fiasco. Vauban had in 1689 fortified La Tour Dorée, at the end of the breakwater, and 1200 men died trying unsuccessfully to take it. The bell-tower of the seventeenth-century chapel, Notre-Dame de Roc'h Amadour, also on the breakwater, was carried away by an English shot and is still missing. The chapel had been given its odd name by pilgrims returning by sea from the famous shrine of Rocamadour in the Dordogne. In the 1790s an American, Robert Fulton, later the first successful builder of a steamboat, came to Camaret to perfect his torpedo submarine. With articulated oars five men could propel themselves under water at 2 knots and place a clockwork-driven 100-lb bomb on the side of an enemy ship. An English frigate moored off Camaret was the chosen victim in this trial, but as the submarine approached, the frigate, though quite oblivious of what was in store, set sail and left.

The walk to the Pointe de Penhir is almost obligatory. You climb up out of the town, past the Alignements de Lagatjar, a cromlech, or three-sided rectangle of menhirs, and on through the heather south-westwards, with the sea on both sides. At the end, weather permitting, you can enjoy a superb view: in front, the Tas de Pois ('heap of peas'), three great granite lumps sticking out of the sea; to the right, the Pointe de St-Mathieu and Ushant; to the left, the Pointe de Dinan, the Cap de la Chèvre and, further off to the south, the Pointe du Raz.

There are six major headlands on the Crozon peninsula and the sea can sluice quite dangerously around them, so even accomplished swimmers should be prudent beyond the recognized beaches – there is a small sand and shingle beach at Camaret, and a much finer, larger beach at Morgat. Everywhere there are cliffs pocked with caves – at Morgat the Grandes Grottes; by the Pointe de Dinan, the Grottes des Korrigans (*Korrigans* are leprechauns – the little people). From Morgat it would be an energetic but satisfying walk south to Cap de la Chèvre, 8 kms away. The small town of Crozon is nearer, and Brest can be reached via Le Fret, to the north, and a ferry.

On the way out of the peninsula to Douarnenez look at Argol, up to the left on the D163. A statue of King Gradlon is a reminder that this legendary sixth-century monarch ruled from the city of Ys, now lost beneath the sea somewhere, perhaps in the Bay of Douarnenez. Turn off again to the left, up the D83, for Ménez-Hom. It is only a short walk from the end of the road to Brittany's highest point, at 330 m, with magnificent views of the peninsula you have just left, together with both jaws of the roaring animal and the Monts d'Arrée behind.

Drive south through Ste-Marie-du-Ménez-Hom, with fine woodwork in its church, and take the D47 south through the region of Porzay to Locronan. On the shores of the bay to the west is a tiny village, Ste-Anne-la-Palud. Quiet enough for most of the year, it is thronged by thousands on the last Sunday in August, for the *pardon* there is a very important one. A painting of it by Boudin hangs in the Le Havre museum. Perhaps because of Duchess Anne of Brittany, veneration of St Anne, mother of Mary, is very strong in these parts. Legend has it that she was born in Brittany and fled to Palestine to escape a brutish husband.

Another important *pardon* takes place in Locronan, a little further south, and in Cornouaille, on the second Sunday in July. Locronan worries me. It is just a shade too perfect. Its seventeenth-century prosperity came from sail-making, for the French East India Company among others, and the houses of its rich master weavers have been converted now into the establishments of rich *crêperie* and souvenir shop owners. The seventeenth-century square, with a tiny well in the centre and the splendid ensemble of church and chapel of the Pénity along one side, is magnificent. The fifteenth-century tomb of St Ronan, the fine pulpit, stained glass and bas-reliefs in the chapel should certainly be seen. Yet the whole town lacks authenticity and looks too much like a Walt Disney set. Ronan, a sixth-century hermit, lived here – it means 'Holy place of Ronan' – and the *pardon*, known locally as the Troménie, re-enacts his daily walk, barefoot and unfed, from the town to a nearby mountain top. Every six years they have a Grande Troménie, lasting a whole week, in which processions encircle the Montagne de Locronan and each parish on the 12-km route brings out its holy relics. The next one is in 1989.

12 From Cornouaille to the Grande Brière

The South Brittany Coast

All roads lead to Quimper, once capital of Cornouaille, and it is a fine town to make a centre for excursions. The Breton word *kemper* means confluence, in this case of the Steïr, the Jet and the Odet. The Steïr flows through the old town with its half-timbered houses overhanging the banks. The Odet is canalized, formal and flanked by tree-lined boulevards near the cathedral precincts. A Roman road ended here, but the fifth-century King Gradlon is the town's traditional founder, and his colleague, St Corentin, built the first cathedral and was its first bishop. A delightful tale has it that he was sustained by a miraculous fish of which he would consume half and throw the rest back into the Odet. The obliging fish would present itself to him next day, whole and ready to be half-eaten again.

It is an imposing cathedral, the oldest Gothic structure in south Brittany, and was rebuilt between 1240 and 1515 – or 1856 if you include the two nineteenth-century spires. In Brittany, where money was tight and construction costs – in granite – were high, cathedrals were a long time a-building. Even the spires were paid for by a special five-year tithe. The unusual feature is the cathedral's asymmetrical choir and nave. As to be expected, it has fine decorations, excellent stained glass and a superb sixteenth-century organ reconstructed by Robert Dallam, an Englishman who from 1642–1660 sat out the Civil War and Commonwealth in Brittany, and recently restored.

The former Bishops' Palace contains an extremely good museum given over to local history, folklore, furniture and costume. In Quimper on quite ordinary days you can still see women in the traditional black dress, white apron and sabots, though only on feast days will you find them with the cow-bell-shaped lace coif on their heads. The grandest of these occasions is the annual arts festival, the Grande Fête de Cornouaille, which occupies the week prior to the fourth Sunday in July. During this week *manifestations* might include a work by a Breton playwright such as Pierre-Jakez Hélias; Breton music galore; *bombarde* and organ in the cathedral; an overseas folklore groups from, say, Romania or Polynesia; Breton song and dance; a traditional *Fest-Noz*; groups from Scotland and Ireland; a parade of Breton dress – eighty groups and three thousand costumes; ballet and traditional Breton wrestling. The *Fest-Noz* (night-festival) is very characteristic. The *bombarde, biniou* and *batterie* (oboe, bagpipes and drums) make the whole thing predominantly instrumental. Brittany and Wales diverge here, for there is no great choral tradition in Brittany. The *biniou* and *biniou koz* (the old *biniou*, which is smaller, has just one drone and is an octave higher) indicate a link with Scotland and Ireland; the *bombarde* has more affinity with Galicia and Andalusia in Spain, and even with North Africa. The music is plaintive, strident, insistently repetitive and strangely compelling even to my non-Celtic ear.

Dancing, too, is central to the *Fest-Noz*. It is all very informal and communal: no pairing off, but mainly large circles of people linked arm in arm and shuffling round sideways to the haunting, rapid rhythms, while little children run in and out through the fence of legs. The only note that I found disturbing was that the proceeds of the *Fest-Noz* might well go to a fund for IRA prisoners in the H-blocks. Sometimes Celtic nationalism is so powerfully felt that a blind eye can be turned to the enormities of the Provisionals in Northern Ireland and an anti-English stance maintained. This may be only the expression of a tiny minority, however, and my contacts with Bretons on these and other occasions have been entirely friendly.

There is a pleasing genuineness about the Grande Fête de Cornouaille. Nothing is done specifically for tourists, in fact zealots in the Breton movement despise the interest that tourists evidently take in the week's proceedings. It is a festival to manifest the deeply held convictions, sentiments and traditions of Bretons today. Thousands take part spontaneously, in a spirit of comradely competition. Tourists are incidental.

As I strolled by the quays of the Odet I saw a street sign that

Two old women in traditional Breton dress (Victoria Southwell)

The author (Victoria Southwell)

rang a distant geographical bell – the Boulevard de Kerguélen. Kerguélen, one of a number of French islands in the southern Indian Ocean, was discovered by Yves-Joseph de Kerguélen-Trémarec in 1772. Another *Quimpérois* with an equally luxuriant name was the inventor of the stethoscope, René-Théophile-Hyacinthe Laënnec. He was born in the city in 1781, became an army doctor and did much work on lung diseases. He is buried at Douarnenez. Max Jacob, an influential poet of the early twentieth century, was born in 1876 in a corner house on the Rue du Parc.

The Musée des Beaux-Arts (open mornings and afternoons except Tuesday) contains paintings by a string of great names – Rubens, Mignard, Boucher, Fragonard, Corot and Boudin. Then there are the *faïenceries*: tin-enamelled earthenware has been made at Locmaria, a south-western suburb, since 1690, and you can visit the workshops in working hours.

Quimper is a pleasant drive from Roscoff over the Monts d'Arrée, but you could perfectly well fly in. From Quimper-Pluguffan there are daily links with Jersey, Paris and London, via Morlaix. And even though it is 15 kms down to the sea at Bénodet you can sail up the Odet practically into the heart of Quimper.

Bénodet is the first of those large resorts that will appear in greater numbers as the route goes further eastwards into southern Brittany. It is a pleasant 44-km run by car from Quimper, taking perhaps two hours. Leave by the D785 and then turn left on to the D20. The road runs past a succession of manor houses – Kerlagatu, Keraval, Kerdour, Kerbernès and Kerembleis – then at the V5 turn left. You can walk to the ruins of an old mill and a point overlooking the narrows of the Odet at Les Vire-Court. The D20 continues, with pleasant views of the river, to Combrit. Bénodet, across the Pont de Cornouaille toll bridge, is an important yacht station and has fine sand beaches. The country is flat and wooded all round, and you can climb up the Pyramid lighthouse for a good view over the estuary. The D34 carries you back to Quimper.

For another perspective and a memorable one, take one of the many *vedettes* that run down the Odet to Bénodet, or half an hour further on to Loctudy. You could even go out to the Iles de Glénan, a ninety-minute trip. There are nine islets, on three of which, Perfret, Cigogne and St-Nicolas, are the premises of a famous sail training school. Three islets are inhabited and there is an hotel.

A longer but very exciting tour from Quimper is to Douarnenez and the Pointe du Raz and round the fringes of the old county of Cornouaille – the Circuit du Cap-Sizun as it is often called. Douarnenez, reached via Locronan or by the more direct D765, is a big fishing and commercial port. I have never lingered long there but there are some attractive steep lanes in the old quarter of the town. Wagner enthusiasts will be interested in Ile Tristan, named after the nephew of King Marc'h of Cornouaille and the lover of Isolde (Iseult), which lies close offshore at the mouth of the Pouldavid. We are on firmer historical ground with La Fontenelle, who made the island his base during the Wars of Religion (see pp. 244–5) and was the notorious ravager of Penmarc'h until Henri IV trapped him in 1602.

There are at least two routes from Douarnenez to the Pointe du Raz. The northern one, by minor roads, passes the seabird sanctuary of Cap-Sizun, which is open during the nesting season, from mid-March to the end of August. Further on, the headland becomes more attenuated and wild and the Pointe du Raz attracts thousands of tourists in summer. It is not, however, as some have said, the westernmost point on the French mainland; that is the Pointe de Corsen, a gentler protuberance north of Le Conquet. The press of other visitors and the accompanying apparatus of tourism, shops, coach parks, *crêperies* and snack bars is much the same as at Land's End. When I was there I had hoped to try the vertiginous guided walk down the narrowing spur past the Enfer de Plogoff to its final tip, but felt that this excitement could be better experienced at a bleaker, less crowded time of year than midsummer.

I retreated from the noisy Pointe du Razmatazz to the nearby Pointe du Van which looks north, gives much the same amazing views, but is less majestic. It has a chapel dedicated to St-They, however, and the attractive connecting road to Van leads past the gloomy-sounding Baie de Trépassés, the Bay of Departed Souls, from which the corpses of Iron Age priests were taken to burial on the Ile de Sein. Inland of the marshy bay is another supposed site of Ys, King Gradlon's vanished city. In fine

weather there is an occasional ferry service and you could yourself make the fateful journey to the Ile, 8 kms to the west, from
the tiny Port de Bestrée at the Pointe du Raz. Alternatively there
is a more certain service from Audierne, daily in the season. But
the weather and the tides govern all. Just off Raz (which means
'strait' or 'race') vessels can experience the worst seas for miles.

Things moderate nearer the Ile de Sein, however, and yachtsmen can visit it reasonably safely by day. This really is the outer
edge of civilization. Flat, treeless and not quite a kilometre
square, there is a small drying port, a tiny *bourg* with streets
sometimes only a metre wide to conserve space, and a few fields
of potatoes and barley tended by the black-clad women. Once
the islanders made a dishonest living as wreckers, but in the last
century dedicated themselves to saving endangered ships. In
1940 they earned true glory. After the fall of France de Gaulle
issued from London his famous call to resistance. All the men of
Sein decided to join him and carry on the struggle from England.
Over the next few days boats carrying 130 reached Cornwall.
When de Gaulle inspected the five hundred Free French in London he was able to say, 'So Sein is a quarter of France.' He later
awarded the island the Croix de la Libération.

Leaving the Pointe du Raz on the road to Audierne you will
come quite soon to Plogoff, with its sixteenth-century church of
St-Kea. This quiet village shot into the news in 1980 when the
government announced plans to build a huge nuclear power
station there. The project was eventually cancelled, but not before the staunch Breton villagers, admittedly reinforced by outside ecologists and left-wingers, had held riot police and *paras*
at bay.

Six kilometres further on, it is worth turning off to the tiny
village of St-Tugen which has a good Flamboyant Gothic
church, interestingly furnished. St-Tugen (or Eoghan – he was
Bishop of Derry and died in 618) is portrayed holding a large
key as he stands beside two dogs, one of which is biting the
head off the other. He is a thaumaturgical saint, like St-Méen
who deals with madness or St-Yvertin who soothes migraine.
Tugen's speciality is hydrophobia. If bitten by a mad dog, just
touch his key with your own and all will be well. I was there in
June and it must have been the Sunday in Trinity before 24
June because it was the day of the *pardon*. At mass, which was
half in Breton, half in Latin, almost every pew and chair was

filled. Afterwards a procession emerged from the church. Aco-lytes carried crosses and banners, followed by grave village eld-ers, little girls bearing effigies of the Virgin Mary and young boys with bow ties on, their hair slicked down, carrying votive ships, given – perhaps modelled – by thankful survivors of marine disasters. The procession and all the church's treasures circled the village, stopping occasionally to pray. Then it wound back into the church for the concluding rites. Outside, in an open space adjoining the north aisle, a noisy fair was in full swing. Pop music blared out in competition with the church bells, and after I had rather hesitantly joined in the last canticles in Breton the priest's prayers were punctuated by the smashing of glass at the coconut shy. It was a curious blend of piety and gaiety.

Audierne, the nearest town, lies 5 kms east, a quiet, attractively sited holiday centre and lobster fishing port straddling the es-tuary of the Goyen. It is of great importance to yachts as it is the only safe harbour between Morgat and Douarnenez and St-Guénolé on the Pointe de Penmarc'h. From Raz to Penmarc'h is 40 kms of rocky cliffs and dunes broken only by the Goyen estuary with Audierne and the anchorage at nearby Ste-Evette. In the 1870s the famous actress Sarah Bernhardt used to take her holidays hereabouts, and went on sketching expeditions to the Baie des Trépassés, where the hotel now is. Audierne was then a flourishing tunny-fishing port and so she probably sketched the gaff-rigged *thoniers*, their tall net suspension booms waving in the air like an insect's antennae, as they slipped out under sail. The big trawlers have ended all this now, and only lobster fishing survives.

As you return towards Quimper on the D784 you will enter the northern fringes of the Pays Bigouden, a distinctive piece of Brittany which includes Penmarc'h, Pont-l'Abbé, its chief town, and Loctudy, and reaches as far as Quimper. Here the Breton costume is more evident than anywhere else and the very tall lace coif known as the *coiffe bigoudène*, associated with this particular area of Brittany and a veritable 'menhir' 25 cm tall, is its most prominent feature. Oddly, this head-dress has grown in size in the last fifty years or so.

Although the country seems flat and unremarkable and the villages very ordinary, a great deal has been written of this area. Ronald Millar recounted his experiences with the tunny fisher-men of Audierne in the 1970s in *A Time of Cherries*. In *Le*

Cheval d'Orgueil the veteran Breton author Pierre-Jakez Hélias writes movingly and in meticulous detail of his childhood in Pouldreuzic during World War I. And a detailed picture of life in the Pays Bigouden in the 1960s is offered in Edgar Morin's evocative study in depth of a Breton village, *Plodémet*. This distillation of several months' research is consistently accurate and perceptive and gives a good feel of a traditional yet changing society. Actually Plodémet does not exist, but it is clearly Plozévet. Morin fictionalized the names of the village and its immediate neighbours – Pors-Ensker is in reality Pors-Poulhan, Armez is Brumphuez – but the broader setting of Audierne, Pont-Croix, Quimper and so on is exact.

Beyond Audierne there are quiet beaches off the D784. At Plouhinec you should turn off down to the sea at Pors-Poulhan. From Plozévet the D784 heads for Quimper, but the full tour of the Pays Bigouden is recommended. Penhors, on the coast near Pouldreuzic, has an especially good *pardon* on the first Sunday in September. After Plonéour-Lanvern, near which be the atmospheric ruins of the chapel of Languivoa, it is worth heading towards the sea and hunting among the dunes for the chapel of Notre-Dame de Tronoën. Here is what is reputed to be the oldest calvary in Brittany, built in the 1450s and now weather-worn but unrestored. It even shows Mary bare-breasted and suckling Jesus, which has usually attracted the censorious chisel of the prude. You will now be near the Penmarc'h peninsula, which is full of interest. St-Guénolé, named after St-Winwaloe, is a port for use by yachts *in extremis*, though full of local fishing boats. Its sights include an old church tower, the Museum of Prehistoric Finistère (open in summer at the usual times) and the sixteenth-century chapel of Notre-Dame de la Joie nearby. The Pointe de Penmarc'h, the point of Brittany's 'chin' and the northern end of the Bay of Biscay, is dominated by the massive granite Eckmühl lighthouse, with a throw of some 50 kms. Its Germanic name comes from the Marquise de Blocqueville, daughter of the Prince of Eckmühl, General Davout, she paid for it, and named it after her father, in 1897. Penmarc'h, a third possible site of the lost city of Ys, was once a prosperous cod-fishing centre, but the fish fled and the dreaded La Fontenelle butchered the populace in the 1590s and seized their possessions.

The tiny fishing harbours along the coast get grander as you go east – Kérity, Guilvinec, Lesconil, Loctudy and Bénodet. The first four are full of trawlers, *sardiniers* and *thoniers*. Loctudy is a working port but a favourite with yachtsmen too. It is at the mouth of the Pont-l'Abbé river and on the other bank is the attractive Ile Tudy: not in fact an island but a finger of land fringed by a magnificently long, golden beach with the town at the end. 'Loc' and 'L'Ile', as they are known, are linked by ferry.

Five kilometres up river, and worth a short visit up the well-marked channel, is Pont-l'Abbé. Motorists returning to Quimper will equally have to pass this way, but it is no imposition. The manor of Kerazan is of the sixteenth and eighteenth centuries and now a school of embroidery. The building with its modest art collection is open at the usual times (except Tuesday). Pont-l'Abbé is full of character, with a château guarding the bridge first built by the abbot of Loctudy. The château houses the Musée Bigouden, which exhibits costumes and furniture of the region. But the costumes are still in use here and can often be seen outside the museum. From Pont l'Abbé the N785 takes you in 19 kms, past the airport and back to Quimper.

A good excursion from Quimper in a south-easterly direction would be to the Baie de la Forêt and the resorts of Beg-Meil and Concarneau which face each other across the bay. Fouesnant and La Forêt Fouesnant are at the head of the bay in country heavily wooded and decidedly fruity – apple and cherry trees abound and good Breton cider is made here. Beg-Meil is already recognized in Britain as a first choice for a traditional seaside holiday. It would be a good place to bring a dinghy – there are sailing schools, a clubhouse and launching slipway. There are excellent sand beaches (the rocks and cliffs of Finistère began to thin out east of Audierne) and each is wrapped round with its mantle of pinewoods.

Concarneau is more animated, a deservedly popular family holiday centre of the classic south Breton kind. It is a mecca for yachts, too, with a beautiful, easily entered, well-protected marina. La Ville Close, Concarneau's glory, is a crescent-shaped island fortified by Vauban, with an old town of cobbled streets, ancient houses and smart shops. A walk around the ramparts (a small charge is made, but they are open into the early evening in high season) is a favourite preliminary to a seafood dinner in the main town. The Musée de la Pêche, in the Ville Close, is full of fascinating things and well worth a look. After

Douarnenez Concarneau is Brittany's biggest fishery, and it is an education to get up early (or stay up late) and watch the landing, sorting and auctioning of the fish along the Avenue Pierre Guéguin and the Quai Carnot. Proceeds from the Fête des Filets Bleus (Blue Nets), a sort of piscine *pardon* on the penultimate Sunday in August, go to a fishermen's benevolent fund. It is a colourful occasion. Concarneau, it is tempting to say, has everything – there are beaches too, on the western side of the town proper.

Those who base themselves in Concarneau have some interesting places to explore down the coast to the south-east. The Pointe du Cabellou, only 7 kms away, affords good views of Concarneau. The Pointe de Trévignon is further, and Raguenès-Plage, Kerascoët and Port-Manech are all quiet places on the way to the Aven estuary. This can best be enjoyed from the river and yachts often stage at Port-Manech and motor upstream past stunning corners of rural Cornouaille to Pont-Aven. This prettily sited town grew up where the Aven ceased to leap down over rocks and suddenly became tidal and navigable. Once there were as many mills as houses. It lies on a busy road which executes an awkward turn on to the bridge, but away from this danger spot it is a very pleasant retreat. There is a famous and pricey restaurant here, the Moulin Rosmadec – I dined and lodged at the more modest Mimosas by the port. There was no traffic here, I could watch the considerable rise and fall in the river and it was the best find of the trip. Ambitiously my companion and I ordered *araignée de mer* which, of course, is a spider-crab with the thinnest and reddest of legs, and it required the skills of a micro-surgeon to get into. We struggled for minutes, fragments of inexpertly crushed shell flying about the restaurant. Eventually the waitress took pity and came over and deftly filleted it for us.

You can also eat very well at Chez Mélanie in Riec-sur-Belon, just 5 kms down the D783, The Belon, like the Aven, has many picturesque corners, though it is less easy to penetrate from the sea as it has a tricky sandbar at its mouth, as also has the next river, the Laïta, which starts in Quimperlé. Highly confusible with Quimper, this town, very appealing indeed and two towns in one really, is so called because it is at the confluence of the Ellé (*kemper-ellé*) and the Isole. There is an upper town and a lower, more interesting, one. The beautifully rounded church of Ste-Croix, in the lower town, contains some of the best Romanesque work in Brittany.

The obvious excursion from here is south, parallel to the Laïta, through the Forêt de Carnoët, to Le Pouldu, a small port at the river's mouth with some cottages leading down to the sea. The painter Paul Gauguin moved to La Pouldu and lived in one of them in 1889 after three years, on and off, in Pont-Aven. Between 1886 and 1891 he was doyen of an artists' colony there and ranged between Quimperlé and Concarneau capturing typical aspects of Breton social and religious life. A painted wooden Christ in the chapel at Trémalo on the fringes of Pont-Aven is the model for his *Yellow Christ*, now in Buffalo, New York. In its foreground are Pont-Aven peasant women wearing their characteristic coifs and unique lace collars which turn up at the shoulders.

The Laïta is a department boundary – the roads east out of Quimperlé leave Finistère and enter Morbihan. They also enter the magnetic field of Lorient. This is a large town but not really a place to stay in or even visit when there is so much else of charm or interest near at hand. It was founded in 1664 when the French East India Company was being strengthened by Colbert. Because of the depredations of the English on ships using Le Havre, Colbert sought an Atlantic coast base and decided on a stretch of empty land on the banks of the Scorff. Lorient was once L'Orient (the East) and in Breton it is An Oriant. Various companies operated from here until the French were ousted from India in the late eighteenth century. Napoléon then made it a military port. In World War II it suffered the same double blow as Brest – bombed steadily by the allies in 1940–4, then the scene of a bitter slog between Germans and Americans until it was liberated as late as May 1945. Now it is a thriving military, commercial and fishing port, best seen from the railway viaduct. Only French citizens may go round the cumbersomely named Ingénieur-général Stosskopf Submarine Base.

The Ile de Groix, three-quarters of an hour away from Lorient by ferry, is high, flat and almost treeless. Port-Tudy is a good harbour of some interest to yachtsmen. Groix and Locmaria, another port, are simple, away-from-it-all places but the island suffers from having far less appeal than its larger neighbour Belle

Ile: if you are going to an offshore island it might as well be the best.

The Lorient, Lanester, Hennebont conurbation on the banks of the Blavet is to be avoided. Most motorists' sights will be set on Carnac, Quiberon, Belle-Ile, Auray, Vannes and the Gulf of Morbihan.

Carnac is the prehistoric capital of Brittany, famous for its megaliths, or 'great stones', which have been mentioned earlier but are found in greatest profusion here. These are of three kinds – menhirs, or single standing stones, literally 'long stones' in Breton, sometimes up to 7 m long; dolmens, or 'table stones', an arrangement of three or more stones in which a horizontal one is supported by the others; and cromlechs, which are menhirs formed in a square or circle (in Wales, just to confuse things, cromlechs are called dolmens). Much controversy has been generated over why, when and how they were put up. The peoples who preceded the Gauls must have built them, perhaps between 3000 and 750 BC. The dolmens were burial chambers, once covered by earth to form a tumulus which has since eroded. The menhirs are more difficult to account for, especially isolated examples. Those that are arranged in rows, the *alignements*, probably had some astronomical function, to enable the druids to observe sun, moon and stars and determine seed-time and harvest.

Sometimes the past has been inconsiderately lavish in the way it has left us its monuments. There are almost too many megaliths in the Carnac area for easy viewing: with over three thousand of them one does not know where to begin. It is not really much use looking at a few menhirs and then getting back in the car, because the impact of Carnac lies in its sheer extent. They begin at Etel in the west and stretch as far as the eastern side of the Gulf of Morbihan – some 30 kms away.

If you are coming in from the Lorient side you can start keeping an eye open from Erdeven onwards, and one of the biggest of its kind is the Dolmen of Crucuno, just off the D781 to the left. Once in Carnac it is probably best to go to the Tumulus Hotel first and ask to see the Tumulus of St-Michel nearby. This is a long barrow, 120 × 12 m, whose internal chambers can be explored. On the top stand a chapel, a small calvary and an orientation table which will enable you to look at the countryside and get your bearings. Reassured in this way, you could set out to see the *alignements*. It is really only possible to get some sense of the spirit of the place by wandering among the stones on foot. A reasonable figure-of-eight tour would take a full morning or afternoon. If you cannot manage it on foot, a quick spin down the D196 in a car will give a general impression. Walkers should make for Ménec, on the north-west side of Carnac, where there is a cromlech whose stones are built into local houses and gardens. Keep alongside the D196 and walk northeastwards (a compass is quite useful here) through the sometimes ten or eleven parallel lines of stones, which seem to get smaller as you move east. The *alignements* of Kermario, 'the house of the dead', follow those of Ménec. Divert to the Tumulus of Kercado, then north to the *alignements* of Kerlescan, then up the D186 to the Tumulus of Moustoir and back to Carnac. This is about 9 kms, but if you have had enough you could peel off at Kercado or Kerlescan and head for Carnac or nearby La Trinité-sur-Mer.

Unless you make this walk at some very odd time of day or night or in foul weather, you will not be alone. Late on a summer's night under a full moon might be the most atmospheric time of all. A July or August afternoon is impossible. Even in June I have found coach parties of children swarming about, many of them climbing up and leaping off the taller menhirs.

To understand it all fully you should visit La Musée Préhistorique J. Miln – L. Le Rouzic. A Scots enthusiast, James Miln, began to excavate at Carnac in 1874 and was joined by a young school-leaver, the eleven-year-old Zacharie Le Rouzic – a strange partnership. When Miln died suddenly in 1881 his young colleague took on the work and subsequently ran the museum until World War II.

A great many visitors, wholly unconcerned with archaeology, nowadays take their holidays at the lively and growing resort of Carnac-Plage. In fact, for a holidaymaker there who has no more than a passing interest in prehistory, there is a dolmen nestling among pine trees next door to a postcard shop.

There are many more standing stones on the Quiberon peninsula which projects, a Breton Portland Bill, for 14 kms into the Bay of Biscay. It was once an island but sand has built up to form an isthmus which at one point is 40 m wide and only just permits

road and railway line to squeeze over. La Grande Plage at Penthièvre, on the west coast, is now a great centre for sand-yachting. A marked contrast can be seen between east and west
coasts – the east tranquil, with neat little bathing beaches dotted
with villas and summer homes; the west, the Côte Sauvage,
lashed by waves, indented and reef-strewn. Lifebelts, which are
placed every two hundred metres or so, tell their own story, and
notice-boards say 'Bathing forbidden even in a calm sea. Fishing
dangerous, life-jacket recommended'. Quiberon, the town at the
southern tip, is certainly worth a visit.

The roads from Carnac and Auray (D781 and D768) both
converge on Plouharnel and the Abbeys of Kergonan, twin
establishments, both going concerns – Ste-Anne, rather confusingly, housing monks and St-Michel nuns. Gregorian chant may
be heard here at mass or verpers (1000 and 1630 on Sundays,
1130 and 1800 weekdays). After Plouharnel the isthmus begins.
Before long you will see moored on the sheltered eastern side
a curious reproduction galleon which offers an exhibition of
shells. The Fort de Penthièvre, still used for training French soldiers, soon looms up on the right. A monument reminds us that
59 men of the resistance were shot here in World War II. You
can then take a circuitous and ill-signposted coast road down
the Côte Sauvage with startling views of the wild sea if there is
any sort of wind, or press on through St-Pierre-Quiberon to the
end. Quiberon itself has a lively harbour and the usual quayside
crêperies and bars. The coast road to the Pointe de Conguel and
Port-Haliguen is worth taking. Ferries run from Port-Maria in
Quiberon, or Port-Haliguen in rough westerlies, to Belle-Ile in
forty-five minutes and to the smaller, wilder Ile de Houat and Ile
de Hoëdic in rather longer.

Near Port-Haliguen stands an obelisk recalling those ill-fated
Royalists who did not escape the bungled attempt to reverse the
French Revolution in 1795. Ten thousand of them landed on
Carnac-Plage and joined the waiting Chouans, but the other
side had been forewarned and bottled them up in the Quiberon
peninsula. Only two thousand got back to the waiting English
fleet; the rest were killed, or captured and then shot.

Belle-Ile is worth a few days. Like Quiberon, its history is
chequered, having been over-run by almost all France's enemies
from the Romans onward. Like Quiberon it has a Côte Sauvage,
like the Ile de Groix it has a Locmaria and a Plage des Grands-

Cornouaille to the Grande Brière

Sables, and like north Wales it has a Bangor. The old town and port of Sauzon takes its name from the Saxons that once occupied it. The main town, and a delightfully remote retreat, is the oddly named Le Palais. Nicolas Fouquet, Sebastien Vauban and Sarah Bernhardt all built different kinds of forts on it. For others it has been a prison – Georges Cadoudal, the Chouan leader; Barbès and Blanqui after the 1848 Revolution; several Germans after its final fall in 1945 and Ben Bella, the Algerian rebel leader, in 1959.

There is a wide range of things to see – lighthouses, forts, ports, menhirs and caves. Cars can be hired in Le Palais, as can mopeds, bicycles and even tandems. It is clearly a favourite with tourists, especially yachtsmen. For both it offers variety – the animation ashore and the busy little harbour of Le Palais, or the solitude of the hamlets in the interior and the quieter anchorages round its coasts, such as the remarkable Port du Vieux-Château, near Sauzon, a fiord unique in Brittany.

Yachtsmen heading back to the mainland will very likely make for La Trinité-sur-Mer. For those whose hearts beat faster at the sound of halyards thwacking against steel masts this is the place. It seems that everything converges on the harbour – it is a *port de plaisance* which just happens to have a town attached to it. The reason? It is on the estuary of the Crac'h – so gentle that oysters can be cultivated there – and at the head of Quiberon Bay, sheltered by the natural breakwater of the peninsula and scene of a British naval victory over the French in 1759.

Much earlier than this the bay had been the scene of great naval activity. Of all the Celtic tribes that resisted the Romans, the Veneti were the most redoubtable. Gaul fell to Julius Caesar in 57 BC – except for the land and harbours of the Veneti, who were essentially a sea power. Caesar built a fleet of oared galleys in the Loire estuary and his admiral, Brutus, set out in 56 BC to confront the Veneti in their high-sided, tough little galleons with their leather sails. In rough conditions they would have had the advantage over the less stable galleys, but a flat calm fell and even with 220 galleons they were no match for the Romans, who approached, threw grappling hooks into the rigging and then rowed away hard, tearing down masts and sails.

Caesar watched this unexpected victory from the shore, probably from the Bronze Age Tumulus de Tumiac, near today's entrance to the Gulf of Morbihan. In Caesar's day the gulf may not have been quite so extensive – a double cromlech on the islet of Er Lannic, just inside the entrance, is now half under water and the land is slowly subsiding. But the gulf was there, for the very name 'Mor-bihan' means 'little sea'.

Two headlands, like the two claws of a crab, one bigger than the other, close it in from the bigger sea beyond, and these are only $1\frac{1}{2}$ kms apart at the sea's entrance. Port-Navalo. On the western arm, the headland of Locmariaquer, there are many notable megaliths: the Table des Marchands, a dolmen with a colossal capstone and fine engravings; Mané Lud, a passage grave under a long barrow which makes an excellent vantage point over the gulf; and, most astonishingly, the Menhir Brisé, now broken into five great chunks but formerly over 20 m high and weighing well over 300 tons. As you approach Locmariaquer down the D781 these three, all very well worth searching out, are off the road to the right. Rather more difficult of access, but the finest of its kind, is the Tumulus of Gavrinis, on the island of the same name, just inside the gulf's entrance. You can go out to it by canoe from Larmor-Baden.

But the gulf, which Cyril Connolly called 'the green and violet ocean of the Morbihan', has attractions other than prehistoric ones. The best way to see it is by boat – either your own or a vedette from Locmariaquer, Auray or Vannes (the Vedettes Bleues operate from here). It is worth spending a whole day doing this. You will see the Ile d'Arz, the Pointe d'Arradon and the Ile aux Moines, 6 kms long and the gulf's largest island. It also has the largest cromlech of all – at Kergonan. If you have no time for a boat trip, the best viewpoint reachable by car is the Pointe d'Arradon, 9 kms south-west of Vannes.

At the head of one of the long arms of the gulf is the old town of Auray, which would make a suitable centre from which to look at this part of the Morbihan coast. It has an attractive port area by the Promenade du Loc, overlooked by the main town, and an old quarter called St-Goustan, with fifteenth-century houses, on the east bank of the river. It is often a congested little town, though, despite being by-passed by the N165.

North-east of the town is the Chartreuse d'Auray, the site of a monastery founded to commemorate a battle fought near here in 1364. It was rebuilt in the eighteenth century and later housed the tomb of the Royalists shot after the 1795 Quiberon landing.

It is open to the public. An odd event occurred in 1776 of which the Café Franklin and the Boulevard Franklin are reminders. Benjamin Franklin, headed for the Loire, was forced by adverse winds to come ashore here on his way to Paris for talks which were two years later to bring France into the War of American Independence against Britain. It is near the Boulevard Franklin that you might come to anchor in a yacht. At the right state of the tide you can slip all the way up-river to St-Goustan, past the famous beds where baby oysters (*naissains*) are cultivated on white tiles.

A spectacular *pardon* occurs at Ste-Anne d'Auray, 6 kms to the north, on 25 and 26 July each year. For Breton costumes and Christian pageantry this is the best of them all, and it is another manifestation of the power of the cult of Ste-Anne, the mother of Mary. On the way into the town, on the D19, is a monument to a man who had the last realistic chance of becoming King of France. In 1873, if he had been prepared to give up the Bourbon flag in favour of the revolutionary tricolour, the Comte de Chambord could have become Henri V.

All roads now begin to lead to Vannes, which, though it is attainable, like Auray, from the Gulf of Morbihan, has the feel of an inland place and so has been dealt with in Chapter 7. In the attractive gardens which foot the ramparts you will find a plaque marking the spot where twenty-two of the Royalists taken at Quiberon were shot in 1795. Among them was the last Bishop of Dol, Mgr de Hercé, who, since his hands were tied, asked for someone to take off his hat while he said his final prayers. A soldier of the Revolution approached, but a Royalist general next to the bishop said, 'Leave it, you aren't worthy of it,' and took the hat off with his teeth.

From Vannes an excellent outing would be to the eastern claw' which almost encloses the Gulf of Morbihan – the Rhuys peninsula. Once forested, this is now flat, bosky, broom-covered and rather Dutch in feel. East of Vannes, leave the Michelin tyre plant behind and take the D780 southwards past the Noyalo oyster beds. The classical lines of the eighteenth-century Château de Kerlévenan are visible on the left just after the dual carriageway begins. Shortly after this turn right for Sarzeau, the 'capital' of the Rhuys peninsula and a rather crowded little town with a handsome eighteenth-century church. It was the birthplace in 1668 of Alain René Le Sage, the playwright and novelist who borrowed freely from Spanish writers but made his name with *Gil Blas*. The quiet D198 leads across the main road down to St-Gildas-de-Rhuys with its part-Romanesque, part-seventeenth-century abbey church. Two men make this rather exposed little place famous: St-Gildas and Abbot Abélard. Gildas came from Glastonbury to Armorica and founded an abbey here; in the 550s he wrote almost the only history of the Dark Ages in Britain, the period just before his birth, between the Roman evacuation and the coming of the Anglo-Saxons. Abélard, after his involvements with Heloise, came to the abbey in the 1120s but found it a barbarous place: the umbrageous monks and the incomprehensible Breton language led to his flight in 1132. The abbey is now private but the church is worth a visit. It was a Celtic foundation which took the Benedictine rule in 818. The choir is much as Abélard would have remembered it, with the relics of St-Gildas behind the high altar. The transepts have some fine Renaissance work and you will notice also a giant votive ship there and the rather grisly remains of St-Goustan in a reliquary.

If you rejoin the main D780 you will come to Arzon, Port-du-Crouesty – a fine new marina that can offer over a thousand yachts the best of facilities, and Port-Navalo at the peninsula's tip. If it happens not to be Thursday, L'Escarpolette at 13, Avenue Géneral-de-Gaulle, would be a very agreeable place to have lunch. Port-Navalo looks across to the Pointe de Kerpenhir on the western 'claw' and has a harbour and beaches with a very Cornish air. On the way back you will see to the north of the road the Tumulus de Tumiac, Caesar's vantage point in 56 BC and known now as the Butte de César. The view from the top makes the stroll up well worth while, however full of lunch you may be.

Do not leave the peninsula without seeing its greatest treasure, the fine *Château-féodale* de Suscinio, towards the coast south of Sarzeau and once the summer residence and hunting lodge of the Dukes of Brittany. It was built to guard the approaches to the Gulf of Morbihan and its moat was once filled tidally by the sea. Now it is surrounded by reedy marshland and the sea lies some distance away behind rolling dunes. In 1373 Bertrand du Guesclin successfully took it from the English after a siege. In the years following Dukes Jean IV and V rebuilt and enlarged it. Henry Tudor, later Henry VII, spent twelve years in exile here. It lapsed into ruin after the Revolution, but the walls, with six towers still standing, have recently been very imaginatively restored and are open to public view. Tours are not guided and a glossy explanatory folder is given free.

Further east there are a number of small holiday centres tucked into the corners of Quiberon Bay. Damgan, for example, is a pleasant, out-of-the-way place with no history but plenty of scope for sailing, fishing and the usual beach pursuits. Just inland at Muzillac, off the busy N165, I once lunched at La Taverne. It was a chance call and I would not go out of my way to return, but Brittany is full of these simple, cheap places where one can stop for a *galette*, a *crêpe* or, in my case, fish soup and *côte de porc*. There is little to detain visitors in Muzillac, but just off the D20 to Péaule, the D139 to Le Guerno leads on to the zoological park of the Château de Branféré – an attractive, creeper-clad Renaissance structure, restored in 1848 and now the home of two thousand free-ranging birds and animals accommodated in an extensive park. Another château open to view can be found at Léhélec, 8 kms further along the D20 east of Péaule in the Vilaine valley.

But we are on the edge now of another rich and varied region made up of the Grande Brière and the Guérande peninsula and must cross the broad estuary of the Vilaine to enter it. This you can do by the D139, which is carried over the river to Camoël on the top of the Arzal dam, or by the main Vannes–Nantes road, the N165. The Barrage d'Arzal has a lock which opens from early morning to mid-evening and admits yachts to many miles of carefree, tideless river – 36 kms before the mast has to be lowered at Redon, the Clapham Junction of the Breton inland waterways system. The N165 crosses the Vilaine on a handsome new suspension bridge to the old town of La Roche-Bernard.

It is worthwhile stopping on the northern end of the bridge for a general view of the pleasantly wooded Vilaine valley and the many yachts in La Roche-Bernard's marina. The rock after which the town is named looms over the marina entrance – Bernard was its tenth-century lord. It has three good little hotels and would make a sensible short-term base. Many of France's best-known wooden warships were built here, for instance *La Couronne* in 1634, designed to counter Britain's first *Royal Sov-*

ereign, launched three years before. There are some fine old streets and houses in the town, and afternoon boat trips, every hour on the hour, to the Arzal dam. The châteaux at Branféré and Léhélec, described above, are in easy reach, as is the imposing fifteenth-century (restored) Château de la Bretesche at Missillac, 12 kms down the N165, which may only be seen from the outside.

My favourite town, from which the Grande Brière and the Guérande peninsula can equally well be visited, is Guérande itself. This is a miniature Carcassonne, surrounded by an unbroken ring of fifteenth-century ramparts, which are much less a tribute to the restorer's art than are those at Carcassonne. The plan of the old town is classic: the walls are circular, with six towers and four gates, and were begun by Jean de Montfort in 1343. The streets inside form a cross, the arms of which are interlinked by tiny lanes. It is a pleasant walk round the outside of the walls, with water still filling parts of the moat, and takes only a brisk twenty minutes. Sadly, one cannot yet climb to the parapets and circle the town that way. The Porte St-Michel, at the eastern side, once the home of the governor, now houses the very helpful syndicat d'initiative and a local history museum on three upper floors. The collegiate church of St-Aubin has a twelfth-century Romanesque nave with later Gothic additions, and a typical Breton exterior pulpit (as well as interior ones) at the western end, from which sixteenth-century priests were wont to combat the Protestant heresies. I drove into the walled town in March, but later in the season it becomes pedestrianized. If you are in Guérande in July or August, try to be there on at least one Friday night when there will be an organ recital – or maybe organ and *bombarde* – in the church.

On the way to Guérande, shortly after leaving La Roche-Bernard, you enter the department of Loire Atlantique and also Brittany's second regional park, the Parc Naturel Régional de Brière. Most of this is made up of the Marais de Grande Brière, an extraordinary region of flat, reedy marshland, second only to the Camargue, intersected by canals and scattered with islets on which are ancient villages of thatched cottages. Here live the *Briérons*, a tough and fiercely independent people whose ancestors cut peat and reeds, hunted, fished and defended the autonomy granted them by Duke François II in 1462 and confirmed in 1492 by the Duchess Anne. They continue these activities (though commercial peat cutting ceased about 1950) and have latterly combined them with working in the shipyards of nearby St-Nazaire or the metallurgical works at Trignac.

Neolithic men lived here before the waters of the Loire and the Vilaine rolled in and flooded them out, laying down rich deposits of alluvium, to which was added the decaying vegetation, which formed the peat. Dead trees have also been prised out, five thousand years old and iron hard, to make beams and joists for cottage roofs. In recent centuries the marsh has been drained and developed but has always remained a private wilderness for the use of the *Briérons*, unmindful of all the activity on the coastal belt that surrounds it. Even now the attitude of the Grande Brière to the rest of France is reluctant and cautious, and the area remains a secret domain.

From Guérande the obvious plan for the motorist is to spend a day slowly encircling the Marais and penetrating it at various points, many of which offer the chance of a short spin on the canals, guided or self-drive, in a *chaland*, a kind of punt but with pointed ends, the standard runabout in the Grande Brière. Take the D51 past the Dolmen de Kerbourg. The adjacent hamlet of Kerhinet has been carefully restored to represent traditional *Briéron* life, with eighteen thatched cottages, several open to visitors at roughly normal opening hours. The life of the *Briérons* can be savoured to the full at the Auberge de Kerhinet, which has a menu offering such marshland fare as frogs, eel and duck – *cuisses de grenouille, anguilles de Roquefort* and *canard aux pêches*. The road through Le Brunet to Bréca brings you right to the west end of the main lateral canal. Return to Le Brunet and take the D47 to St-Lyphard. There is a fine panorama from the church tower here and in July and August a twenty-five minute commentary tells the story. *Chalands* can be hired at Le Clos d'Orange. Go further on to Les Fossés-Blancs and you can punt down, or just look down, the long Canal du Nord. At La Chapelle-des-Marais there is an enormous fossilized tree on view, and the Maison du Sabotier (Clogmaker's House). Take the D50 south through Camer and Camerun, two typical 'islet-villages', but better is to come – Fédrun, off the road to the right at St-Joachim. In these villages the houses form a ring and face inwards, but outside them is an encircling *curée*, or small canal,

linked to the main system, on which each house has a landing
stage for its *chaland*. Here, on the Ile de Fédrun, is the Park
headquarters, the Maison de la Mariée (Bride's House), where in
a typical *Briéron* interior there is a collection of wax orange-blos-
som headdresses as made locally to be worn by brides, and the
Chaumière Briéronne (Briéron Cottage). Further down at Rosé (or
Rozé), at the east end of the lateral canal, is the Maison de
l'Eclusier (Lock-keeper's Cottage), now a small museum of
Briéron life. Moored nearby is a *blin* of the kind which once
transported peat.

After Rosé, with its *parc animalier*, you come to one of the
highest points in this flat land: at St-Malo-de-Guersac you are
13 m above the marsh. Before reaching Montoir-de-Bretagne
and being drawn past St-Nazaire airport into the swirl of ex-
pressways and St-Nazaire itself, turn off right on a tiny road to
Le Pin, Loncé and Trignac. That way you can creep between the
Marais and the northern fringes of the city and thread through
to St-André-des-Eaux, where the D127 leads to La Chaussée-
Neuve and more *chalands*, and the D247 leads back to Guérande.

Another pleasant tour from Guérande is up the coast to the mouth
of the Vilaine. Take the D99 to Clis and stop to enjoy the fine
views over the salt marshes to La Grande Côte. That long ridge
which now accommodates the thickly populated conurbation of
holiday resorts from Le Pouliguen to Le Croisic must have been
an island not so long ago. But the magnificent beach at La
Baule, the only considerable one in Brittany to face south, now
closes the eastern end, and from the west the sea is let in
through the lattice-work of levées to flood the salt pans. La Tur-
balle, with the sixteenth-century calvary of Fourbihan, one of
the finest in the region, is a modern sardine port, rather difficult
of access for yachts, but it is an attractive drive to the Pointe du
Castelli and Piriac-sur-Mer. Piriac is a fishing harbour with an
old-established air and the bird sanctuary of Dumet, with its
ruined Fort de Ré, lying offshore. The D452 runs along a piece
of savage coastline and some quieter beaches before the D52
turns inland to Mesquer, another fishing harbour. Thread round
more salt pans to Assérac and the Château de Kerouga. The D82
and D201 take you into a little-visited headland with a succession of tiny hamlets where lanes lead down to minuscule beaches
in between the rock promontories. At Pénestin turn inland again

on the D34 to Camoël and Férel. Five kilometres away is Herbignac where, by way of contrast, I recommend a half-hour's wander over the atmospheric twelfth-century ruins of the *château-féodale* at Ranrouët, which is being patiently restored by voluntary enthusiasts. Six towers remain, linked by a curtain wall and surrounded by moats. There is a barbican and vestiges of three drawbridges. The D774 takes you quickly back to Guérande.

Even if primarily bound for La Baule few visitors to Guérande can surely fail to drop down from the town, on the same D774 but heading south now, into Les Marais Salants, the salt marches on either side of Saillé. This is Guérande's original and continuing industry and explains its name (*Gwen-Ran* means White Land in Breton). Since Gallo-Roman days men have raked salt from the sea here, and the way it is done has not changed over the centuries. Le Pays Blanc is made up of three large salt marshes – the *traicts* of Le Croisic, Le Pouliguen and Mesquer, to the north.

From Guérande it would be a pleasant and interesting afternoon's expedition of about 9 kms to walk to Saillé, where you can learn about the past and present of Les Marais Salants in a small folk museum, La Maison du Paludier (the House of the Marsh-man). Then go westwards on the D92 past the salt pans to Pradel and Quentquen, and from there back to Guérande. It looks best if the sun is setting over the marshes as you get back on to the higher ground. Longer tours can be made by car along the sinuous roads.

This ancient business looks simple, but has its technical subtleties and its private language. In essence the *paludier*, in summer and at high tide, lets seawater in along an *étier*, or conduit, into the *vasière*, the first of three flat reservoirs sub-divided into smaller pans by banks of earth. The water is gradually purified and heated by the sun as it is slowly let through little sluice gates from one reservoir to the other. In the final and cleaner pans, called *oeillets*, it crystallizes and can be raked with a long wooden *las* into heaps. Women can also skim off *la fleur de sel*, the fine salt on the surface of the water, for their own use, but men generally rake *le gros sel* or *sel gris* (there is always a trace of mud in it) and carry heavy loads of it off in *jèdes*, or wooden tubs, balanced on the head. This can be seen going on every day in July, less often in other summer months.

*   *   *

La Grande Côte, or La Côte d'Amour as the tourist leaflet writers now like to term it, is the rocky headland, in times past an island, now linked to the interior by La Baule and the salt marshes. Here are the justifiably popular resorts of Le Croisic, Batz-sur-Mer and Le Pouliguen. On a blowy March day it showed me its two faces: on the southern coast road, the D45, fronting the Bay of Biscay, a few rosy-cheeked townsfolk half turned into the wind as they watched the seas pounding the rocks off the Pointe du Croisic; 500 m away, in the lee of Le Croisic itself, the flag outside the *mairie* hung limp and yachts lay peacefully at their moorings on the northern side of the peninsula. In general the houses and hotels of Le Croisic present their backs to the prevailing westerlies and look north-east across the open water of the Grand Traict first and then Les Marais Salants.

It is an unpretentious, active place, an important fishing port and popular with yachtsmen who can get in at most states of the tide. The harbour is sheltered by a man-made promontory opposite, Pen Bron. Fishing boats tie up in great numbers by the Poissonnerie, or old fish market, in basins or *chambres* at the heart of the town. Just short of the rail terminus there is an artificial tumulus from which a good view can be had from 30 m up. Nearby stands the fine seventeenth-century belfry of the older Notre-Dame-de-Pitié church. In the other direction a similar but larger bell-tower rises from among the rooftops of Batz-sur-Mer, giving the landscape a very Dutch look. I have never seen a coelacanth and would rather like to, but I did not discover until I had left Le Croisic that there is a stuffed one in the Côte d'Amour aquarium there. Also for that rainy day, there is a naval museum in the Hôtel d'Aiguillon, where the French generously show how they lost the battle of Quiberon Bay to the British Admiral Hawke in 1759 just off Le Croisic.

Batz prefers to face the Bay of Biscay and has three little sand beaches hemmed in by rocks (there is a tiny one also at Port-Lin, 500 m from Le Croisic). St-Guénolé church is the great feature of Batz – and especially its belfry, all 60 m of it, built in 1677. The oldest part of the interior dates from 1428 and, like Quimper Cathedral, it is out of alignment. From the top of the tower you will see how Batz has the best of two worlds: from the busy beach of St-Michel, protected by its jetty, the main street, Rue de la Plage, runs through the town clear across the peninsula, past the station, to the salt marshes, where you can walk alone along the levées among the avocets, lapwings, godwits, sand-pipers, land-rails, golden plovers and a whole lot more.

A certain added refinement creeps in at neighbouring Le Pouliguen, where big houses often hide behind high walls. It is the fringe of affluent La Baule. Once just a fishing village on the west bank of a broad *étier* which at high tide brings seawater into the salt marshes behind, Le Pouliguen has grown into a fashionable resort since the mid-nineteenth century.

Cross the *étier* and you are in La Baule and another world again. It is a *station internationale* and in no way Breton – a moonshot away from the thatched cottages of the Grande Brière. It equates more with Biarritz or Juan-les-Pins, and its *raison d'être* is its stunning 5 kms of golden sand beach behind which, over the last hundred years, a series of parallel avenues have grown up, whose trees shade impressive villas and the most *soigné* of hotels. Along the complete length of the beach runs an esplanade, the west end of which is peacefully pedestrianized, the rest – from the main casino eastwards – open to Lamborghinis, Porsches and the like. Some astonishingly modernistic apartment blocks, on the lines of Port-Grimaud, have recently sprung up on it. Le Baule has everything in profusion: seven thousand villas, six thousand apartments, two thousand hours of sunshine a year, fifteen hundred hotel rooms, two hundred horses in two equestrian centres, fifteen beach clubs, six discos and night clubs, four sailing schools, four cinemas, three tennis clubs, three casinos, two eighteen-hole golf courses and two miniature ones, a diving club and a conference centre. It is a mecca for wind-surfers and water-skiers.

Yachtsmen are catered for at both ends of the bay – Le Pouliguen to the west is both fishing port and sailing centre, but dries out; to the east is Pornichet, which has a recently built, well appointed, deep-water *port de plaisance* for a thousand yachts. Pornichet is a very well-organized resort, lively in places, tranquil in others, with a wide range of hotels, restaurants, water sports and individually waymarked suburban walks. Just behind La Baule, off the road to Guérande, is the Château de Careil, a pleasant inhabited manor house which offers a half-hour guided tour of its late fourteenth-century *corps de logis* and two later wings, one Renaissance.

The last of the holiday centres of this coast before St-Nazaire and the mouth of the Loire is St-Marc-sur-Mer, just near the

Modern apartments at La Baule

Pointe de Chémoulin on the D292 coast road to St-Nazaire. It is in the middle of a chain of eleven sandy beaches and creeks, all prettily wooded behind. St-Marc is for nature lovers, for there is little else but sand, sea, sun and cliffs. A system of walks on paths once patrolled by coastguards is offered.

Round the corner lurks St-Nazaire, a big industrial town. Interest in it is centred almost wholly on its port, which grew up in the mid-nineteenth century when some larger ships found it hard to get up the Loire to Nantes. It has been reconstructed after being badly damaged in World War II and has lately become a great shipbuilding centre. Since it achieved fame as the German submarine base which was the objective of an audacious commando raid by Canadians and British in 1942, I had always wanted to visit the place. I came in by road from Pornichet, keeping the sea on my right all the way. Soon after the Boulevard Albert Ier becomes the Boulevard Président Wilson a commemorative monument faces out over the estuary.

The Germans built a vast concrete hangar with fourteen separate pens to protect up to twenty U-boats, which thus remained undamaged by Allied bombing. The best views can be had from the opposite side of the Bassin de St-Nazaire, where there is another interesting and rather spooky war relic, the covered lock. So that U-boats could come and go secretly and safely from their pens the Germans protected the exit lock from the basin by a big concrete shed. It is alongside the uncovered lock used by fishing craft and yachts today. On top of the covered lock is a fine terrace with a panorama, open from June to September except on Mondays. Here is the best place from which to see the vast Louis-Joubet lock leading into the Bassin de Penhoët, used by the biggest of tankers and *transatlantiques*.

It was here that the old destroyer *Campbeltown* came in 1942, rammed down the gates of the Louis-Joubet lock, manoeuvred in and deliberately sank herself, thus putting the lock out of action for the rest of the war. As St-Nazaire had the only dry dock on the Atlantic coast capable of taking the German battleship *Tirpitz* she had to remain in Norwegian waters until sunk there in September 1944. But the U-boat pens were not greatly damaged and Allied casualties incurred during the raid were high.

Now the submarine bays have been put to various other uses,

cold storage, for example, but there is little that can be done with them. Shipbuilding has declined worldwide and St-Nazaire, a hotbed of union militancy and known as 'Red St-Nazaire', has suffered more than most. It has a languid, forlorn air as plant rusts on the empty quaysides.

There is, however, one great symbol of progress and engineering skill visible from the *terrasse panoramique*. The elegant St-Nazaire suspension bridge across the Loire was opened in 1975, eliminating the long haul round by Nantes. It is 3,356 metres long overall, and gives 61 metres clearance at high water. It is expensive to use, but its claim to be 'the most beautiful bridge in Europe' may not be so outrageous.

The bridge carries traffic to St-Brévin, Retz and the Vendée. Here you are not so convincingly in north-west France any more: still in Loire Atlantique, certainly, but this is now part of the Pays de Loire region. Spiritually it is still Brittany, but the evidence begins to thin out. There is a dolmen (in fact a trilithon) in St-Nazaire, even La Baule has arranged for itself a *pardon*, and, as if they felt they had to prove the point, Breton zealots have painted BZH (Breizh equals Brittany, in Breton) on boulders on the way in to Batz-sur-Mer. But south of the Loire is somewhere else.

Practical Information

HOW TO GET THERE

Sea

Townsend Thoresen	Portsmouth– Cherbourg	Up to three sailings a day, 24 May to 2 September. Day crossing $4\frac{1}{2}$ hours, night crossing 8.
	Portsmouth– Le Havre	Two sailings a day, occasionally three in January and February. Day crossing $5\frac{1}{2}$ hours, night crossing $8\frac{1}{4}$.
Brittany Ferries	Portsmouth– Ouistreham	Starts June 1986. Up to six sailings a day.
	Portsmouth– St Malo	Two sailings a day, 18 May to 24 September. Crossing time, 9 hours.
	Plymouth–Roscoff	Up to three sailings a day, 20 April to 16 September. Crossing time, 5 to $6\frac{1}{2}$ hours.
	Cork–Roscoff	One sailing a week. Crossing time, $13\frac{1}{2}$ to 17 hours.
Sealink/ SNCF	Weymouth– Cherbourg	April to October inclusive. Up to three sailings a day in mid-summer. Day crossing 4 hours, night $6\frac{1}{4}$.
	Newhaven–Dieppe	Up to six sailings a day in high summer. Crossing time $3\frac{3}{4}$ hours.
Irish Continental	Rosslare– Cherbourg	Every Tuesday and Saturday, April to September.

Except for Sealink's Weymouth–Cherbourg service and one or two others in the post-Christmas period, car ferries operate on all these routes at least once a day in both directions all the year round. Pound for mile the Channel crossing is still a very expensive one, especially at the height of the season, but it has increasingly become a much more pleasurable one. Good food is provided at appropriate times, there are plenty of bars, duty-free shops, video-games, films and television, and after all that either a reclining seat or a decently appointed cabin. At off-peak times I have enjoyed some excellent crossings in recent years, especially with Brittany Ferries and Townsend Thoresen. One word of warning: Brittany Ferries' cabin accommodation on night crossings is frequently fully booked months in advance. Ships' facilities with these companies and Sealink are fairly standard and it is difficult to distinguish between them. I note that most Brittany Ferries vessels have a children's playroom while Townsend Thoresen offer waiter-service restaurants and Club Class facilities. It is always refreshing to find, as I did with Townsend Thoresen, that at the very end of a crossing the loos are still serviceable and sweet-smelling and the roller machines still produce clean towelling.

Air

A quick, if expensive, way of getting to Normandy or Brittany would be by one of the short-haul air routes. Brit Air (c/o Air France, 158 New Bond Street, London W1Y 0AY; tel. (01)499 9511) run regular, year-round flights between Gatwick, Le Havre and Caen, and between Gatwick, Rennes, Morlaix and Quimper. From April to September Air France operates a service from Heathrow to Nantes. Lucas Air Transport (Gatwick Handling Reservations desk, Gatwick Airport, Horley, Surrey; tel. (0293) 531631) fly in season from Gatwick to Deauville. Jersey European Airways (10 Conway Street, St Helier; tel. (0534) 45661) fly in season from Gatwick to Dinard; from the Channel Islands they offer a year-round link between Jersey and Dinard. Aurigny Air Services (Town Office, Victoria Street, St Anne's, Alderney; tel. (048 182) 2886) fly regularly to Cherbourg from Guernsey and in the season from Jersey and Alderney. Brymon Airways (City Airport, Crownhill, Plymouth Devon; tel. (0752) 707023) operate services from Plymouth to Brest and Morlaix.

Rail

Once in France, it would be perfectly feasible to tour Normandy and Brittany by rail, but the options are, of course, fewer than they were since SNCF cross-country routes have been reduced. The traveller on a radial line from Paris is more fortunate.

Four principal lines slice across Normandy: Paris–Rouen–Dieppe, Paris–Rouen–Le Havre, Paris–Caen–Cherbourg and Paris–Argentan–Granville. Brittany can be reached from Paris via Rennes or circumnavigated from St-Malo, Dol and Dinan to Morlaix and Brest, then south to Quimper (a very scenic route) and on through Morbihan to Nantes. Some spur lines remain – to Lannion, Roscoff, Pontivy, for example – and the *Thomas Cook Continental Timetable* is the Bible here.

Rail travel in France is crowded but comfortable. Platforms and carriages are clean and station restaurants generally excellent – many discerning Frenchmen, not necessarily travellers, head for the Buffet de la Gare. The food can be just as good on board the trains: one of the most memorable meals I ever had in France was crossing the Jura courtesy of SNCF. If the train has no restaurant snacks can often be bought from a *buffet ambulant* in the corridor.

WHERE TO STAY

Hotels

Of classified hotels (with one to four stars, which is the top French rating) there are over 1,000 in Brittany and 790 in Normandy, with 160,000 rooms. Booking by letter, telephone or telex is prudent but I have almost always found it possible to secure a room even in summer by arriving in good time and shopping around.

Leaflets giving comprehensive lists of hotels can be had from the French Government Tourist Office in London, or from offices in each of the ten departments and local Syndicats d'Initiative (addresses from the Tourist Office). The red *Guide Michelin* is invaluable, but many modest but acceptable establishments are not included in it. Not to be listed does not imply cockroaches in the bathroom or cigarette burns on the bedside table. The following selection gives two or three hotels in places in which I have suggested a visitor could well base himself. I have generally avoided most of the prestigious, well-known hotels listed in gastronomic guides (though some are mentioned in the text) but offer instead some examples in the middle range, organized under chapters.

1 Inland from Dieppe

Dieppe Overlooking the spacious lawns on the seafront are several well-liked hotels along the Boulevard de Verdun. Among them, at number 18, the Hotel Windsor (tel. (35) 84.15.23) is quiet and dignified. You are expected to eat in. Cheaper, more cheerful, more French is the Hotel de la Jetée in the old quarter between dockside and seafront. It has no restaurant, but there are plenty on the nearby quay.

Eu On the road from Le Tréport to Eu is the highly recommended Pavillon de Joinville (tel. (35) 86.24.03) and in the centre of Eu one of the reliable Logis et Auberges de France chain, Le Relais (tel. (35) 86.14.88).

Fécamp There are no very good hotels and restaurants in this town, but try the Hotel de la Mer on Boulevard Albert 1er, overlooking the sea (tel. (35) 28.24.64). There are plenty of adequate seafood restaurants along the nearby harbourside.

Etretat The Dormy House (tel. (35) 27.07.88) is modern, slightly out of the town centre and overlooks the beach and rooftops. In the centre but off the main through road there is L'Escale (tel. (35) 27.03.69), cheap and cheerful.

2 Le Havre, the Pays d'Auge and the Seine Valley

Le Havre For those who prefer to spend their first or last night near the ferry the Petit Vatel (tel. (35) 41.72.07) is recommended and has a restaurant next door. In the Rue Emile Zola pleasant proprietors run the clean, good value Séjour Fleuri (tel. (35) 41.33.81). Les Vikings (tel. (35) 42.51.67) is similar and near the Townsend Thoresen boats.

Honfleur The Cheval Blanc (tel. (31) 89.13.49) is an old established place in a most attractive site by the harbour. In the nearby Place Ste Catherine is the cheaper, good value Hostel-lerie Lechat (tel. (31) 89.23.85). Both these hotels, and many others elsewhere, expect you to eat in, which by all accounts is a loss here only of independence.

Trouville-Deauville Vogue described the St-James (tel. (31) 88.05.23) as a 'nice, small hotel'. It is near the beach in Trouville. Over the river in Deauville is the Pavillon de la Poste (tel. (31) 88.38.29), central and quiet, or the Trois Canards (tel. (31) 88.30.68), less exorbitant than most in this smart resort.

Cabourg Shades of *A la Recherche du temps perdu* at the Grand Hotel PLM and Restaurant Le Balbec on the Promenade Marcel Proust (tel. (31) 91.01.79) and it's four-star and pricey. Peace and quiet and good food can be had at the Hostellerie Moulin du Pré (tel. (31) 78.83.68) off the D513 towards Gonne-ville. It is more a restaurant with rooms than a hotel.

Caen There are plenty of good hotels in this bustling city. I have tried the Central (tel. (31) 86.18.52) which is a business-like post-war rebuild in the area south of the castle. Parking is just possible. There is no restaurant, but several nearby. Le Dau-phin (tel. (31) 86.22.26) is one of the France Accueil chain and offers very good food.

Orbec The France, in the main street, (tel. (31) 32.74.02) is an old coaching inn, higgledy-piggledy inside, where I have found good rooms and friendly service.

Pont l'Evéque The only one worth considering is the Lion d'Or (tel. (31) 64.00.38).

Pont Audemer The Hotel de la Risle (tel. (32) 41.14.57) is regularly and highly recommended by British visitors off the Le Havre boat. It's modern and relatively inexpensive. But there are also the Cloches de Corneville (tel. (32) 57.01.04), just 6 kms south-east up the Risle, and the Auberge du Vieux Puits (tel. (32) 41.04.48), the latter really a superb restaurant with rooms.

Brionne Le Logis (tel. (32) 44.81.73) is anglophile and sen-sibly priced, while the Auberge Vieux Donjon (tel. (32) 44.80.62) is convivial and keeps a good table.

Caudebec-en-Caux The Normandie (tel. (35) 96.25.11) overlooks the Seine and its good value makes it deservedly popular, and the Manoir de Rétival (tel. (35) 96.11.22) is a house in a park up above the town. It is small and quiet and light meals are available.

Rouen Of the plethora of hotels in this city these are recommended: Hotel des Carmes (tel. (35) 71.92.31) is in the heart of the old quarter, Grand Hotel du Nord (tel. (35) 70.41.41) is also central but quite quiet and the Normandie (tel. (35) 71.55.77) is small and reasonably priced.

3 Cherbourg and beyond

Cherbourg　Not renowned for top-class hotels. Between the Basilique Saint-Trinité and the Avant-Port is the Rue de la Marine. Try the Grand (tel. (33) 43.04.02) at number 42 or the Moderna at number 28 (tel. (33) 43.05.30).

Bricquebec　The Hôtel du Vieux Château (tel. (33) 52.24.49) is just inside the castle, very attractive and with plenty of parking space. The restaurant is in the thick-pillared Salle des Chevaliers. Armies of waitresses give efficient service. Menus are reasonably priced and there is one for children.

Coutances　At the northern end of this little city the Moderne (tel. (33) 45.13.77) is peaceful, friendly and good value. To the south, on the road out to Granville by the viaduct over the Soulles, is the Relais du Viaduc (tel. (33) 45.02.68), cheerful, cheap but noisy.

Granville　The Normandy-Chaumière (tel. (33) 50.01.71), in the heart of the lower town, is a restaurant with rooms: good food and good value.

Avranches　The Croix d'Or (tel. (33) 58.04.88) and the Auberge St-Michel (tel. (33) 58.01.91) are both very close to the Patton memorial on the south side of the town and good places to eat and stay, but 11 kms to the south is the highly recommended Auberge de la Sélune (tel. (33) 48.53.62) in a former hospice at Ducey.

4 Norman Normandy

Falaise　The Normandie (tel. (31) 90.18.26) is central and within walking distance of the castle. (Hotels in other Norman centres appear in the other chapters).

5 D-Day Normandy

Bayeux　This is the best, and really almost the only good base for a few days' look at the June 1944 landing beaches. The Lion d'Or (tel. (31) 92.06.90) is the place most highly spoken of (though the décor worries some people). It is full of Norman character and very quiet. La Tour d'Argent (tel. (31) 92.30.08) is smack between Cathedral and Tapestry and handy for both.

Recommended also for its food is a Logis de France, the Notre Dame (tel. (31) 92.87.24), hear Tourist Office and Cathedral.

6 Innermost Normandy

Mortain Hotel des Cascades (tel. (33) 59.00.03) is a peaceful corner where you can eat well (closed Sunday evenings and Mondays).

Domfront Of the eight hotels in this hill-top town probably the best are the France (tel. (33) 38.51.44), down by the station and the Poste (tel. (33) 38.51.00) up on the ridge.

Bagnoles de l'Orne There are thirty-two hotels in this small spa town so there should be no problem finding a place between March and September. La Bruyère, 2 kms north at St-Michel-des-Andaines (tel. (33) 37.22.26), is one of the few open all year (except Mondays in winter).

Sées The Cheval Blanc (tel. (33) 27.80.48) is a small, inexpensive member of the Logis de France chain.

Alençon The Grand Cerf (tel. (33) 26.00.51) is good, and near the birthplace of Ste-Thérèse and the Cathedral.

Conches-en-Ouche Try either the Normandie (tel. (32) 30.04.58) or the Grand'mare (tel. (32) 30.23.30) – both equally well recommended.

7 St-Malo, the Pays du Rance and the Emerald Coast

St-Malo It would be a pity not to stay inside the walls. The Chiens du Guet (tel. (99) 40.87.29), named after the mastiffs that used to roam round the walls, is full of character and its rooms and meals are sensibly priced. The Quic-en-Groigne (tel. (99) 40.86.81) is in the Rue d'Estrées in the north-west quarter of the town. It is new and clean and popular with English.

Dol-de-Bretagne The two principal hotels here are constantly recommended for their welcome and their food – Logis de la Bresche-Arthur (tel. (99) 48.01.44) and Bretagne (tel. (99) 48.02.03), which is tucked away north of the main throughway.

Dinan The Ramparts (tel. (96) 39.10.16) is near the castle and the Place du Guesclin and full of atmosphere, as is the Marguerite, which is traditional and reasonably priced.

Dinard There are thirty-three hotels in Dinard. Among them, the Altaïr (tel. (99) 46.13.58), centrally placed on the main north-south boulevard, deserves its frequent mentions. The two-star Dunes (tel. (99) 46.12.72) is nearer Casino and beach.

Le-Val-André The Grand Hotel (tel. (96) 72.20.56) overlooks the sea from Rue Amiral Charner and is excellent value, well above its two-star rating.

8 Rennes and the Eastern Argoat
Rennes Six hotels cluster around the station square and the Avenue Janvier leading south to it. Try the Brest (tel. (99) 30.35.83).
Josselin The Château (tel. (97) 22.20.11), across the bridge over the Oust, gives good views of the castle; it is the only place.
Malestroit The Aigle d'Or (tel. (97) 22.40.10) is central, by the river and has a pleasant ambience – a simple hotel in an unsophisticated part of France.
Vannes The Bretagne (tel. (97) 47.20.21) and the Colonies (tel. (97) 47.22.05) are both one-star hotels and well placed near the ramparts. Or you could try another modest establishment, the Marée Bleue (tel. (97) 47.24.29) in Place Bir-Hakeim in the upper part of the town, where the food is very good and not expensive.

9 The Way in from Roscoff
Roscoff The Gulf Stream (tel. (98) 69.73.19), on a quiet road leading out to the west, is one of the most comfortable. Less expensive is the Bains (tel. (98) 61.20.65), in the square by the church.
Morlaix The Europe (tel. (98) 62.11.99) is well worth the short drive from the Plymouth – Roscoff ferry and is the only hotel regularly recommended in this town.

10 The Western Argoat
Carhaix-Plouguer The Gradlon (tel. (98) 93.15.22) is simple and central. The D'Ahès (tel. (98) 93.00.09), almost next door, is a little cheaper.
Huelgoat The L'Armorique (tel. (98) 99.71.24), at the entrance to the Place Aristide-Briand, looks good, and I also recommend the Hotel du Lac (tel. (98) 99.71.14) which is unpretentious and well sited.
St-Nicolas-du-Pélem The Hotel de l'Ouest (tel. (96) 29.51.34) is a quiet, congenial hotel right next to the church. Its restaurant, overlooking a pleasant garden, offers good food-courteously served. I found it a useful staging point.

Moncontour   On the road out south-west, the France (tel. (96) 73.41.37) offers good fare in a pleasant rustic setting.

11 From Trégor to Porzay

Paimpol   Near Paimpol are three superb establishments which could be most easily booked as part of a Brittany Ferries holiday: the Relais Brenner (tel. (96) 20.11.05), one of the Relais and Châteaux group, has superb gardens overlooking the Trieux near Lézardrieux, and thirty very modern rooms; the Château de Coatguelen (tel. (96) 22.31.24), at Pléhédel, 9 kms due south of Paimpol, just off the D7, is an older house in a large park; and the Repaire de Kerroc'h (tel. (96) 20.50.13) is a seventeenth-century house overlooking the port of Paimpol.

Tréguier   The Estuaire (tel. (96) 92.30.25) is down by the Jaudy and reasonably priced.

Perros-Guirec   Thirty-five to choose from here and in nearby Ploumanac'h. If you like to watch yachts coming and going, try the Bon Accueil (tel. (96) 23.24.11) or the Levant (tel. (96) 23.20.15), both by the port.

Lannion   The best, most central places are the Terminus (tel. (96) 37.03.67) and A l'Arrivée (tel. (96) 37.00.67), both, naturally, near the station.

Brest   A good, centrally-placed hotel with a reputation for fine cooking is the Voyageurs (tel. (98) 80.25.73).

Camaret   The France (tel. (98) 27.93.06) is a bright, modern, slate-roofed hotel wedged among the shops alongside the port. Excellent, good value food.

12 From Cornouaille to the Grande Brière

Audierne   Le Goyen (tel. (98) 70.08.88) and Cornouaille (tel. (98) 70.09.13) are both by the attractive fishing port – the first, rather smarter and offering good fish dishes, the second, simpler but with no restaurant.

Quimper   The Tour d'Auvergne (tel. (98) 95.08.70) is generally recommended, but you could try Le Transvaal (tel. (98) 90.09.91), south of the Odet but still convenient.

Bénodet   The Ker Moor and Kastel Moor (tel. (98) 91.04.48 and (98) 91.05.01) are twin establishments, on the expensive side, but attractively placed in a park overlooking the sea. Otherwise, the Ancre de Marine (tel. (98) 91.05.29) is a good choice near the port.

Concarneau   The Grand (tel. (98) 97.00.28) is very central, on the corner of a tree-lined avenue by the port and looking across to the walls of the Ville Close. For the seaside rather than the port, try the Sables Blancs (tel. (98) 97.01.39), looking west.

Quimperlé   The Auberge de Toulfoën (tel. (98) 96.00.29) is the best of a not very rich choice around here – 3 kms south of the town on the D49. It is a restaurant with rooms.

Carnac   The Alignements (tel. (97) 52.06.30) would be the one for archaeologists – in the town rather than on the beach, no-nonsense, comfortable. The Celtique (tel. (97) 52.11.49) is near the sea-front and not so pricey as the hotels that line it.

La Roche-Bernard   The name of the Deux Magots (tel. (99) 90.60.75) attracted me; it is an old house in the old quarter and serves good food. Equally good, but smaller and quieter is the Auberge Bretonne (tel. (99) 90.60.28).

Guérande   As with St-Malo, you really have to be within the walls. The Roc Maria (tel. (40) 24.90.51) is a fifteenth-century house opposite the church. Just outside the walls, by the northern gate, there is the Voyageurs (tel. (40) 24.90.13).

Le Baule   In high season you should go, if unbooked, to the Tourist Office at 8 Place Victoire to enquire where there are vacancies. La Palmeraie (tel. (40) 60.24.41) is in attractively wooded surroundings and quite near the beach.

Camping and Caravanning

There is plenty of scope for this in Normandy and Brittany. In fact, camping and caravanning in France is generally a delight. The roads seem wider and more open for your caravan and camping is altogether easier. There is no law against putting up a tent anywhere you like in unrestricted areas and the country is so well-endowed with woods and heathland that I have never found it a problem to tuck the car up some quiet forest track and erect a small tent. You should, of course, respect *Propriété Privé* signs and not try to penetrate cultivated fields or wired-off woodland.

For greater security and for all the amenities they offer, organized campsites are the answer. These abound – practically every town exhibits the familiar blue and cream metal sign with its tent and caravan, and they lead you unerringly to the site. The standards that you will find there are often astonishingly high for no great outlay – hot water, shops, sometimes swimming pool and tennis courts. It is not necessarily the best thing to plan your itinerary too thoroughly. Indeed, it would add a pleasurable element of surprise to your holiday to allow seren-dipity to come into play by just happening on a camping ground by chance.

Of course, sites on the coast near sandy beaches tend to be packed full in high season and if you want a place by a beach it is imperative to book beforehand or else to arrive about ten in the morning in the hope that other campers may be leaving. You should if possible avoid August, though after the week in which the Assumption of the Blessed Virgin Mary falls, France's last public holiday of the summer, campsites begin to thin out per-ceptibly and places become available. September is even better.

Sites further inland are less crowded and often more agree-able, especially those in small towns where the camp is within easy walking distance of the town centre. It is infinitely pleas-anter to stroll into town to dine in a restaurant and then sway back under the shining moon than to have all the fag of driving in. The Camping and Caravanning Club, the AA, the RAC and Michelin all publish handbooks about touring abroad in this way and the French Government Tourist Board offers a brochure of sites. Here are a few which have been found of good quality:

Arromanches-les-Bains Camping Municipal (tel. (31) 22.36.78) in the Avenue de Verdun. Handy for a look at the Normandy beaches.

La Baule Les Ajoncs d'Or (tel. (40) 60.33.29) is two camps – one for caravans, the other, rather simpler, for tents. La Baule's excellent beach only 1 km away.

Cabourg Plage (tel. (31) 91.05.75) is right on the dunes and usually full.

Caen Camping Municipal (tel. (31) 73.60.92) is south-south-west of the city on the D212B to Louvigny by the west bank of the Orne. A useful overnight stop.

Carnac La Grande Métairie (tel. (97) 55.71.47) is Carnac's only 5-tent establishment (in the Michelin classification system) and is off the D196 near the Tumulus de Kercado.

Dinard Camping Municipal du Port Blanc (tel. (99) 46.10.74) is 1 km west of the town and right alongside the beach.

Erquy Pins (tel. (96) 32.31.12) is in a pine forest 1 km north-east of Erquy, on the way to the Plage du Guen. A clean site with a good restaurant and a sand beach near.

Guérande   Pré du Château de Careil (tel. (40) 60.22.99) is for caravans only and you need to book. It is a very good site, kept spotless by a diligent dragon. Quite near La Baule beach.

Mont-St-Michel   Mont-St-Michel (tel. (33) 60.09.33) is a good, clean site 2 kms south of the abbey. Usually plenty of room. Good sunsets.

Quiberon   Municipal de Penthièvre (tel. (97) 52.00.14) is almost at the narrowest part of the isthmus, on a fine, quiet sandy beach. Good site for touring Carnac and Quiberon.

St-Malo   Camping de la Grande Grève (tel. (99) 34.93.27) is on the Avenue de Moka and close to a sand beach. An easy walk into St-Malo. Usually crowded.

SIGHTSEEING

Opening times are varied and often complicated, and only general guidance is given in this book. There are certain patterns, however: Tuesday tends to be closing day; and where there are references to 'normal hours' these are 1000 to 1200 and 1400 to 1800.

There are notable exceptions, but the deplorable habit of insisting on tours being guided has become increasingly evident in France. This is often unsatisfactory: the information given, where it is comprehensible to non-French, is sometimes too thin, too romanticized, too tailored to an understanding of French history or too little understood by the guide herself. There is the depressing business of being shepherded along at an even pace with no time to browse and no chance to distance oneself from a crowd of other tourists, some of whom would equally prefer to go at their own speed. The guide locks and unlocks doors and the sheep trail through. Sometimes a tedious wait is involved, too. Tours may leave only hourly. I once made a special visit to the Château d'Eu, billed as being open until 1700. I arrived at 1605, but the last tour of the day had left at 1600 and I was not allowed to join it. There are notable exceptions, like Mont-St-Michel, to whom these strictures do not apply and where the guides are excellent. The price of admission is generally between 20 and 30 francs, rather less than the going rate in Britain.

Museums and monuments which are owned by the state are free to: the under-sevens and anyone with them; seven to eighteen-year-olds; teachers and art or architecture students (proof of identity or student cards required); professional artists, journalists, tourist guides.

The eighteen to twenty-five and over sixty-five age groups get in for half price, as do holders of the Council of Europe Identity Card, obtainable from the Central Bureau for Educational Visits and Exchanges, Seymour Mews House, Seymour Mews, London W1H 9PE (01-486 5101).

The state-owned properties in Normandy and Brittany are:

Abbaye du Bec-Hellouin (Eure)
Château de Carrouges (Orne)
Abbaye de Jumièges (Seine-Maritime)
Château de Kerjean (Finistère)
Tour d'Oudon (Loire-Atlantique)
Abbaye de Mont-St-Michel (Manche)
Maison de Renan, Tréguier (Côtes-du-Nord)
Tour Solidor, St-Malo (Ille et Vilaine)

HOLIDAY READING

Books

In 1840 the novelist Anthony Trollope's brother, Thomas Adolphus, published *A Summer in Brittany*, which must be one of the first travel books written about the area in English. In Victorian and Edwardian times several effusive, rather self-indulgent works of the 'Strolling through Tuscany' kind appeared. The best I know is Emil Davies' *Off Beaten Tracks in Brittany* (1912) which describes the adventures of two bright young men walking from Brest to Dinan (see page 236). There are two nice collector's pieces – *Brittany* (1902) by S. Baring-Gould, the Devon clergyman who wrote 'Onward, Christian Soldiers', and *Normandy* (1906) by Cyril Scudamore MA. An old Baedeker is always interesting – I have the fifth (1909) edition of *Northern France*. *Normandy* by Camille Mauclair is full of sepia photographs of churches, châteaux and fishermen, with barely a motor car to be seen.

But these are really only of historical interest, and not of much

300

practical use today. Books produced just after World War II are not very helpful, as Normandy and Brittany had not yet been rebuilt. In Hodder and Stoughton's 1947 series, *The People's France*, Alan Houghton Brodrick's *Normandy* suffers from this but is nevertheless of interest, being, unusually, an alphabetical gazetteer of places. In 1984 the AA produced a new gazetteer of places, *Brittany*, translated from the French and superbly illustrated. Evans brought out two companion volumes in 1951 – George Renwick's *Sea-Girt Brittany* and Vivian Rowe's *Return to Normandy*, but the best is an early example of Batsford's excellent topographical series, Ralph Dutton's *Normandy and Brittany* of 1953.

A later version in the same series was Mary Elsy's somewhat sketchy *Brittany and Normandy* which covered the two provinces department by department in 1974. A Blue Guide, *Loire Valley, Normandy, Brittany*, followed in 1978 and, equally thorough and strong on history and architecture but devoted to only one province, Nesta Roberts' *Companion Guide to Normandy* from Collins in 1980. Two carefully researched, well-written volumes cover the historical, literary, social, political and economic aspects: Peter Gunn's *Normandy – Landscape with Figures* of 1975, and Keith Spence's *Brittany and the Bretons* of 1978, both from Gollancz. Elisabeth de Stroumillo's *The Tastes of Travel: Normandy Brittany* (Collins Harvill, 1979) tours the region in a very readable manner, but gives less emphasis to its culinary glories than the title suggests. *The Visitor's Guide to Brittany*, by Neil Lands, is a well illustrated though somewhat inaccurately printed guidebook (Moorland, 1984). Unique and quite indispensable, of course, are the Michelin Green and Red guides.

There has been a recent crop of paperback guides which deal specifically with the hinterland behind France's cross-Channel arrival ports. Some of them are simply expanded lists of hotels and restaurants in the area and concentrate heavily on the creature comforts. Arthur Eperon, who admits to enjoying these comforts hugely, presents a very useful personal view in *Le Weekend* (Pan, 1984). He originally struck gold with his highly popular *Travellers' France*, easy-to-follow descriptions of seven routes, most of which ran from Channel ports southwards. *Encore Travellers' France* describes seven more (both Pan again). *Just Across the Channel* by Charles Owen (Cadogan Books,

1983) describes tours made in summer 1982 and suggests routes, including hotels and restaurants, for those who wish to follow in his path. It has good indexes and offers a mass of information. Patricia Fenn's *French Entrée 3 – Normandy* (Quiller Press, 1985) is a Townsend Thoresen gazetteer of places with most space given to descriptions of hotels and restaurants. It is now rearranged alphabetically, rather than by Townsend Thoresen ports of entry, and much simpler to use than in earlier editions. *French Leave*, by Richard Binns (Chiltern Books) is regularly updated. Brittany and Normandy feature, as they do in his *Hidden France*. Both are aimed at the enthusiastic gastronome and *bon viveur*.

Guides also exist for other sorts of holiday. *Walking in France* by Rob Hunter (Hamlyn, 1983) has a chapter on Brittany and Normandy, and Adam Nicolson and Charlie Waite's beautiful *Long Walks in France* (Weidenfeld and Nicolson, 1983) features one walk in each province. Topographical guides for walkers are available from the FFRP–CNSGR – Fédération Française de Randonnée Pédestre – Comité National de Sentiers de Grande Randonnée, 92 Rue de Clignancourt, 75883 Paris. *Fat Man on a Bicycle* is Tom Vernon's jokey account of the bicycle ride to the south of France on which he based a number of BBC radio programmes. He arrived in Dieppe and cycled across the Pays de Caux to the Seine at, naturally, Vernon. Rob Hunter has also produced *Cycle Touring in France* (Muller, 1984).

For visitors to the Normandy battlefields – there are thousands of them every year, and not only in commemorative years such as 1984 – I recommend two excellent books. Patrice Boussel's *D-Day Beaches Pocket Guide* (Macdonald, 1964) was written to cash in on the twentieth anniversary. It takes the enthusiast on seven tours of the landing zones, tells plenty of good stories, is well furnished with maps and photographs but is, inevitably, a bit out of date now. *Holt's Battlefield Guides: Normandy – Overlord* (Leo Cooper, 1983) is a complementary booklet, slimmer, neater and easily carried in a top pocket, with three principal itineraries and a mass of other information. Virtually every vestige of the 1944 battles is referred to by Major Tonie and Mrs Valmai Holt, who organize and conduct tours of the area.

For a close look at a little-regarded war I turned to *The Rouen Campaign, 1590–2* by Howell A. Lloyd (Clarendon Press, 1973), but more familiar, recent and crucial action is described in *The Battle for Normandy* by Eversley Bellfield and H. Essame (Batsford, 1965). The best insight into the 1944 invasion comes from two other sources – John Keegan's magisterial survey of various parts of the battle in *Six Armies in Normandy* (Cape, 1982) and an excellent collection of officers' experiences there in *Brightly Shone the Dawn* by Gary Johnson and Christopher Dunphie (Warne, 1980).

Yachting enthusiasts are offered a wealth of titles, among which I have noted David Jefferson's *Brittany and Channel Islands Cruising Guide* (Stanford Maritime, 1981) and for Normandy harbours the *Normandy and Channel Islands Pilot* by Mark Brackenbury (Adlard Coles, 1986). Both have excellent guidance in getting into the havens between Calais and St-Nazaire and give you some idea of the facilities available.

For the early history of the two provinces there is P. R. Giot's *Brittany* in Thames and Hudson's series *Ancient Peoples and Places* (1960), and Glyn Daniels' *Lascaux and Carnac* (Lutterworth, 1955). Neil Fairbairn's *A Traveller's Guide to the Kingdom of Arthur* (Evans, 1983) has a section on Arthur in Brittany. *Roman Gaul* by J. F. Drinkwater (Croom Helm, 1983) puts the region in its perspective – the further, quieter end of vast, west European Roman provinces. On the events of 1066 I found *William the Conqueror* by David Douglas (Eyre Methuen, 1964) particularly useful, as well as two books both called *The Norman Conquest* – H. R. Loyn's (Hutchinson, 1965) and D. J. A. Matthew's (Batsford, 1966). *The Bayeux Tapestry and the Norman Invasion* by Lewis Thorpe (Folio Society, 1973) is also valuable. There is no good, easily accessible book on castles in Normandy, but for Brittany Roger Grand's *L'Architecture Militaire en Bretagne* is found in the *Bulletin Monumental* for 1951–2. The murky comings and goings of armies in the medieval centuries can be somewhat enlightened by Lt. Col. Alfred H. Burne's *The Crécy War* (Eyre and Spottiswoode, 1955); Froissart's *Chronicles* and *The Hundred Years' War* (Folio Society, 1966) help here too.

Much pleasure and a deeper understanding of the peoples of Normandy and Brittany past and present can be derived from reading novels set in the region. Notable examples are:

| Honoré de Balzac | *Les Chouans* | Fougères |
| | *Beatrice* | Guérande |

Alphonse de		
Châteaubriant	*Le Brière*	Le Brière
Tristan Corbière	*Armor*	Roscoff
	Gens de mer	
Gustave Flaubert	*Madame Bovary*	Pays de Caux
Victor Hugo	*Quatre-Vingt-Treize*	Fougères
Pierre Loti	*Pêcheur d'Islande*	Paimpol
Guy de Maupassant	*Boule de Suif*	Normandy
	La Maison Tellier	
	Une Vie	
	Bel Ami (and others)	
Marcel Proust	*A La Recherche du*	
	temps perdu	Cabourg
	A l'Ombre des jeunes	
	filles en fleur	Trouville

Finally there are two very illuminating works of autobiography: Ronald Millar's *A Time of Cherries: Sailing with the Breton Tunnymen* (Cassell, 1977) and Pierre-Jakez Hélias's *Le Cheval d'Orgueil* (Plon, 1975) which is an evocation of a childhood spent in the Pays Bigouden.

Maps

The most popular for ordinary overland touring are the yellow Michelin maps. Their scale of 1:200,000, or 1 cm to 2 km, enables the whole of metropolitan France to be covered in thirty-seven maps. They are not difficult to intrepret, and offer a great deal of detail: you will easily find your way down that uncoloured *voie ordinaire* to the thin blue line of a stream by which to picnic. As new express-ways and autoroutes are built the maps are constantly being updated.

Also very good, though less readily available, are the *Cartes – Institut Géographique National* (IGN). Their *Série Rouge* are of a scale 1:250,000 and you only need two for north-west France – 102 for Normandy and 105 for Brittany. They offer also the excellent *Série Verte* at 1:100,000. For the two provinces you will need 3, 6, 7, 8, 13 to 18 inclusive, and 24. They also have even larger scale 1:50,000 and 1:25,000 maps. Street plans of several French towns are produced by Plans Guides Blay of 14 Rue Favart, 75002 Paris.

For long-distance walkers the Fédération Francaise de la Randonnée Pédestre publish the *Topo-Guides des Sentiers de Grande Randonnée*, though their maps are rather grey and not too clear. Yachtsmen will have sea charts of their own in plenty, but Claude Vergnot's *Carte Guide Navigation Cotière* covers the French coastline at a scale of 1:50,000 and is offered byEditions Cartographiques Maritimes. The same house has invaluable guidance for those following inland waterways – M. Sandrin's *Carte Guide Navigation Fluviale: Voies Navigables de Bretagne*. All these maps can be found at Edward Stanford, Long Acre, London WC2.

Outdoor Activities

GOLF COURSES

Normandy

Bagnoles de l'Orne (Orne)	Golf d'Andaines	9
Bréhal (Manche)	Golf Municipal de Bréhal	9
Cabourg (Calvados)	Golf de Cabourg	18
Cherbourg (Manche)	Club de Cherbourg (1973)	9
Coutainville (Manche)	Golf Club de Coutainville	9
Deauville (Calvados)	New Golf Club (1929)	18 and 9
Dieppe (Seine-Maritime)	Golf de Dieppe	18
Etretat (Seine-Maritime)	Golf Marin d'Etretat (1908)	18
Granville (Manche)	Club de Granville (Manche)	18
Le Havre (Seine-Maritime)	Golf du Havre	18
Houlgate (Calvados)	Golf du Clair Vallon	18
Rouen (Seine-Maritime)	Club de Rouen	18
St-Aubin-sur-Mer (Calvados)	Club St-Aubin (1976)	18
Le Vaudreuil (Eure)	Golf du Vaudreuil	18

Brittany

La Baule (Loire-Atlantique)	Golf de la Baule – St Denac	18

Dinard–St Briac (Ille et Vilaine.)	Golf de Dinard	18
La Forêt-Fouesnant (Finistère)	Golf de Quimper et de Cornouaille (1959)	9
Landerneau (Finistère)	Golf de Lann Rohou	18
Missillac (Loire-Atlantique)	Country Club de la Bretesche	18
Nantes (Loire-Atlantique)	Grand Golf de Nantes – Vigneux	18
Paimpol (Côtes-du-Nord)	Château de Coatguélen	9
Perros-Guirec (Côtes-du-Nord)	Golf de Saint-Samson	18
Ploërmel (Morbihan)	Golf de Saint-Laurent	18
Pornic (Loire-Atlantique)	Golf de Pornic	9
Rennes (Ille-et-Vilaine)	Golf de Saint-Jacques-de-la-Lande	9
Sables d'Or – Fréhel (Côtes-du-Nord)	Club des Sables-d'Or-les-Pins	9
Saint-Cast-le-Guildo (Côtes-du-Nord)	Golf de Pen Guen	9
Saint-Quay-Portrieux (Côtes-du-Nord)	Golf des Ajoncs d'Or	18

BOAT HIRE

Normandy

Boats can be hired in season from a great many places on Normandy's long coastline. Here are some of them:

> CABOURG – Chantiers ACM, 14390 Cabourg (tel. (31) 91.06.37)
> COURSEULLES-SUR-MER – Marine, 4 Quai Ouest (tel. (31) 97.43.17)
> DEAUVILLE – Krischarter, Port Deauville (tel. (31) 88.67.32)
> GRANVILLE – Lepesqueux Voile, 3 Rue Clement Desmaisons (tel. (33) 50.18.97)

Some indication of competence is often necessary. Learners will find sailing schools in practically every coastal centre. There are yacht marinas at the following places: Barneville–Carteret, Cabourg, Cherbourg, Courseulles-sur-Mer, Deauville–Trouville, Dieppe, Fécamp, Honfleur, Le Havre, Le Tréport, Ouistreham–Riva Bella, Portbail, Quinéville, St-Valéry-en-Caux. Sailing craft may be hired for use on the Seine et Les Andelys, Poses, Venables and Vernon.

Brittany

Brittany has a long, deeply-indented coastline and an ancient sea-faring tradition, and so you can expect an immense number of sailing schools and boat hire firms. Write to the Comité Regional du Tourisme de Bretagne, 3 Rue d'Espagne, 35022 Rennes (tel. (99) 50.11.15). It also has 600 kms of navigable inland waterways and boats can be hired for use on them from at least fifteen firms. Information is available from the Association Bretonne des Relais et Itinéraires, 3 Rue des Portes Mordelaises, 35000 Rennes (tel. (99) 79.36.26). There are yacht marinas at: Belle Ile (Le Palais), Bénodet, Binic, Brest, Concarneau, Dinan, Dinard, Douarnenez, Gulf of Morbihan (several), Ile de Groix, L'Aberwrac'h, La Forêt-Fouesnant, La Roche-Bernard, La Trinité-sur-Mer, Lézardrieux, Lorient, Morgat, Morlaix, Paimpol, Perros-Guirec, Pléneuf-Val-André, Plougasnou, Port du Crouesty, Port-Haliguen, Port-Louis, Redon, Roscoff, St-Malo.

CANOE HIRE

Normandy

Normandy is a good province for canoeing. Offices in these towns could help you to explore its various rivers (in brackets):

CARENTAN (Douve, Taute) – Club Nautique Carentanais, 17 Route des Périers (tel. (33) 42.17.56)

ST HILAIRE-DU-HARCOUËT (Sélune) – M. Ponchon, 62 Rue de Mortain (tel. (33) 49.15.39)

THURY-HARCOURT (Orne) – SIVOM du Val d'Orne, 15 Rue de Condé (tel. (31) 79.61.61).

TORCHAMP (Varenne) – Maison du Parc, Parc Naturel Régional de Normandie–Maine, Carrouges (tel. (33) 27.21.15)

EVREUX (Andelle, Charentonne, Epte, Eure, Risle) – Direction de la Jeunesse et des Sports, Cité Administrative (tel. (32) 39.52.09)

CAEN (Orne) – Comité Départemental, Stade Nautique, Avenue Albert-Sorel, (tel. (31) 86.04.12)
ROUEN (Seine) – Canoë Club Rouennais, Ile Lacroix, 76000 Rouen.
LE TRAIT (Seine) – Union Sportive du Trait, Mairie, Le Trait (tel. (35) 97.94.32)

Brittany

In Brittany Morbihan is perhaps the best department for canoeing on rivers and canals. Try the Comité Départemental de Canoë-Kayak, 14 Rue de Blavet, 56650 Lochrist (tel. (97) 36.09.05) or the Comité de Promotion Touristique des Canaux Bretons et des Voies Navigables de l'Ouest, 3 Rue des Portes-Mordelaises, 35000 Rennes (tel. (99) 79.36.26).

HORSES

Normandy

There are two nationally-renowned stud farms – the Haras de St-Lô and the Haras du Pin (near Argentan) – and over ninety *centres hippiques* where horses may be ridden. Tourist offices will give information on those most convenient for you.

Holidays in horse-drawn caravans (*roulottes*) or carriages (*calèches*) can begin at four centres in Normandy – Tessé-la-Madeleine (near Bagnoles-de-l'Orne), Cambremer and Hotot-en-Auge (near Caen) and Thury-Harcourt. Apply to Jean Dinard, BP 6, Tessé-la-Madeleine, 61140 Bagnoles-de-l'Orne (tel. (33) 37.00.56), Les Roulottes de Valdoré, Route de Manerbe, 14340 Cambremer (tel. (31) 31.14.97). M. de Cressac, Manoir d'Auvillars, Hotot-en-Auge (tel. (31) 79.28.86) or SIVOM du Val d'Orne, 15 Rue de Condé, 14220 Thury-Harcourt (tel. (31) 79.61.61). The west coast of the Cotentin is a good place for dune-riding on ponies.

Brittany

For riding holidays apply to the Association Régionale pour le Tourisme Equestre en Bretagne, 1 Rue Gambetta, 56300 Pontivy (afternoons only) (tel. (97) 25.31.36). For a horse-drawn caravan holiday in the Monts d'Arrée get in touch with Roulottes de Bretagne, Gare de Locmaria–Berrien, 29218 Huelgoat (tel. (98) 93.73.28). Two other useful addresses in this field are the Centre Equestre de la Côte d'Eméraude, 35800 Dinard (tel. (99) 46.23.57) and the Centre Equestre de La Baule, 44500 La Baule, (tel. (40) 60.39.29).

BICYCLES

Bicycles can be hired (*location vélos*) in almost any self-respecting holiday centre – whether it be Caen, where the two abbeys are awkwardly far apart for foot exploration, or Lampaul on Ushant, where you can bowl out to the giant lighthouse at Creac'h. French Railways cater very sympathetically for cyclists and on many trains bicycles travel free and can be loaded and unloaded by the rider. At several stations bicycles can be hired in advance (*trains-vélos*). In Normandy, for example, this can be done at Bayeux, Caen, Bueil, Vernon, Granville, Pontorson, Argentan, Dieppe and Le Tréport. At several others they can be hired on arrival but they may also often be rented from the Syndicats d'Initiative, cycle shops or individuals.

OTHER SPORTS

Tennis is possible almost everywhere. Walking is coming into vogue again and there are numerous references in the text and on the maps to the Sentiers de Grande Randonnée (GR) and the topo-guides which go with them (these topo-guides can be bought from Edward Stanford Ltd, 12/14 Long Acre, London WC2). Wind-surfing, water-skiing and scuba-diving grow in popularity. Sea and river fishing attract enormous numbers in France as elsewhere. Even rock-climbing is on offer in the Suisse Normande region of Normandy at Clécy, and sand-yachting at Penthièvre near Quiberon and in the Baie de Kernic near Plouescat.

Among more exotic sports pot-holing, flying, gliding and parachuting can all be practised somewhere in Normandy and Brittany and on the Etang au Duc near Ploërmel there are even races occasionally in the summer between waterborne Citroën 2CVs.

Index

Normandy

Brittany

319